OFF THE BEATEN PATH® SERIES

Kentucky

FIFTH EDITION

Off the Beaten Path®

by Zoé Ayn Strecker

Edited
by Teresa Day

The
Globe
Pequot
Press

Guilford, Connecticut

Cover and text design by Laura Augustine
Cover photo by Craig W. Davis
Maps created by Equator Graphics © The Globe Pequot Press
Illustrations on pages 20, 59, 62, 92, 107, 127, 133, 152, 167, 195, and 215 by Richard Gersony.
Illustrations on pages 162 and 211 by Julie Lynch.
Excerpt from "Outdoor Lore" reprinted with the permission of the estate of Nevyle Shackelford.

ISSN: 1535-8038
ISBN: 0-7627-1038-1

Manufactured in the United States of America
Fifth Edition/First Printing

To those Kentuckians who,
with lots of love and humor,
continue to guide me off the beaten path
in all realms of life

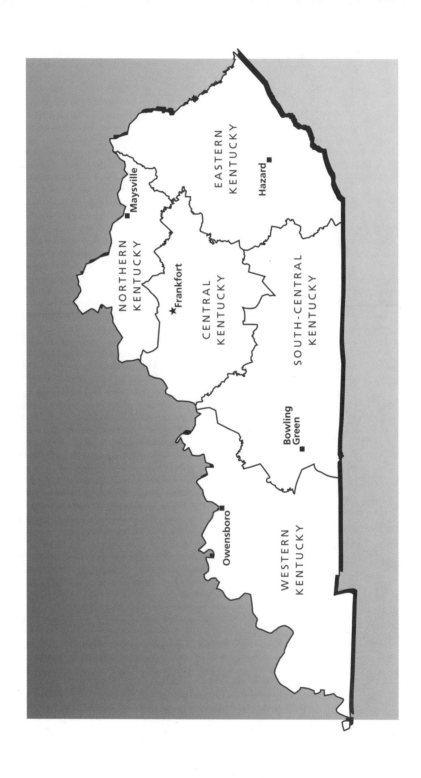

Contents

Introduction

In an age when *Vive la difference!* is our cultural rallying cry, Kentucky should be a traveler's sheer delight. This 40,000-square-mile stretch of land is home to a greater variety of distinct cultures than any other rural state in the United States. Our landscapes vary wildly, our accents fluctuate county to county, and we're downright contradictory, always have been. This contradictory nature is a quality that is both enjoyable and educational for locals as well as inquisitive outsiders. Despite being a longtime victim of simplified stereotypes, the Commonwealth of Kentucky doesn't include a single "typical Kentuckian." Where the edges of Kentucky's cultures overlap, delightful contrasts abound. Where else can you find hitching posts for horse and buggy rigs in a Druther's fast-food parking lot? Where else do you hear English spoken with a heavy German lilt and a thick Southern twang? Or an Elizabethan dialect with a drawl?

Maybe the contradictions started with Daniel Boone (what didn't?), who was torn between settling the land he loved passionately and, not trusting his fellow pioneers, merging with the native people who loved and adopted him. Maybe Kentucky's contradictory nature proved itself in bearing both Civil War presidents into the world within a year and fewer than 100 miles apart. The same waters that produce the world's smoothest bourbon and worst bootleg also sustained the life of Carrie Nation and continue to fill the teetotalers' baptismal fonts. Stereotypes of illiteracy are at loggerheads with a remarkable history of erudition and fine literary accomplishments, and the lack of national recognition for Kentucky's contributions to the high arts is suspect upon examination of the state's almost unequaled tradition of music, dance, and fine craft.

Then there's our geography, as erratic as Colorado's, yet older and more diverse in terms of flora and fauna. Vast, big-sky country dominates the western regions, where acre after fertile acre fan out, making a flat, midwestern horizon, ending in swampland and rich arable bottomland by the banks of the great Mississippi and Ohio Rivers. Central and northern Kentucky ride on a high, fertile plateau, where game has always grazed and where livestock continue to make the region wealthy and world famous for equine and bovine bloodlines. Eastern Kentucky's lush mountains are well rounded with age, well supplied with precious seams of coal and iron ore, and laced with clear, beautiful streams. The south-central region has a touch of it all, including some of the world's most spectacular caverns.

In this book I'm just giving you leads to places that you may not have otherwise found. Your job is to immerse yourself and explore everything with fresh eyes and an open heart. The people here are so friendly, you'll get tired of smiling.

The pleasure of traveling in Kentucky begins with studying the map. Read the names of our towns and you'll begin to believe that Kentucky soil grows poets (and humorists) even better than tobacco: Bear Wallow, Horse Fly Holler, Cat Creek, Dog Town, Dogwalk, Dog Trot, Maddog, The Bark Yard, Monkey's Eyebrow, Possum Trot, Terrapin, Otterpond, Buzzard Roost, Pigeon Roost, Beaver Bottom, Beaver Lick, Rabbit Hash, Chicken Bristle, Chicken City, Ticktown, Scuffletown, Coiltown, Gold City, Future City, Sublimity City, Preacherville, Fearsville, Shuckville (population 7), Spottsville, Jugville, Blandsville, Pleasureville, Touristville, Wisdom, Beauty, Joy, Temperance, Poverty, Chance, Energy, Victory, Democrat, Republican, The Mouth, Mouth Card, Dimple, Nuckles, Shoulderblade, Big Bone, Back Bone, Wish Bone, Marrowbone, Cheap, Habit, Whynot, Pinchem Slyly, Mossy Bottom, Needmore, Sugartit, Hot Spot, Climax, Limp, Subtle, Geneva, Moscow, Bagdad, Warsaw, Paris, London, Athens, Versailles, Ninevah, Sinai, Buena Vista, Key West, Texas, Pittsburg, Omaha, Yosemite, Two Mile Town, Four Mile, Ten Mile, Halfway, Twenty-six, Seventy-six, Eighty-eight, Bachelor's Rest, Belcher, Brodhead, Oddville, Waddy, Wax, Dot, Empire, Embryo, Factory, Tidal Wave, Troublesome Creek, Vortex, Princess, Savage, Clutts, Decoy, Thousand Sticks, Gravel Switch, Quicksand, Halo, Moon, Static, Nonesuch, No Creek, Slickaway, Slap Out, Sideview, Nonchalanta, Fleming-Neon, Hi Hat, Go Forth, Alpha, Zula, Zoe, Zag, Zebulon, Zilpo, Yamacraw, Yeaddis, Yerkes, Uz (YOOzee), Wooton, Tyewhoppety, Kinniconic, Willailla, Whoopflarea, Symsonia, Smilax, Escondida, Cutshin, Cubage, Dongola, Nada, Nada (NAdee), Nebo, Slemp, Se Ree, Gee, Gad, Glo, Guy, Ono, Uno, Ino, Elba, Ulva, Ula, Ep, Eden, Devil's Fork, Paradise, Hell'n Back, Kingdome Come, Hell Fer Certain.

Kentucky Travel at a Glance

Kentucky Tourism
Dept. KVG, P.O. Box 2011, Frankfort 40602; (800) 225–8747 or www.kentuckytourism.com

Regional and Local Tourism Offices
Ashland Area Visitors Bureau, 1509 Winchester Avenue, P.O. Box 987, Ashland 41105-0987; (800) 377–6249 or (606) 329–1007

Bardstown-Nelson County Touristand Convention Commission, 107 East Stephen Foster Avenue, Box 867, Bardstown 40004; (800) 638–4877 or (502) 348–4877

Berea Welcome Center, 201 North Broadway, Berea 40403; (800) 598–5263 or (859) 986–2540

Bowling Green-Warren County Tourism, 352 Three Springs Road, Bowling Green 42104; (800) 326–7465 or (270) 782–0800

Carroll County Tourism and Convention Commission, 515 Highland Street, P.O. Box 293, Carrollton 41008; (800) 325–4290 or (502) 732–7036

Cave City Tourism Center, 502 Mammoth Cave Street, Box 518, Cave City 42127; (800) 346–8908 or (270) 773–3131

Corbin Tourist Bureau, 101 North Depot Street, Corbin 40701; (800) 528–7123 or (606) 526–6390

Danville-Boyle County Tourism, 304 South Fourth Street, Danville 40422; (800) 755–0076 or (895) 236–7794

Elizabethtown Tourism Bureau, 1030 North Mulberry Street, Elizabethtown 42701; (800) 437–0092 or (270) 765–2175

Frankfort Tourist Commission, 100 Capital Avenue, Frankfort 40601; (800) 960–7200 or (502) 875–8687

Georgetown/Scott County Tourism, 399 Outlet Center Drive, Georgetown 40324; (888) 863–8600 or (502) 863–2547

Harlan County Chamber of Commerce, 117 North Cumberland Avenue, P.O. Box 268, Harlan 40831; (606) 573–4717

Harrodsburg Tourist Commission, 103 South Main, Harrodsburg 40330; (800) 355–9192 or (859) 734–2364

Henderson Welcome Center, 2961 U.S. 41 North, Henderson 42420; (800) 648–3128 or (270) 826–3128

Hopkinsville-Christian County Convention and Visitors Bureau, 2800 Fort Campbell Boulevard, P.O. Box 1382, Hopkinsville 42241; (800) 842–9959 or (270) 885–9096

Lexington Convention and Visitors Bureau, 301 East Vine Street, Lexington 40507; (800) 845–3959 or (859) 233–7299

Louisville and Jefferson County Information Center, Third and Market Streets, Louisville 40202; (800) 792–5595 or (502) 584–2121

INTRODUCTION

Maysville Visitor Center, 115 East Third Street, Maysville 41056;
(606) 564–6986

Morehead Tourism Commission, 150 East First Street, Morehead 40351;
(800) 654–1944 or (606) 784–6221

Murray Tourism Commission, 805 North Twelfth Street,
P.O. Box 190, Murray 42071; (800) 651–1603 or (270) 759–2199

Northern Kentucky Visitor Center, 605 Philadelphia Street,
Covington 41011; (800) STAY–NKY or (859) 655–4172

Owensboro-Daviess County Tourist Commission, 215 East Second
Street, Owensboro 42303; (800) 489–1131 or (270) 926–1100

Paducah-McCracken County Tourism, 128 Broadway, Box 90,
Paducah 42001; (800) 723–8224 or (270) 443–8783

Paris-Bourbon County Chamber, 525 High Street, Suite 114,
Paris 40361; (888) 987–3205

Richmond Tourism, 345 Lancaster Avenue, Richmond 40475;
(800) 866–3705 or (859) 626–8474

Somerset-Pulaski County Convention and Visitors Bureau, 522 Ogden
Street, P.O. Box 622, Somerset 42502; (800) 642–6287 or (606) 679–6394

Winchester/Clark County Chamber, 2 South Maple Street,
Winchester 40391; (800) 298–9105 or (859) 744–6420

Woodford County Chamber of Commerce, 141 North Main Street,
Box 442, Versailles 40383; (859) 873–5122

In an Emergency

All regions of the state use the 911 emergency number. Also, if you're
involved in an accident, call (800) 222–5555, the emergency dispatcher's
number for the Kentucky State Police.

Current Road Conditions

Call (800) 459–7623 for the Kentucky Transportation Cabinet's prere-
corded road report. Note: The highest speed limit in the state is 65 mph.

A Few Facts about the Commonwealth

Capital: Frankfort

Largest city: Louisville, population approximately 1 million (metro
area)

State bird: Kentucky cardinal

State flower: goldenrod

State fish: Kentucky bass

State horse: thoroughbred

State song: "My Old Kentucky Home" by Stephen Collins Foster; written 1853

State bluegrass song: "Blue Moon of Kentucky" by Bill Monroe; copyright 1947

Land area: 39,732 square miles; rank, 37

Highest elevation: 4,145 feet at Black Mountain

Lowest elevation: 257 feet, near the Mississippi River in Fulton County

A Few of the Many Famous Kentuckians

Bobbie Ann Mason, writer

Cassius Marcellus Clay, abolitionist, ambassador to Russia

Crystal Gayle, country singer

Dwight Yoakam, country singer

Gus Van Sant, award-winning movie director

Harry Dean Stanton, actor

Henry L. Faulkner, artist and poet

James Bowie, Texas Ranger who designed the Bowie knife

Jean Ritchie, folk singer/songwriter

Johnny Depp, actor

Kit Carson, agent for Native Americans

Lee Majors, actor

Loretta Lynn, country singer

Muhammad Ali, boxer

Ralph Eugene Meatyard, photographer

Tom T. Hall, country singer

Tom Cruise, actor

Wendell Berry, writer

Central Kentucky

Like nowhere else in the world, central Kentucky seems to have been created for horses. For this we can thank the rocks. Water percolates through the limestone strata and brings phosphates into the soil that, in turn, enrich plants like bluegrass (actually green with a subtle blue tint), which give our thoroughbreds strong, lightweight bones—perfect for racing. The same water is the magic ingredient in this region's world-famous bourbon whiskey.

Central Kentucky is also a kind of Mesopotamia of the South, a cradle of civilization west of the Allegheny Mountains. Modern buildings and businesses revolve around the region's direct links to the past. Antiques malls and bed-and-breakfasts in restored homes are ubiquitous in central Kentucky, and many of the humorous sites, like old country stores, are funny precisely because of their anachronisms. But there's nothing homogeneous about an area that can comfortably be home to everyone from Trappist monks to soul food chefs, jockeys, millionaires, Amish farmers, sculptors, and yoga teachers. And there's no chance you'll be bored exploring it all.

Bluegrass on the Rocks

Wherever there is bluegrass, there are horse farms. To get a good long look at some of the world's best-known horse farms, start in **Lexington.** Take a drive on Harrodsburg Road, Old Frankfort Pike, Iron Works Pike, Paris Pike, Danville Road, or Versailles Road. Many of these and the smaller lanes that weave through them make wonderful bicycling routes. The miles of wooden-plank fences are dizzying; these days most are sprayed with a black, creosote-based paint instead of the traditional white. Dotting the countryside are ostentatious mansions and lavish horse barns where handmade wainscoting and brass chandeliers are not unheard of.

Lexington is surrounded by hundreds of horse farms. The most famous are the thoroughbred farms, where the top racehorses in the world are

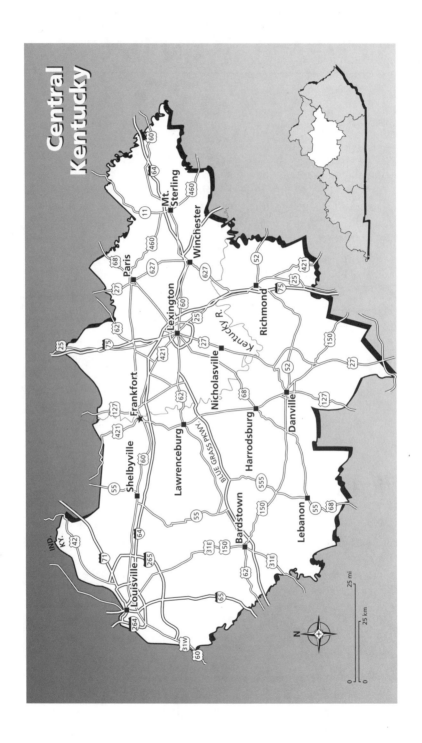

Central Kentucky

Mt. Sterling
Winchester
Paris
Lexington
Richmond
Frankfort
Nicholasville
Danville
Shelbyville
Lawrenceburg
Harrodsburg
Lebanon
Bardstown
Louisville

BLUE GRASS PKWY.
Kentucky R.

IND.
KY.

25 mi
25 km

N

bred, born, trained, and retired. Amid those gangly-legged foals you see romping in the fields in the spring may be a future Kentucky Derby—or Epsom or French Derby—winner.

Thoroughbreds are just one of many horse breeds raised on farms in and around Lexington. Standardbreds, American saddlebreds, draft horses, miniatures—all kinds of equines call Lexington home. Visitor policies on farms vary widely. Several local tour companies, including *Historic and Horse Farm Tours, Inc.* (859–268–2906) and *Blue Grass Tours* (859–252–5744) offer horse farm tours. An excellent option for independent types is the tour of the stallion division of *Three Chimneys* (859–873–7053), located on Old Frankfort Pike between Lexington and Midway. Notable racing champions, including 1977 Triple Crown winner Seattle Slew, reside at Three Chimneys, and during the tour you'll meet some of them up-close. Tours are offered February through November, strictly by appointment. Call (859) 873–7053 for reservations and directions to the farm.

The best way to find out which farms are currently open is to call or stop by the *Lexington Convention and Visitors Bureau* (859–233–7299 or 800–845–3959), which keeps updated information. The bureau is in downtown Lexington at 301 East Vine Street. There's no admission charge to tour individual farms, but keep in mind that it's traditional to tip the groom who shows you around, at least $5.00 to $10.00.

ZOE'S TOP PICKS IN CENTRAL KENTUCKY
Abbey of Gethsemani, New Haven; (502) 549–3117
Actors Theatre, Louisville; (502) 584–1205 or (800) 428–5849
American Printing House for the Blind, Louisville; (800) 223–1839
Bernheim Forest Arboretum, Bardstown; (502) 543–2451
Harry C. Miller Lock Collection, Nicholasville; (859) 885–6041
Kentucky History Center, Frankfort; (502) 564–3016
Peace Roots Studio, Harrodsburg; (859) 734–5271
Rhodes Hall Art Gallery, Nerinx; (502) 865–5811
Shaker Village of Pleasant Hill, Harrodsburg; (800) 734–5611
Weisenberger Mill, Midway; (859) 254–5282

True Blue

Lexington was such a cultural center in the early 1800s that it was known as the "Athens of the West."

While you're at the visitors center, pick up a free copy of the *Lexington Walk and Bluegrass Country Driving Tour* guide, which directs your attention to specific histories while you absorb horse-farm aesthetics. The visitors center also offers special guides on more than a dozen topics of special interest, from antiques stores to area museums.

The *Kentucky Horse Park* (859–233–4303), located a few miles north of downtown on Iron Works Pike, is not off the beaten path in any

True Blue

sense, but it is a great place to see all kinds of real horses, from thoroughbreds to rare breeds. There are some lesser-known aspects of this 1,032-acre park. Everybody stops at the Man o' War statue and grave, but take time also to visit the grave of Isaac Murphy. Here's a reminder of the important and largely unheralded role African-Americans played in the early days of thoroughbred racing. Fourteen of the fifteen riders in the first Kentucky Derby were Black. Murphy, born in Lexington in 1861, remains the all-time most winning jockey, achieving victory in 44 percent of his races.

The Kentucky Horse Park is an educational center as well as a tourist attraction. So in addition to watching the films and looking at the antique carriages and other exhibits in the museum, be sure to walk through the Big Barn. You might find future horse trainers or veterinarians hard at work or meet some members of the Mustang Troop, Lexington inner-city youngsters who come to the park to care for once-wild western mustangs. The Mustang Troop rode in the 1997 Presidential Inaugural Parade.

Horses have been a favorite subject of artists, and the William G. Kenton Gallery, part of the park's *International Museum of the Horse,* is host

Jot 'Em Down

*S*top by the **Jot 'Em Down Store** *at the intersection of Iron Works Pike and Russell Cave Road. Once called Terrell's Grocery, this little store has long been a favorite hangout for horse-farm employees. Founder Robert Terrell remembered the late 1930s, when his father and uncle listened for fifteen minutes every night to a radio show called* Lum and Abner, *a comedic series about two store owners much like themselves. Lum was tall and savvy, while Abner was short, dim-witted, and funny. The fictional characters ran a grocery called the Jot 'Em*

Down Store in Pine Ridge, Arkansas. The Terrells' customers got into the habit of calling them Lum and Abner and began adopting character names from the show, like Mousie and Grandpappy Spears. Once when the real Lum and Abner were in Lexington buying horses, they heard about the tradition at Terrell's Grocery, so they dropped in for a visit, bringing with them a sign that read Jot 'Em Down Store. The rest is history. Come by for sandwiches and beers and you will meet Robert Terrell II ("Robey"), who has run the store since his father's death in 1998.

to fascinating exhibits from around the globe. A world-exclusive exhibit planned for 2003, "All the Queen's Horses: History of the Horse in the British Isles," will include $150 million worth of artifacts from Roman times to the present. Something interesting is always on display, so don't skip over the gallery.

The Kentucky Horse Park is open from 9:00 A.M. to 5:00 P.M. daily April through October and from 9:00 A.M. to 5:00 P.M. Wednesday through Sunday November through March. There are many special shows and events throughout the year. Admission is $12.00 spring through fall, $9.00 in winter.

True Blue
Kentucky has more than 1,500 miles of marked hiking trails.

To experience other important aspects of Kentucky's equine industry, go to the races or one of the big sales. Late April through May, and in late September and early October, standardbred horses race at the ***Red Mile Harness Track*** (859–255–0752 or 800–354–9092), located off South Broadway, just a few blocks from the downtown business district. Great trotters and pacers have been racing this track and provoking bets since 1875. Tattersalls Sales holds a variety of standardbred auctions at the track throughout the year.

Across the street from the Red Mile at 711 Red Mile Road, Lexington 40504 (859–252–3481), is a small riding apparel store called ***Le Cheval Ltd.*** Paige Kahn tailors custom-made riding apparel for clients from coast to coast. The store is open weekdays and Saturday mornings. Even if you're not in the market for a $1,500 riding suit, the fine designs are worth seeing.

About 43 percent of all the thoroughbred horses sold in North America are sold at public horse sales in Kentucky. And the most prestigious horse sale in the world is the July Selected Yearling Sale at

The Mysterious Castle

*J*ust west of Keeneland on Versailles Road (Highway 60) is a castle surrounded by stone walls and mysterious rumors. According to the rumors, a slew of celebrities have owned it, including actor Lee Majors, but the truth is that the original owner and builder, Rex Martin, still owns the property but is looking to sell it. He and his ex-wife had the castle built as a residence in 1969; inside the turreted wall is a 10,400-square-foot, six-bedroom house complete with a huge library and swimming pool. Add chickens, goats, and peasants, and you'd have a medieval village fort.

Keeneland Race Course (4201 Versailles Road, Lexington 40510; 859–254–3412 or 800–456–3412) in Lexington. This sale dates to 1943, and the horses sold must meet high bloodline and conformation standards. The bidders are an impressive group, too. From sheiks and film stars to international business moguls and Texas cowboys, you just never know who you'll see at the Keeneland sales pavilion. But you can bet that they will have one thing in common: the means and the desire to spend big bucks on horses. The world-record price for a horse ($13.1 million) was set at this sale. You don't have to be a millionaire just to watch the sales from the pavilion lobby, or to walk through the barns while the horses are being shown to potential buyers. It's a fascinating and surreal experience. Additional sales are held at Keeneland in January, September, and November.

Race meets at Keeneland are brief (just three weeks in April and three weeks in October), but they usually attract the top echelon of the thoroughbred world. The spring meet includes the Blue Grass Stakes, an important preparatory race to the Kentucky Derby. The atmosphere is relaxed and genteel (until 1997, the track didn't even have a public address system), and this is one of the few tracks in North America where the public is allowed access to the barn areas. Keeneland is worth a visit at any time of year. The old stone buildings and grounds are lovely, and at the track's training center, you can catch early morning workouts year-round. Plan to have breakfast at the track kitchen.

Lexington boasts plenty of beautiful mansions, many dating to the early 1800s. One of the historic houses open for tour is *The Hunt-Morgan House* (201 North Mill Street, Lexington 40507; 859–253–0362). This lovely Federal-style brick house was built in 1814 by John Wesley Hunt, an early Lexington entrepreneur believed to be Kentucky's first millionaire. Later residents included Thomas Hunt Morgan, who won a Nobel Prize for medicine in 1933. Civil War buffs will be interested in the collection of uniforms, weapons, pictures, and other items relating to its most flamboyant occupant, Confederate general John Hunt Morgan. The escapades of Morgan and his "Morgan's Raiders" are recounted to this day in many a Kentucky community. Tour guides tell visitors that Morgan is reputed to have ridden his horse into the front hall of the house, kissed his mother, and galloped out the back door, with Union troops in hot pursuit. Morgan must have had a thing about riding his horse in the house, because there's a similar story attached to a house Morgan and his troops occupied in Lebanon, Kentucky. If you like old houses, you'll enjoy strolling in the surrounding Gratz Park neighborhood, Lexington's most posh address in the early 1800s.

Several historic Lexington homes operate as bed-and-breakfasts. At *The Brand House at Rose Hill* (461 Limestone Street, Lexington 40508; 859–226–9464), you can enjoy nineteenth-century charm along with modern comforts such as whirlpools. Pam and Logan Leet bought the 1812 house at auction in 1994, then painstakingly renovated it into a luxurious city getaway. The house is within easy walking distance of most downtown attractions. The five rooms, each with private bath, range from $109 to $259 per night. The five guest rooms at *A True Inn* (467 West Second Street, Lexington 40507 859–252–6166 or 800–374–6151) are named for historic Lexingtonians, from statesman Henry Clay and First Lady Mary Todd Lincoln to Belle Brezing, the city's most famous madam (thought to be the inspiration for the Belle Watling character in *Gone With the Wind*). The inn itself, an 1843 Romanesque-style brick house, is named for owners Bobby and Beverly True. Rates start at about $95 per night.

Consider a man who was a jewelry designer known to drape diamond necklaces around the stubby red neck of his dachshund, Ernie, then send the dog out to model them for potential clients who were sunbathing by the swimming pool at the Bel Air Hotel. Try to imagine what kind of museum such a man would build. When you give up, take a drive west from downtown on the Old Frankfort Pike to the *Headley-Whitney Museum* (859–225–6653). Originally, the late George W. Headley III established the space at his home to privately display his jewel collection, but in 1968 he and his wife opened the place to the public. Headley died in 1985, but the legacy of his museum continued. In the dramatic setting of the Jewel Room, visitors could once marvel at Headley's unusual jeweled boxes and bibelots, ranging from a ruby-encrusted abalone horse head to a scene of the moon landing in semiprecious stones. Unfortunately, in a sensational 1994 heist, burglars made off with many of the pieces. Since the robbery, the museum has increased its focus on fine decorative arts and features changing exhibits of clothing, textiles, and furniture. There are still many Headley creations on display, loaned by private owners, and if you need further evidence of his eccentricity, you need only step into the Shell Grotto—an entire room encrusted with thousands of seashells. The museum is open from 10:00 A.M. to 5:00 P.M. Tuesday through Friday and from noon to 5:00 P.M. Saturday and Sunday. It's closed in January. The grounds are elegant for picnicking. Old Frankfort Pike is a great place for biking; part of it is an official National Scenic Byway.

For more art, the Lexington Art League has its offices and a small gallery in a strange, castellated 1852 Gothic villa in downtown Lexington, one of five designed by the architect A. J. Davis. The exhibitions at the *Loudoun House* provide a taste of the work of some visual artists in the area. A national juried exhibition every January called (and featuring) *The Nude* is the most popular event. From downtown go north on North Broadway and turn right (east) on Loudon Avenue, then bear left when you reach a V in the road. Turn right onto Castlewood Drive. Hours are noon to 4:00 P.M. Tuesday through Friday and 1:00 to 4:00 P.M. on weekends (859–254–7024). Ask about upcoming fourth Friday "Alternative Happy Hour" events.

Despite being central Kentucky's second-largest tourist attraction (the largest is Kentucky Horse Park), the *Lexington Children's Museum* is something of a hidden treasure. It is hidden to adults because we might assume it's not for us. Think again. I found myself replanning the design of my shower stall after playing in the "bubble area," where you stand in a funny little booth and pull a giant vertical bubble completely around you, while watching it all in a fun-house mirror. Being confronted with "kid" information is also humbling. The ever-changing display areas range from cultural exhibitions about the Ukraine to a hands-on exhibit about how animation works. The favorite educational area is a walk-through human heart, a series of sculpted and marvelously painted plaster chambers representing ventricles and auricles, all vibrating to the constant beat of our most powerful muscle. This megaheart was designed (and made, in part) by medical illustrator Rick Gersony, who is also one of the pen-and-ink illustrators for this book. This museum is an all-day treat at the price of $3.00 per person; children under two admitted free.

The museum is located downtown, in Victorian Square, a complex of renovated nineteeth century commerical buildings at the corner of Vine and Broadway. Call (859) 258–3253 for more information.

Lexington is Kentucky's second largest city, so there are all manner of eateries and shops, but there are a few special places, oddballs, or old standbys that you may miss. *Flag Fork Herb Farm Gift Shop* at 900 North Broadway, Lexington 40505 (859–233–7381), has transplanted a little bit of country into the city. In 1994 Mike and Carrie Creech moved their gardens from a farm in rural Franklin County to Lexington. Behind the shop, a 1790s carriage house, are large herb, perennial, and everlasting gardens. The shop carries live plants, dried herbs, jellies, potpourri, and handmade soaps. Hours are 10:00 A.M. to 6:00 P.M. Tuesday through Saturday. You can have lunch or afternoon dessert at The

Garden Cafe, which overlooks the bird-feeding garden. Cafe hours are 11:00 A.M. to 2:00 P.M. for lunch and 2:00 to 4:00 P.M. for beverages and dessert Tuesday through Saturday. Call (859) 252–6837 for reservations.

The *Atomic Cafe* (859–254–1969), located in an old corner building near downtown at 265 North Limestone, Lexington 40507 (across Third Street from Transylvania University), is definitely a hot place to eat. Guinness on tap and a huge basket of spicy sweet-potato chips are reasons enough to go. The whole menu is Caribbean, ranging from a savory chicken pot pie to spicy lime shrimp. In good weather there's outdoor patio seating. Indoors, the cafe tends to be loud and lively. Island murals cover the walls from floor to ceiling. Dinner only; closed on Monday.

In most parts of the world, more business is done over tea than martinis. So contends Gay Redding, an owner of *Greentree Tearoom* at 521 Short Street, Lexington 40507. The Greentree was designed to be the kind of tearoom even the business crowd could appreciate—elegant, stylish, and impressive. "There's not a touch of Victoriana anywhere," Redding says proudly. Instead, there are crisp white tablecloths, fresh flowers, fine porcelain, and five courses of delicious food served in a bright and airy atmosphere. A recent menu featured artichoke soup, cheese scones with sun-dried tomatoes, penne pasta with cream sauce, tea sandwiches, and a choice of desserts, including Italian cream cake and tiramisu. (With food like that, who needs martinis!) Located in a renovated 1901 cottage near downtown, the Greentree shares space with Greentree Antiques and L. V. Harkness, a home accessories and gift shop. So if you're not on a tight schedule, you can browse amid a collection of fine (and pricey) furniture, china, crystal, and decorative items. Tea is $15.95, with seatings at noon and 3:00 P.M. Wednesday through Saturday. Call (859) 455–9660 for reservations.

A co-owner of Greentree is the chef, John Martin, who has a devoted following of fans in Lexington. He's also responsible for the wonderful gourmet box lunches served at *The Gingko Tree,* a seasonal eatery located on the grounds at Ashland, the Henry Clay Estate, a historic home east of downtown Lexington. The components sound ordinary— choice of sandwich, side, dessert, and beverage— but you'll never think so after tasting the curried chicken salad, spicy tomato aspic, or absolutely addictive brown sugar cake. You get all for around $9.00, and the lovely setting is free. Before or after lunch, stroll through the formal English parterre garden. Or pay a few dollars and tour the restored eighteen-room mansion, home to descendants of nineteenth-century statesman and presidential candidate Henry Clay. The Gingko Tree is open from 11:00 A.M. to 4:00 P.M. daily April through October, weather permitting. The garden is open dawn to dusk daily, year-round. House tours are given from 10:00 A.M. to 4:30 P.M. Monday through Saturday and from 1:00 to 4:30 P.M. Sunday. The house is closed in January and on Mondays November through March. Ashland is located at 120 Sycamore Road, Lexington 40502, off Richmond Road. Call (859) 266–8581 for more information.

True Blue

Kentucky became a state in 1792, as the fifteenth state.

Alfalfa Restaurant was probably one of thousands of health-food cooperative restaurants that opened on extremely limited budgets in the early 1970s. But it survived. With varnished shipping pallets for wainscoting and big chalkboards for menus, it's a good, unpretentious place to eat. Although it is not purely vegetarian, it does emphasize meatless health food, not to mention potent deserts and cinnamon coffee. Come hungry. There's live music right by your table, ranging from jazz flute to Irish bouzouki. Alfalfa's is across from the main gate of the University of Kentucky, 557 South Limestone Street. Open for lunch daily and for dinner Tuesday through Sunday (859–253–0014).

Another university-area eatery, *Joe Bologna's* (606–252–4933) has been a favorite Lexington hangout since the early 1970s, and not just for students. In the early 1990s it moved across the street from its original location to a restored church building at 120 West Maxwell Street—the bar is sacrilegiously located right where the altar used to be, and televisions are everywhere. Joe B's is the place to go for pizza and other Italian dishes. You must order the famous breadstick, served in a sinful pool of garlic butter. For a dinner that's a bit more expensive, but much more Italian, try *Giuseppe's Ristorante Italiano.* Go south out of town on Nicholasville Road ½-mile beyond Man o' War, and look for the sign on the left. A great wine list dominated by Chianti is featured. Call (859) 272–4269 for reservations, a recommended practice.

Almost directly across Nicholasville Road is the *Waveland State Historic Site* (859–272–3611), a grand Greek Revival mansion that was built in 1847 by Joseph Bryan, the grandnephew of Daniel Boone. Guided tours cost $6.00 and are offered between March and December, Monday through Saturday from 10:00 A.M. to 5:00 P.M. and on Sunday from 1:00 to 5:00 P.M. You'll see all aspects of life on an antebellum plantation, from the smokehouse and icehouse to the servants' quarters and some remarkable period furnishings. The most intriguing object is a hickory ladderback chair that originally came from the home of Daniel Boone's parents in Pennsylvania. The chair was tied to the side of a packhorse in 1779 to make a seat for the two-year-old Rebecca Boone Grant, Daniel's niece, as her family traveled to Kentucky from North Carolina.

For an unusually intimate look at the workaday world of thorough-bred training, plan to tour the ***Kentucky Horse Center,*** 3380 Paris Pike, Lexington 40511. From downtown Lexington take North Broadway out of town, which becomes Paris Pike (or Highways 68 and 27). After a few miles, look for the horse center on your right. Since 1969, when this business was started, it has been one of the most prestigious, privately owned thoroughbred training centers in the world. More than 1,100 stalls are leased to individual horse owners, who supply their own trainers and riders.

The tour takes you through a barn, by the rail where you can talk to a trainer, and into the sales pavilion, where you'll be amazed at the complexity of yet another aspect of the business—horse sales. Tours take one and a half hours and cost $10.00 for adults, $5.00 for children. They're given at 10:30 A.M. Monday through Friday. Call ahead, because tour space is limited (859–293–1853). Either before or after the tour, stop by the extensive tack shop, where you may luck into an opportunity to watch leather workers in action.

We all love to experience a time warp, and now that everyone's into retro, campy fashion, you have to love the ***Bourbon Bowl,*** just south of Paris on Highway 68. This place has not changed since it opened in the 1960s. Owner Sue White swears that she will never install an automatic scoring system or radically alter the decor. This place is super clean, and people say that the snack bar serves the best cheeseburgers in town. Saturday is "red-pin night" (if the red pin comes up in your lane as the head pin and you get a strike, then you win a free game and the admiration of your fellow bowlers). Call (859) 987–3161.

True meat-and-potatoes fans will want to check out ***Van Hoose Steak and Tavern*** (859–987–6180), where only fresh steak is served. The meat, which is never frozen, is cut in the kitchen, so it's as tender as a steak can be. There isn't a steak knife in the house. Prices are fairly reasonable. After 9:00 P.M. on weekends, there is live country music. Go to downtown ***Paris*** on Main Street and watch for it on the right. The bar is open from 4:00 P.M. to 1:00 A.M. Monday through Saturday, and the dining room is open for lunch Monday through Friday and for dinner Monday through Saturday.

Van Hoose would have had a serious competitor in the late eighteenth century when the ***Duncan Tavern,*** at 323 High Street, Paris 40361, was in its heyday. Major Joseph Duncan built the huge inn out of native limestone on High Street in 1788, four years before Kentucky was a state. Everything else in town was built of logs, so the tavern was an eye-catcher as well as a social catchall. Originally there was a ballroom, a bar, a billiards room, dining rooms, kitchens, and bedrooms. Daniel Boone slept there. So did frontiersman Simon Kenton.

Today the Duncan Tavern and Anne Duncan House is a historic site owned by the Kentucky Society of the Daughters of the American Revolution, which has acquired enough period furniture and significant artifacts to fill the huge building gracefully. Much of the original large furniture was built on-site. Its tradition as a tavern is maintained by keeping it active as a party place: People can rent the Duncan Tavern for parties and receptions. The D.A.R. hosts small events in the original dining room and serves meals on a long, cherry, boardinghouse-style table, valued at $30,000. Normally the tavern and genealogy library are open to visitors Tuesday through Saturday from 10:00 A.M. to noon and from 1:00 to 4:00 P.M. Tours are given Tuesday through Saturday at 10:30 A.M., 1:30 P.M., and 3:00 P.M. Admission to the tavern is $4.00; the genealogy library is $2.50. However, in late 2000 the tavern closed temporarily for extensive exterior and interior restoration work, and may be closed for most of 2001. Call (859) 987–1788.

Another historic building being kept alive by means of regular use is the *L&N Depot,* between Tenth Street and Winchester Road. Built in the early 1800s, this station saw lots of Civil War action, and Theodore Roosevelt is said to have made a whistle-stop speech here. Today it houses the *Iron Rail Restaurant,* the dubiously self-proclaimed "Home of Home Cooking." Buffet only. Closed Monday. Call (859) 987–4422.

Learn about area history at the *Hopewell Museum* (859–987–7274), in a proud little building at the corner of Eighth and Pleasant Streets. Admission is $2.00, and hours are Wednesday through Saturday from noon to 5:00 P.M. and Sunday from 2:00 to 4:00 P.M. Closed in January. Just up the street is the *Nannine Clay Wallis Arboretum,* 616 Pleasant Street, Paris 40361, at the headquarters of the Garden Club of Kentucky (859–987–6158). A "study guide" for tree identification is available. Admission is free, and hours are Monday through Saturday from 10:00 A.M. to 6:00 P.M. and Sunday from noon to 6:00 P.M.

Another way to travel into the past and yet satisfy the desires of your contemporary senses is to spend some time at *Amelia's Field Country Inn,* 2 miles north of downtown Paris on Highway 27. First, you should know that the farm functions as an all-organic CSA (community supported agriculture) project, basically a massive kitchen garden that supplies nongardening members with fresh produce on a weekly basis for a set rate, paid in advance at the beginning of the season. In this way, the customers are intimately connected with the grower, even taking the seasonal financial risk. The risk is small, however, and the rewards are great in this and other such operations. You may be taking a greater risk by buying produce at the grocery store, which may have been sprayed with unspeakable chemicals or irradiated, probably grown in ways that are detrimental to the land.

Amelia's Field is co-owned by Joseph Clay and chef Mark May, who make wonderful use of the fresh produce and free-range chickens by serving classy, beautiful French Provençal meals either indoors or outdoors on the garden terrace. You must make reservations to dine, or

Moonshine and Woodcarvings

You'd better sit down for this one: The father of bourbon whiskey was a Baptist preacher. According to legend, the good Reverend Elijah Craig ran a distillery, a hemp rope walk, and a paper mill (the first in the state). A fire swept through a building where barrels were being stored, and being something of a tightwad, Reverend Craig decided to put new corn whiskey into the charred barrels despite the damage. The color of the whiskey changed, the flavor mellowed, and a tradition was born. Eventually this new sour mash was named bourbon because large quantities were made in nearby Bourbon County. Baptists, don't despair. In the late eighteenth century, Baptists were not as concerned with temperance. Drunkenness among preachers was prohibited, but drinking was not. In fact, clergy often were paid in whiskey. Gambling, dancing, and going to barbecues, on the other hand, were considered serious crimes.

*Elijah Craig's sundry enterprises were all built near the **Royal Spring**, a steady water source gurgling up from under a huge bed of limestone, discovered in 1774. Georgetown was built around the spring, and the city still gets its water from it. A small park around the spring is the site of an 1874 log cabin built by a former slave, Milton Leach, and a 1997 wooden statue of Elijah Craig by Georgetown artist Sandy Schu. This is no typical woodcarving; it was created using a chainsaw from a tree still rooted in the park grounds. Other examples of Schu's noisy yet surprisingly detailed work can be seen throughout the area. He created the buffalo on display at Cardome Centre, north of downtown. His 20-foot eagle inspires golfers at the twelfth hole of Kearney Hill Links golf course in Lexington. For more information about Royal Spring and other Georgetown attractions, call **Scott County Tourism** at (502) 863-2547.*

you might just miss out on the chance to savor poached shrimp in spiced carrot juice or grilled salmon with wild mushrooms. The inn is also a lodging, offering four traditionally appointed rooms in the 1936 Georgian-style country mansion. Rates are $75 or $100 per night. For reservations call (859) 987–5778, or write Amelia's Field at 617 Cynthiana Road, Paris 40361-8859.

Bourbon County has more than eighty-five horse farms, but very few allow visitors. One exception is **Claiborne Farm,** home and burial place of the celebrated Triple Crown winner Secretariat, which generously welcomes visitors by appointment only. Call (859) 233–4252 or (859) 987–2330. From downtown Paris go south on Highway 627 (also called Winchester Road) beyond the edge of town. Watch for the farm entrance on your left.

Cane Ridge Meeting House Shrine is the site of some powerful events and the source of some wild stories. Follow Main Street (Highway 68) north from downtown Paris and go east on Highway 460 to Highway 537 North. Take the latter for 5.6 miles and look left (west) for the shrine. Said to be the largest one-room log structure in the state, the church is impressive.

Two events make this church significant. The first was the Cane Ridge Revival, which took place August 7–12, 1801. It was one of the nation's largest revivals during a period of big ones. Preachers stood on stumps and hay bales all over the yard, talking simultaneously to 30,000 people for seven days and six nights. As the story goes, women's hair stood straight out and crackled like fire; people spoke in tongues, barked, shook, danced, and were moved every which way by the Holy Spirit. The excitement ended only when the food ran out. The second event occurred in 1804, when the new Cane Ridge preacher, Barton Warren Stone, led the people away from the Presbyterian Church and started a new, nondenominational movement that, after linking with the Campbell movement in Virginia, became the Christian Church, Disciples of Christ. Today the denomination (which numbers nearly two million) owns and manages the shrine. In 1957 an enormous limestone superstructure was erected to protect the log building. Later a museum was built nearby. From April through October the whole place is open daily, from 9:00 A.M. to 5:00 P.M. Donations are accepted. Call (859) 987–5350.

Downtown **Georgetown** is chock-full of history. It's also a good place for a walk. *Fava's Restaurant,* established in 1910 on East Main Street (502–863-4383), is a true diner in the old style (which are fast becoming extinct in Kentucky), where you can eat breakfast, lunch, or have three o'clock coffee and argue local issues with politicians and merchants.

If you're interested in antiques, look in any direction. In a state as obsessed with old stuff as Kentucky, any town that dares call itself the Antiques Capital of Kentucky better be able to back up that claim with something substantial. Georgetown does, with five malls all within easy walking distance of the courthouse. If it's old, you probably can find it at the **Central Kentucky Antique Mall, Wyatt's Antique Center, Hoot and Nana's, The Vault** (housed in an old bank building), or the **Georgetown Antique Mall.** In addition to its Main Street building, the latter includes a building around the corner at 199 South Broadway, where Liz Cox does picture framing, custom leaded- and stained-glass work, and what she calls "family heirloom bears." Say your great-grandmother had a fur coat, but it's gotten damaged by moths over the years. You can take what's left to Liz Cox, and she'll transform it into lovable Mama, Papa, or Baby bears. She makes bears from vintage clothing and fabric as well as fur. At press time, the scuttlebutt in Georgetown was that the building housing Liz's business was going to be demolished to become a bank drive-through area. In that event, Liz said, she'll probably move her business, **Heirlooms,** to another downtown location ("but not too far away") and will try to keep the same phone number—(502) 863–2538.

The old buildings on Georgetown's Main Street have seen other changes in recent years. When the post office moved from Main and Mulberry to a new suburban building, many residents were concerned about the fate of the stately limestone building that had housed the post office since the early 1900s. They were thrilled when the county purchased the building as a home for the **Georgetown and Scott County Museum.** The museum features a variety of displays about local history, from bourbon to ballpoints, with special programs on local history every month. The marble-floored lobby of the post office has been left pretty much intact. Museum hours are 9:00 A.M. to 4:00 P.M. Monday through Friday, 10:00 A.M. to 4:00 P.M. Saturday. Admission is free. Call (502) 863–6201.

From downtown Georgetown take Highway 25 North out of town and watch for signs to **Cardome Centre** (502–863–1575), a property that has played a significant role in Kentucky history for hundreds of years. After having been a major hunting ground for Choctaw, Mingo, and Shawnee Indians, it was one of the first areas deeded and settled west of the mountains. It was home to a number of early prominent white families during the 1800s, including James F. Robinson, a Kentucky governor, who gave the place its name, Cardome, after the Latin phrase *cara domus,* or "dear

Lawrenceburg, *county seat of Anderson County, was named for nineteenth-century U.S. Navy captain James Lawrence, who is credited with coining the phrase "Don't give up the ship."*

home." The Sisters of Visitation, a cloistered sect, bought Cardome in 1896 and ran an academy there until 1969. Now Cardome belongs to the City of Georgetown and operates as an educational center and historic site, open for self-guided tours Monday through Friday from 8:00 A.M. to 4:00 P.M. Visitors can walk through the original academy and monastery buildings as well as a science classroom and a "dream house," where the senior girls were finally allowed to have outside visitors and even to smoke. Cardome's pride and joy is the school chapel, which features some gorgeous woodwork, Romanesque vaulted ceilings, stained-glass windows, and a classic bell tower. The whole property can be rented for huge company picnics, or smaller areas can be used for weddings, seminars, meetings, and so forth.

Adjacent to Cardome is a sight you don't see everyday in Kentucky, or for that matter, in most places—a Japanese-style garden. But **Yuko-En on the Elkhorn** is, in fact, "the official Kentucky–Japan Friendship Garden." The garden was envisioned by members of the Scott Education and Community Foundation as a way to commemorate the tenth anniversary of the sister city relationship between Georgetown and Tahara-cho, Japan. Dignitaries from Tahara-cho came to Georgetown for the dedication of the garden in September 2000. At the time, Yuko-En was nothing more than mounds of dirt and a concrete pagoda or two. Since then, the garden slowly has been taking shape and ultimately will include a bamboo grove, an arched bridge over a small pond, various plantings, and a Zen meditation garden. All told it will cover some five acres along Highway 25. By Japanese garden standards, that's huge! Call (502) 863–9097 for more information.

While a Japanese garden may be a new idea in Georgetown and Scott County, growing things certainly isn't. Across Highway 25 from Cardome is **Bi-Water Farm** (502–863–3676), one of a bumper crop of Scott County farm markets. Bi-Water, run by the Fister family, features flowers and herbs as well as homegrown vegetables. The farm's Autumnfest runs several weekends in the fall with hayrides, a corn maze, and other family activities. Another branch of the Fister family runs **Double Stink Hog Farm** (with a name like that, you just have to love it), located at the intersections of Highway 460 and Newtown Pike about 5 miles east of Georgetown (502–863–3437). Double Stink has its own fall extravaganza, Pumpkinfest, and as the name suggests, the huge pick-your-own pumpkin patch is the main attraction here. Not far from Double Stink on Newtown Pike is **Evans Farm Orchard** (502-863-4550), which features tomatoes, squash, and other hot-weather veggies in the summer and dozens of apple varieties late summer through fall. **Amerson Farm Orchard** (502-863-3799) on the Highway 62 bypass also features vegetables and apples. So, summer through fall, this is a great place to load up on farm-fresh food. All are open on weekends; weekday hours vary.

One of the best-selling family sedans in America, the Camry, as well as Avalon sedans and Sienna minivans, are made in Georgetown at **Toyota Motor Manufacturing, Kentucky, Inc.,** on Cherry Blossom Way (exit 129 from I-75). Hour-long guided tours of the plant are given several times a day Monday through Friday, by reservation. Call (800) 866-4485. No shorts, cameras, or children under first grade are allowed. You'll don a hard hat and safety goggles and ride an electric tram through the stamping, body weld, and assembly areas of the plant. The plant is a big—about eight million square feet under roof—bright, and noisy place, all the more mind-boggling when you consider that nearly 400,000 vehicles and 500,000 engines are made here each year. Plant tours usually get booked far in advance, but you can stop by and look at the cars and manufacturing exhibits at the visitors center any time between 8:30 A.M. and 4:00 P.M. Monday through Friday.

In the Beginning

I n the beginning there was **Harrodsburg.**

A friend of mine swears that it takes a Harrodsburg resident, in any conversation, less than four minutes to bring up the fact that the genesis of the American West is Harrodsburg, Kentucky. On June 16, 1774, James Harrod and his company took a great leap of faith and of foot when they chose to settle the fertile strip of land between the Kentucky and Salt Rivers, the "Big Spring"—more than 250 miles of wilderness and mountains away from the nearest Anglo-Saxon settlement to the east.

Today Harrodsburg sports a full reproduction of the 1775 fort in the **Old Fort Harrod State Park,** at the intersection of Highways 68 and 127, a good place to begin your exploration of one of the state's significant historic areas. (Oddly, the reproduction fort is not exactly sited where the original stood.) Inside the park's entrance is the **Mansion Museum,** featuring Civil War artifacts, and the **Lincoln Marriage Shrine,** a red brick building that protects the log chapel where Abraham

Lincoln's parents "got hitched." Inside the fort's walls, people in period costumes demonstrate pioneer crafts during the summer. The fort is open to the public year-round, and from March 16 to November 30 the museum is also open. Hours vary by season. Admission is charged. Call (859) 734–3314.

Behind the fort in the James Harrod Amphitheater, **The Legend of Daniel Boone,** a high-adventure drama, is performed under the stars from mid-June to the end of August, Tuesday through Sunday. Curtain is at 8:30 P.M. except on Sunday, when the performance starts at 7:00 P.M. For those with children, rest assured that this colorful drama easily qualifies as family entertainment, though the screaming Indians throwing torches can set little hearts beating up-tempo. Call (859) 734–3346 for further information.

Follow Chiles Street south to Kentucky's first row house, circa 1800, known as **Morgan Row,** after the builder, Joseph Morgan. The street is

It Runs in the Family

*J*ust a few miles from Shaker Village is a pottery and arts studio that has special significance to me. **Peace Roots Studio** features the work of members of my own family. My mother, Chris Strecker, makes functional, high-fired stoneware – butter bowls, bird feeders, plates, and so forth – that is in such great demand that she can't keep the display shelves filled. Her palette of glossy, reduction-fired glazes includes two hard-to-get copper-based reds as well as a deep green, cobalt blue, white, gray, and a rich range of irons. My husband, Michael Frasca, makes sculptural pots, which are often exceptionally large and have complex undulating rims and dramatic feet and handles. His work is single-fired with wood-ash glazes that range from brilliant rivulets of color to satin black or a saturated crystalline iron. And my sister, Erika Strecker, is a metal sculptor and glassblower. Her metalwork forms are organic derivations of traditional ornamental ironwork; for example, one of her works was a beautiful hand-hammered "corn gate" that suggested the form and flow of cornstalks. In addition to architectural applications, her work includes candelabras, beds, tables, fire tools, playful boxes, and an ever-changing array of nonfunctional sculpture. In recent years, Erika has taken up glassblowing, creating handblown ornaments and small glass vessels. Peace Roots Studio is just a few miles from Shaker Village. If you're coming from Lexington, Coghill Lane is a right turn off Highway 68. If you're coming from Shakertown it's a left turn. Go all the way to the end of Coghill Lane, and you'll see a cabin with the pottery behind it. Someone's home just about every day from 9:00 A.M. to 6:00 P.M. In winter months, you might want to call ahead (859-734-5271).

Sooooooeyyy!!!

*I*f you leave town going northeast on Highway 68, toward Lexington, you will pass my alma mater, Harrodsburg High School, affectionately known as "Hog Town." This nickname harks back to the late 1820s, when hogs out-numbered county residents two to one and on the hill where the school stands now were huge hog corrals, sales rings, and auction blocks that served the whole region. Our official high school sports mascot was a pioneer with a coonskin cap, but our proud rallying cry was Sooooooeyyy!!! *(Self-depre-cating humor is healthy, especially for the adolescent soul.)*

named after Morgan's son-in-law, John Chiles, who ran a famous tavern on the site. In front of Morgan Row, Uncle Will of Wildwood, a promi-nent Mercer County farmer, is said to have been cited for speeding in his one-horse buggy. When Uncle Will went to pay his ticket, he paid double the amount, telling the clerk in a voice loud enough for the whole courthouse to hear, "I'm paying you double 'cause I plan to leave the way I came." Today Morgan Row houses, among other things, the **Harrodsburg Historical Society Museum** and office (859–734–5985).

Another of Harrodsburg's claims to fame is **The Beaumont Inn.** The massive brick Greek Revival building, constructed in 1845, was once a finishing school called the Greenville Institute, then Daughter's Col-lege, and later Beaumont College. It was converted into an inn in 1919 by Annie Bell Goddard and her husband, Glave. The inn has remained in the family and is now managed by Annie Bell's great-grandson, Chuck Dedman. The dining room serves very traditional Kentucky-style meals that include dishes such as two-year-old cured country ham (smoked and cured by the proprietor himself), fried chicken, corn pudding, and Robert E. Lee Orange-Lemon Cake. Be ready for a feast! The antiques-filled sleeping quarters suggest the extravagance of the Old South, with a few modern conveniences. A swimming pool, tennis courts, and a gift shop are also on the premises. Reservations are advisable for meals and lodging. Closed late December though early March. Call (859) 734–3381 or (800) 352–3992.

Acting as a business-savvy alchemist, the City of Harrodsburg trans-formed an unsightly lot where an old building burned down in the first block of South Main Street into a city park, called **Olde Towne Park,** which includes a stage for civic events and a 14-foot-high by 35-foot-wide sculptural wall-water fountain designed and made by me, Zoé Strecker, your author with a double life. The fountain sculpture is a lyrical representation of the historic limestone palisades that line the Kentucky River on the eastern border of Mercer County. This work is made of nearly 700 large, high-fired ceramic tiles, all molded or directly sculpted by hand, featuring high-relief plants, vines, reptiles, and rock-like textures for the falling water to play over. For more information, call (859) 734–6811.

The umbrella tables in the park by the fountain are very popular lunch spots. And if they're not too busy two doors down at *La Fonda Restaurant* of Authentic Mexican Food (859–734–0033), the waiters will actually serve your meal in the park. This little restaurant is very popular for its genuine Mexican dishes (the chiles rellenos are unusually good) and for its reasonable prices. You get the pleasant feeling that the chefs are making the food that they love. Open every day for lunch and dinner.

One of the most unique historical buildings in Mercer County is the *Old Mud Meeting House,* built in 1800 by members of the Dutch Reformed Church. As early as 1781 a group of Dutch settlers immigrated here and formed a community where they spoke Dutch and worshiped as they did in the Old World. The church they built became known as the Mud Meeting House because massive timber walls are chinked with clay, straw, twigs, roots, and gravel. The handsome structure, constructed "for the sole Benefit & use of the said Reformed Church forever," has long outlasted its little congregation. The church was restored to its original form in 1971. To visit the site, drive south

Olde Towne Park—Palisades Fountain

True Blue

from town on Highway 127 to the junction of Highway 68 (Moreland Avenue) and turn right. Follow Highway 68 until you reach Dry Branch Pike; turn left and look for the historical marker. Getting there can be confusing. Here's an even better idea: Call the Historical Society office at (859) 734–5985 to arrange a guided tour.

Mercer County is horse country indeed, but the only place where you can get in a saddle and ride is the **Big Red Stables,** at 1605 Jackson Pike, Harrodsburg 40330, which offers guided or unguided trail rides over 2,000 acres of woodlands and pasture. The cost is $15 per person. Call (859) 734–3118 for directions and reservations.

John A. Roebling, designer of the famous bridges in Cincinnati and Brooklyn, New York, also designed a suspension bridge for the Kentucky River at the site where High Bridge now stands. After the financial panic of 1857, the project was abandoned; his exquisite stone piers were torn down in 1929, after never having been used.

Heading east, you pass the world's most beautiful house of mechanic work, *The Stringtown Garage.* Father and son, Big Jack and Lil' Jack Pearson, have transformed a cement-block eyesore into their own little paradise. If you like their vibrant flowers, stop and see Big Jack's antiques and James Dean memorabilia inside, or just honk and wave. You are now entering real saddlebred horse country. Driving Highway

One Well-Used Cavern

*J*ust behind High Bridge on the Jessamine County side is the mouth of a fabricated cavern that is as big as my farm—thirty-two acres of limestone rooms, 130 feet underground. The 30-foot-high corridors were originally created by the Kentucky Stone company between 1900 and 1972 as it mined commercial-grade limestone. The Civil Defense Department has used the space for the storage of food and equipment during the bomb-shelter era, the Campbell Soup Company once filled the floors with loam and grew mushrooms for soup there, and local hearsay is that the secretive Free Masons continue to conduct rites in the unused, unlighted recesses of the mine. In 1979, when Bill Griffin bought the mine to use for underground commodity storage, engineers advised him to drain the water from an underground spring in order to control humidity. It was going to be a big expense. One day Mr. Griffin glibly commented to his daughter, "Well, why don't we just bottle the stuff and sell it off?" Everyone laughed, but by 1990 the family-run business, High Bridge Springwater, had sold over two million gallons of bottled spring water. It now dominates the local market as bottled water becomes increasingly common in households with unfiltered cisterns and in those with unsavory, chlorinated city water.

True Blue

Transylvania University in Lexington was the first university west of the Alleghenies.

68 will give you an opportunity to fall in love with the miles of hundred-year-old mortarless field-stone fences visible on both sides of the road.

Shaker Village of Pleasant Hill is one of central Kentucky's most significant historic sites. It is located 8 miles east of Harrodsburg off Highway 68. The whole restored village is a museum featuring thirty original Shaker buildings and more than 2,700 acres of manicured farmland (about half of what the Shaker community farmed in its prime). "The United Society of Believers in Christ's Second Appearance" was originally founded by an English Quaker woman, Mother Ann Lee, who came to America in 1774 and claimed to be Christ incarnate (this time as a woman) to herald the millennium preceding the total destruction of Earth, as prophesied in the Book of Revelations. The most publicized doctrine of the sect was that Believers should remain pure by avoiding "the World" (non-Shakers) and all its ways, including the "disorderly" state of matrimony. Instead of procreating, the Shakers adopted orphans and received converts, who were plentiful during America's "Great Revival" period of Protestant faiths in the early nineteenth century. Shakers also avoided "the World" by remaining economically self-sufficient; their products were always of the highest quality, from seeds to silk, and continue to influence modern design. The Shakers' Utopia at Pleasant Hill lasted more than one hundred years, until the death of the village's last resident in 1923.

The village admission fee enables you to take a self-guided tour through the buildings, which, like Shaker furniture, are renowned for their graceful, functional aesthetic simplicity. (The song "Simple Gifts" is associated with the Shakers.) In recent years, this village has expanded its interpretation of historic farming techniques. Draft horses and oxen are used for traction in the gardens of heirloom vegetables and to power an impressive collection of period equipment. Blacksmithing, sorghum growing and making, and seed propagation and sales are among the agricultural practices demonstrated. Be sure to visit the interpretive center, where an excellent video and other exhibits provide insight into the Shakers and their tenure at Pleasant Hill. The village offers fine Southern dining and overnight accommodations in original buildings. Call (800) 734–5611 for more information, special programs, and reservations.

The Shakers traded goods with "the World" in large part by river. The road built by the Shakers in 1861 still accesses one of the most spectacular stretches of the Kentucky River, known as **The Palisades,** where high Ordovician limestone bluffs change color with the time of day. Go east about $1/8$ mile from Shakertown's entrance and turn right where a sign indicates RIVER EXCURSIONS. Shakertown offers one-hour trips on a paddle wheel boat called *The Dixie Belle*. From the boat you have a perfect view of **High Bridge,** the first cantilever bridge in the United States, a miracle of engineering at the time of its completion in 1877. High Bridge stretches 1,125 feet and stands 280 feet high; it is still the highest two-track railroad pass in North America.

For a dizzying view of High Bridge, follow Highway 68 east across from Shakertown, toward Lexington. The road begins to wind dramatically as it descends into the river gorge, crosses the Kentucky River on Brooklyn Bridge, and begins another curvy climb. At the top of the hill, take Highway 1268 into Wilmore, then turn right onto Highway 29 and drive to the little community of High Bridge. There are places to park so you can walk to the end of the underside of the criss-crossing bridge structure. Wait for a train. It's a goofy thrill to feel the frequent trains passing over your head. Notice too the confluence of the Kentucky and Dix Rivers. The Kentucky is the big, usually brown, slow-moving river, while the Dix is often a clearer green. If you were down on the water, you'd also notice that the Dix River's water is much, much colder. Less than a mile away the river is being released from the base of the Dix Dam, which forms Herrington Lake. Often, in the summer, the colliding air temperatures form a low, flat layer of fog, just 3 feet high, right over the water's surface, so that people in boats appear to be floating heads. Swimming in that 48-degree water can stop your heart.

Llamaland

*M*ost people think of horses when they think of the bluegrass region, but at **Seldon Scene Farm,** 1710 Watts Ferry Road in Woodford County (859–873–1622), animal lovers Lindy and Paul Huber offer close encounters with other kinds of fascinating beasts. Their "Llama Trek" is a guided picnic hike along scenic trails and meadows overlooking the Kentucky River in the scenic Palisades area. You don't ride the llamas. Instead, you lead, and your friendly llama carries lunch fixings and other gear. A typical four-hour trek includes a 2- to 3-mile hike, a gourmet lunch grilled in the open air (steak, or chicken, or even emu, if you're daring enough), and a tour of the farm, home to about twenty llamas, thirty alpacas, a yak, miniature donkeys, goats, and reindeer. A trek costs $40 per adult, $10 for children under twelve; the trek is not advised for children younger than six because of the distance covered. Families with younger children would probably enjoy the hour-long animal tour, $5.00 per person. Call in advance to schedule either.

Beginning at the Kentucky River and traveling north on Highway 68, turn west (or left) onto Highway 33 and follow the signs to *Irish Acres Antiques* in *Nonesuch* (population 343), a "downtown" comprised of the smallest freestanding voting building you'll ever see and a cluster of houses, one of which has the greatest number and variety of purple martin houses known to humanity (the owner must be a frustrated urban housing planner). Irish Acres Antiques is a not-to-be-missed 32,000-square-foot antiques gallery and tearoom founded by Bonnie and Arch Hannigan and now run by their daughters Emilie and Jane. Two floors of what was once the Nonesuch School are gracefully crammed with antiques, which range from affordable early American primitives to pricey Asian art, fifteenth-century Chinese lacquered boxes, and nineteenth-century French country furniture. An ornate $38,000 French palace bed is among the treasures.

The old basement cafeteria has been converted into a whimsical, elegant tearoom called The Glitz. Amid a fantasia of lights, grapevines, iridescent paper, and silver cherubim, you can enjoy a lavish four-course meal for $15.95. It's a good place to take your time and not the best place to take your kids. Reservations are required. Lunch is served from 11:00 A.M. to 2:00 P.M., when the gallery is open. Gallery hours are 10:00 A.M. to 5:00 P.M., Tuesday through Saturday. Irish Acres and The Glitz are closed January through mid-March. Call (859) 873–7235.

If you're looking for a getaway with room to roam, or a family retreat that can truly accommodate the whole family, *Western Fields,* about a mile from Nonesuch on Fords Mill Road (Highway 1965), will fill the bill. And quite artistically. Deborah and Tom Westerfield's eighty-acre farm includes a three-bedroom guest house, complete with a big patio, hot tub, and such accoutrements as hand-painted murals and hand-carved raku tile beds and mirrors. As if that weren't enough, you can also feed the llamas and alpacas, visit the art studio, check out the mum and garlic beds, or just take a hike. The cottage rents for $125 a night. Call (859) 879–0066 for more information.

Get back onto Highway 33, which winds through lush horse-farm country, to *Versailles* (pronounced Ver-SALES). You can also get to Versailles by way of Highway 60 or Highway 62, once one of the largest buffalo trails in the United States. From the landscaping and architecture in town, one senses an aura of the wealth and deliberate pace of the Old South. Downtown Versailles is full of well-preserved old Federal and Beaux Arts homes, beautiful churches, and antiques stores, one of which is the *Olde Town Antique Mall,* with two floors of goodies at 161 Main Street, Versailles 40383 (859–873–6326). Not far away is a good lunch and dinner spot, **Kesslers 1891 Eatery, Pub and Catering.** One of the features is country ham croquettes. Lunch is served from 11:00 A.M. to 2:00 P.M. Monday through Friday; dinner begins at 5:00 P.M. Kesslers is at 197 South Main, Versailles 40383; call (859) 879–3344.

People come to Kentucky from all over the country to towns that were early settlements in search of information about their ancestors. Like the Mercer County Public Library in Harrodsburg (859–734–4924), the **Woodford County Historic Society Museum** (859–873–6786) has an excellent library of genealogical data that is free and available for any-one's use. The museum is housed in what was formerly the Big Spring Church, circa 1819, at 121 Rose Hill, Versailles 40383. Hours are Tuesday through Saturday from 10:00 A.M. to 4:00 P.M.

For the toy train enthusiast, Versailles offers a once-in-a-lifetime oppor-tunity to pore over the collection of Wanda and Winfrey Adkins, who have converted an old (1911–1932) Louisville and Nashville (L&N) rail-road station into the **Nostalgia Station Toy Train Museum,** located on Depot Street, a one-way street on the east side of Main. The Adkinses, who do repairs and will find rare parts, can tell you just about anything there is to know about model trains and antique cast-iron and mecha-nized toys. Before meeting the Adkinses, I didn't realize that there are modern versions of the 1950s locomotives, boxcars, switches, coal cars, and crossing lights that we played with every Christmas. Wanda likes to point out a wind-up Mickey and Minnie Mouse hand-pump car, one of L&N's forgotten "cheap" toys from the 1930s, when the company was struggling, and a regular engine and coal car that cost at least $32. Hours are Wednesday through Saturday from 10:00 A.M. to 5:00 P.M. and Sunday from 1:00 to 5:00 P.M. Admission is $3.50. Call (859) 873–2497 for more information.

For enthusiasts of full-size railroad artifacts, follow Highway 62 west to the **Bluegrass Railroad Museum, Inc.** in Woodford County Park. On weekends from mid-May through the end of October, you can take a 5½-mile train ride on the Old Louisville Southern Mainland through quintessential bluegrass country, including a hawk's view of the Ken-tucky River palisades, Wild Turkey Distilleries, and Young's High Bridge. The museum is an actual train car with historic railroad displays. A recent addition to the collection is an original L&N railroad bay-win-dow caboose. For times, rates, and special events, call (859) 873–2476 or (800) 755–2476.

"Here's to Old Kentucky, The State where I was born, Where the corn is full of kernels and the Colonels full of corn," goes an old Kentucky toast.

The abundant corn crops of early Kentucky settlers played an important role in the creation of bourbon whiskey, as did, undoubtedly, its appreciation by Southern gentlemen. When, how, and by whom bourbon was first made remains a matter of debate that may never be settled (Georgetown claims it was Baptist minister Elijah Craig; nearby Bourbon County credits Jacob Spears). There's no disagreement, however, that by the early 1800s whiskey making had evolved into a fine art in bluegrass country. Elijah Pepper started making whiskey near Versailles in 1797. In 1812, in search of a more abundant water supply, he moved his operation to a spot along Glenn's Creek. Today, whiskey is still made at the site of Pepper's early distillery, under the name **Labrot & Graham, The Bourbon Homeplace** (7855 McCracken Pike, Versailles 40383; 859–879–1812).

Brown-Forman, an international beverage company based in Louisville, renovated the property as a showplace of the "old ways" of making premium bourbon whiskey. The bulky old stone buildings strung along the creek, the complex aromas from the mash tank, the 25-foot-tall copper stills (unique in modern American distilling), and the lively presentations by the tour guides make this a premium tour, which ends with a taste of bourbon ball candy at the "bar" in the visitors center. By the way, the bourbon distilled on the day you visit won't be available in a bottle for about seven years. The free tours are given at 10:00 and 11:00 A.M. and at 1:00, 2:00, and 3:00 P.M. Tuesday through Saturday, April through October, and Wednesday through Saturday, November through March. The distillery is about 6 miles from Versailles (so far out that it has its own lake as a source of water in case of a fire). If you're in Versailles, take Highway 60 toward Frankfort, turn left onto Grassy Spring Road, then right on McCracken Pike. Or take Elm Street out of downtown Versailles.

Continue on Highway 1659 past the distillery, then turn left (west) on Highway 1964 and right onto Germany Road, then follow the signs to the 374-acre **Buckley Wildlife Sanctuary,** which offers an appropriately private and meditative way to explore the wooded Kentucky River Gorge. You can hike on loop trails between ¼ mile and 2 miles long, and there's a bird blind that keeps you concealed while birds come within view (or camera range). You're likely to see everything, from warblers to wild turkeys; some people come solely for the hummingbirds. There's an interesting exhibit center, a gift shop, and various events year-round. As a sanctuary should be, it's a peaceful, beautiful place. Admission is $3.00. Hours are Wednesday through Friday from 9:00 A.M. to 5:00 P.M. and on weekends from 9:00 A.M. to 6:00 P.M. Call (606) 873–5711 for event information.

For another worthwhile excuse to take a drive, visit the restored **Jack Jouett House,** circa 1797. This home was built by folks who believe, like Mies van der Rohe, that "God hides in the details." From Versailles go 5 miles west on McCowans Ferry Road, and turn on Craig Creek Pike. Jack Jouett, the original owner, was a legendary Revolutionary War hero who rode all night to save Governor Thomas Jefferson from the British. His son, Matthew Jouett, became a well-known portrait artist. Tours are free April through October on Wednesday from 11:00 A.M. to 1:00 P.M. and on weekends from noon to 5:00 P.M. The house is closed November through March. Call (859) 873–7902.

From Versailles take Highway 62 north toward **Midway,** named so because it is exactly midway between Frankfort and Lexington. At the Nugent Crossroads, where Highway 62 intersects Old Frankfort Pike, you will see the old **Offutt-Cole Tavern building.** The building was constructed in the eighteenth century and has been a tavern, an inn, a stagecoach stop, and a toll gatehouse. Part of the building contains what may be one of the oldest log structures in the state. One of the old inn's most famous tenants was Zerelda Cole James, the mother of the infamous Frank and Jesse. Zerelda was born in the building and lived there with her grandfather, who ran a tavern at the site called the Black Horse Inn. Various businesses have occupied the building in recent times, although at press time it sat empty. You can still park and look around the outside of this charming old structure.

Midway was the first town in Kentucky built by a railroad company. The tracks are both centerpiece and divider of the tiny downtown. These days it is a quaint college town full of antiques shops, beautiful historic homes, and a few surprises.

One such surprise is an operative, century-old, hydropower grain mill on the South Elkhorn Creek. The **Weisenberger Mill** is the oldest continuously operating mill in Kentucky and one of the few in the nation to remain in the same family. In 1866 a German steamboat and mill specialist named August Weisenberger bought the mill that had been built on the site in 1818. He revamped the entire system and began grinding all manner of grain at the rate of one hundred barrels a day.

> ## True Blue
>
> *Frank and Jesse James's mother, Zerelda Cole, once lived in the Offutt-Cole Tavern, located at the intersection of U.S. 62 and KY 1981 between Versailles and Midway.*

His great-grandson, Philip J. Weisenberger, and Philip's son, "Mac," have modernized some of the methods and now grind about 3,000 tons of grain a year. The Weisenbergers introduced the use of the mill's electricity-making capacity by having Kentucky's alternative energy whiz,

True Blue

Zachary Taylor grew up and is buried in Louisville.

Dave Kinlock, rebuild the mill's hydropower turbines and add an efficient generator. Now most aspects of the business are water powered, even the computers. Although visitors are not allowed inside the work area, you can walk around the property. Everything Weisenberger mills is sold by the package in the front office (the 50-pound bags are a very good bargain). As an avid bread maker, I can attest to the excellent quality of the products. Call (859) 254–5282 for more information.

There are several little eateries around Midway. There has been a restaurant in the building at 128 Railroad Street (so named because the tracks run right down the middle of it) since 1840. It was known as *The Depot* then, and it's known as The Depot now (859–846–4745). Crab cakes are a traditional feature, but try the delightful daily specials made with local, organic produce and other fresh ingredients. Lunch is served Monday through Saturday; dinner is served Thursday through Saturday.

From Railroad Street, turn east on Winter Street (Highway 62), veer to the right at the Corner Grocery, and go about ¼ mile. You will find yourself at the *Holly Hill Inn,* an 1830 Greek Revival house that has been home to fine dining for more than twenty years. In 2000 the inn also became home to Ouita and Chris Michel, who came well prepared to add their own special touches to the Holly Hill tradition. Both are graduates of the Culinary Institute of America and have cooked at fine restaurants in the Lexington area. Their Holly Hill Inn serves dinner Wednesday through Saturday, as well as Sunday brunch. The menu changes weekly and is built around locally grown produce, Kentucky-raised beef and lamb, and fresh seafood and pasta dishes. Call (859) 846–4732 for reservations.

In the late 1800s, Kentucky was the third-largest grape and wine producer in the United States. Prohibition, however, uprooted not just the vines but also the industry. Cynthia Bohn and Cynthia Hall are among a new generation of vintners working to help grapes make a comeback in the Bluegrass State. At their *Equus Run Vineyards,* thirty-five-acres located on Moores Mill Road, off Highway 62 between Midway and Georgetown, they've renovated a tobacco barn into a wine-making facility and added a taste of fun to the whole experience. Virtually every month there's some kind of special event— a concert, a barbecue, or an open house. Any day, visitors are invited to go fishing or bring a picnic to enjoy amid the flower gardens or by the old grist mill along the banks of Elkhorn Creek. There's even a life-size art horse, "Vegetariat," part of Lexington's "Horse Mania" community art event from summer 2000. And, of course, there are acres of vineyards, a tasting room, and a gift shop, where Equus Run wines sell for $9.00 to $14.00 a bottle. Regular operating hours are 11:00 A.M. to 5:00 P.M. Tuesday through Saturday; in summer the winery stays open until 7:00 P.M. on Friday and Saturday. Call for information or a schedule of special events (859–846–5284).

Danville is a handsome little college town just south of Harrodsburg. From town take Highway 127; from Shakertown take Highway 33 through Burgin. Drive or walk around Danville and the Centre College campus to admire the architecture. For arts and cultural events, check the gallery and schedule of performances at the Frank Lloyd Wright–style *Norton Center for the Arts* (859–236–4692) on campus.

You know an Italian place is good when there's always a customer at the counter reading an Italian newspaper. *Freddie's Restaurant* (126 South Fourth Street, Danville 40422; 859–236–9884) serves quick, primo cuisine for lunch and dinner Monday through Saturday.

The hospital in Danville was named for a local medical hero, Ephraim McDowell, who performed the first successful removal of an ovarian tumor in 1809. Something should be named for his patient, Jane Todd Crawford, who survived the surgery without the aid of antisepsis or the comfort of anesthetic. The site of the operation, the *Ephraim McDowell House and Apothecary* at 125 South Second Street, Danville 40422, has been accurately restored and is open Monday through Saturday from 10:00 A.M. to noon and 1:00 to 4:00 P.M., Sunday from 2:00 to 4:00 P.M. From November through February it is closed Monday. Admission is $5.00. Call (859) 236–2804.

Across the street is *Constitution Square State Park,* a reproduction of the state's first courthouse square and the site of the first post office in the West, circa 1792. All the buildings are log replicas, and most have recorded interpretations (kids like to push the buttons and run when the voice begins to drone). The lawn is a good place for a downtown picnic, and dessert is right across the street at *Burke's Bakery,* 116 West Main, Danvile 40422 (859–236–5661). Burke's is in its fourth generation of owners and customers and makes good old sweet pastries for those times when you just don't want whole grains and carob powder.

It takes a lot of brass to envision being home to a national museum, and for at least one weekend of the year, Danville has more brass than just about anyplace else. Stop by the stately old Federal Building at Main and Fourth Streets, and you'll see what many Danvillians hope is the future home of a national museum devoted to the rich history of bands in the United States. They figure that since Danville attracts some 40,000 people and dozens of bands from around the world to its Great American Brass Band Festival in mid-June, it's the natural place to locate a *Great American Band Museum* celebrating the role of band music in community life. For information about the festival (a full four-day weekend of everything from Sousa to Civil War songs) or the museum's progress, call (859) 236–4692.

The *Tea Leaf* (230 West Broadway, Danville 40422; 859–236–7456) is strictly for lunch, tea, and gift buying. Rosemary Hamblin and Jane Stevens have specialized in children's books and adult aromas—it's easy to get carried away sniffing teas. The *Antique Mall of Historic Danville* (158 North Third Street, Danville 40422 859–236–3026) is housed in a large brick Presbyterian church, circa 1867, across the street from the public library. The booths are full of goodies—a great place for poets. Hours are Tuesday through Saturday from 10:00 A.M. to 5:00 P.M. and Sunday from 1:00 to 5:00 P.M.

A number of internationally acclaimed visual artists call Danville home. At the *Jones Visual Arts Center at Centre College,* you can see the beautiful blown-glass creations of Stephen Rolfe Powell. Powell, a Centre College professor (and self-proclaimed pyromaniac), is internationally recognized as a master hot glass blower. His glass vessels (some weighing up to 30 pounds) are in museum collections around the world and are coveted by collectors for their vivid colors, elegant form, and fascinating texture (created by the thousands of beads of color applied to the surface). The arts center is open by appointment; call (859)–238–5737.

Just down the street from the Jones center is Brook White Jr.'s *glassbrook, LLC,* on Beatty Avenue. White gives studio demonstrations of his handblown art glass techniques by appointment (859–238–4153). Handmade stained-glass artwork is for sale at *Glass Mountain,* 116 North Second Street, Danville 40422 (859–238–0105), and at *Gautier Stained Glass,* 309 East Main Street, Danville 40422 (859–236–1601). The *C. T. Whitehouse Studio* on Perryville Street features handmade bronzes and is also open by appointment (859–236–5890).

Just a few more miles east on Highway 300 brings you to the *Isaac Shelby Cemetery State Historic Site.* Shelby became Kentucky's first governor in 1792 after having earned a reputation by fighting in Lord Dunmore's War and in the Revolutionary War. He won the gubernatorial race again sixteen years later and victoriously fought the British (again) in the War of 1812. In 1818 he and Andrew Jackson were responsible for the negotiations with the Chickasaw Indians to purchase the land to the west of the Tennessee River for Kentucky, an area now known as the Jackson Purchase. This state-owned site is where his farm, Traveler's Rest, was and where he and his family are buried.

Near Forkland, **Penn's Store** may be the oldest continuously operated one-family-owned store west of the Alleghenies, and it looks like it. Everyone falls in love with the wise, tumbledown appearance of the general store, which was opened in 1852 by Dick Penn. The original building burned, and this replacement is more than a hundred years old. In the winter, the little potbellied stove is stoked up hot, and at least three men are playing checkers on a barrel in the middle of the room at all times. (It takes two to play and one to shake his head and chew on his toothpick.) In the summer there's no better place in the world to have a Dr Pepper than on Penn's front porch, where you can hear the creek rumble by. Because of the death of Penn's great-great-granddaughter Dava Osborn in 2000, the store's hours have been irregular and its long-term future uncertain. Before you go, be sure to call Jeanne Lane to make sure Penn's is open. The store phone number is (859) 332–7706. From Forkland continue on Highway 37 south to Highway 243, turn right, then right again just after crossing a concrete bridge. When you see the store by the creek, cross the new bridge.

Leaving Danville to the west, Main Street becomes Highway 150 (or 52) and leads to the historic town of **Perryville.** Under the shade of massive maple and sweet gum trees on the banks of the Chaplain River

"The Knobs"

*I*f you leave Junction City on Highway 37 south, you will suddenly enter "the knobs," a narrow belt of fairly isolated, wooded hills that encircles the bluegrass region. (Rock lovers: The creeks here are loaded with geodes.) In the heart of this alluring terrain is a little town called Forkland, where there's a good country festival the second weekend of October at the **Forkland Community Center**. Notice the huge, round piece of sandstone in the yard. It measures 51 inches in diameter, is 18 inches thick, and probably weighs over a ton. What in tarnation is it? No one knows. Sandstone is never used for grinding grain, so a millstone is out. Archaeologists say it's not prehistoric. The best guess is that it was a "hemp brake," a heavy rock rolled by hand or by oxen over hemp stalks to break the fibers apart for making rope.

is a quiet haven made ready for rest and high tea. The *Elmwood Inn* is a well-preserved Greek Revival home that has been, over the years, a hospital (during the Battle of Perryville), a private school, a music academy, and a restaurant. (Stains on my prom dress remind me of my first meal in the restaurant as a nervous adolescent trying to eat fried chicken gracefully.) The inn is now a stately tearoom. Owners Bruce and Shelley Richardson have added a creative twist to traditional English tea. Each month, the tea and pastries served reflect a different theme. Past themes have included Irish tea (in March) and Shakespeare. Art exhibits at the tearoom often complement the monthly theme. Whatever the theme, count on it to be delicious. Be sure to make reservations by calling (859) 332–2400. Tea time is 1:00 and 3:00 P.M. Thursday, Friday, and Saturday.

Across the river from the Elmwood Inn, you can see the back of *Merchants' Row,* a small row of renovated buildings that house antiques and gift shops, a pizza place, a dry goods store, and an active saddlery. Moving away from creature comforts, proceed in an appropriately somber spirit to the *Perryville Battlefield State Historic Site.* Go north on Highway 1920 for 3 miles and follow the signs. Eighty thousand men fought for one bloody day on this site on October 8, 1862, when Confederate soldiers in search of water accidentally encountered Union troops who were guarding nearby Doctor's Creek. More than 7,500 soldiers were killed, wounded, or missing by sunset. This battle was the largest ever fought on Kentucky soil and, when the Confederate general Braxton Bragg retreated into Tennessee after the battle, there was no real hope left that Kentucky would ever join the Rebel states.

There's a small museum (859–332–8631) with artifacts and battle displays on the 270-acre grounds. A walking tour introduces visitors to important landmarks. There is also a driving tour of the area; ask for maps. The best time to visit is on the weekend closest to October 8, during the massive annual reenactment of the battle, when people in full period costume, with weapons and horses, stage the long, gory combat. The park is open daily from April through October from 9:00 A.M. to 5:00 P.M. and by appointment the remainder of the year. Admission is charged. Call the Perryville Battlefield Preservation Association at (859) 332–1862 for more information about the ongoing development of the site.

The town of *Stanford* is about 13 miles south of Danville on Highway 150. There's a charming restored railroad depot used as a community meeting center. The *Harvey Helm Museum and Library,* downtown on Main Street, is a repository of local history, from manuscripts and books to old-fashioned clothing. It's open late spring through summer

(606–365–7513). The building that houses the museum was built in 1788 as the town's first church.

The **William Whitley House State Historic Site** is southeast of Stanford on Highway 150. Famous "Indian Fighter" (a dubious claim to fame) William Whitley built the elegant brick house in the mid-1780s, making it one of the oldest brick buildings west of the Alleghenies. It was called "a guardian of the Wilderness Road" because it stood next to the important overland route and served as a place of refuge for white travelers. The high upper windows and barred lower windows, the gun ports, and a hidden staircase were built as precautions against attacks.

Whitley's big contributions to Kentucky (and American) culture were building the first racetrack in the state and running the horses counterclockwise, a practice he encouraged to rebel against the British custom of racing clockwise. Having served as a colonel in the Revolution, Whitley was passionately anti-British. (I'm sure he hated kippers and, if he had been around in the 1960s, would have disliked the Beatles, too.) Whitley died in the 1813 Battle of the Thames River after he supposedly killed the great chief Tecumseh. Tours of the house are given Tuesday through Sunday from mid-March through December 31, 9:00 A.M. to 5:00 P.M. Call (606) 355–2881 for further information.

Downtown **Lancaster** is a small but bustling central square around which you will find a number of antiques malls. One of several worth checking is the **Antique Market** (859–792–4536) at 102 Hamilton Street, Lancaster 40444. The **Garrard County Jail Museum,** at 208 Danville Street, Lancaster 40444, is an interesting building featuring

A Teetotaler with a Mission

*J*ust north of Lincoln County and east of Boyle County is Garrard County, birthplace of a radical antiliquor activist oft neglected by history books. From Lancaster take Highway 27 north to Highway 34 and go east to its junction with Fisher Ford Road to find **Carrie A. Nation's birthplace** at "the jumping-off place," as local folks call it. The house was built about 1840, and Carrie was born there in 1846. In 1900, after a short,

disastrous, and life-changing marriage to a severe alcoholic, Carrie single-handedly wreaked havoc on the saloon at the Hotel Casey in Wichita, Kansas, and, consequently, spent seven days in jail, her first of more than thirty jail sentences on similar charges. I've seen fearsome pictures of Ms. Nation in her prime: hatchet in one hand, Bible in the other, purse to the front, and a glare that would make any bartender's blood run cold.

local historic artifacts. It is free and open to the public from noon to 4:00 P.M., Monday through Friday. A local historic home that is open for tours is **Pleasant Retreat,** at 516 Stanford Road, Lancaster 40444, the 1804 home of Governor William Owsley, after whom the ninety-sixth county was named. Hours are noon to 4:00 P.M. Monday, Thursday, and Friday; 10:00 A.M. to 4:00 P.M. Saturday. Call (859) 792–2500 for more information.

Tradition Meets Invention

An old jail, a lot of used furniture, 12,000 locks, and a cemetery—that is what **Nicholasville** has to offer. Go almost due south of Lexington, via Highway 27, then take the business loop into downtown Nicholasville. Make a quick stop at the Chamber of Commerce office at 611 North Main Street, Nicholasville 40356, for a list of the many antiques malls and maps for walking the historic district. The **Old Jail,** 200 South Main Street, Nicholasville 40356, is actually interesting, though it would not have been a good place to spend the night after committing a crime. There are no regular tours of the restored 1870 building, but if you go to the county judge's office in the Jessamine County Courthouse, at the corner of Main and Maple, you can pick up the key and take a look around.

Without doubt, the most fascinating site to visit in town is the **Harry C. Miller Lock Collection,** south on Main Street inside Lockmasters, Inc. (859–885–6041). From the time he was a locksmith's apprentice at the age of twelve to the years he traveled the world developing locks for the State Department's classified materials, Harry Miller collected an astounding variety of locks in order to study their designs. The oldest lock in the collection is Arabic and dates to 1303. A lock removed from the Oval Office during Lincoln's presidency and a key to the Capitol's 16-ton doors are in the collection. Many of the locks were invented by Miller himself; he holds some fifty-four lock patents. Some locks have been donated to the Smithsonian Museum, but the rest are on view for free on Monday, Wednesday, and Friday from 1:00 to 4:00 P.M.

Head south of town on Highway 27 for 5 miles to the **Camp Nelson Civil War Site,** a large Union supply depot and recruitment center. Founded in 1863, Camp Nelson was the preeminent recruiting and training ground for Black soldiers. Over a thousand slaves were "impressed" to construct the camp, its roads, and its railroads, and many of the same men subsequently enlisted. Any Kentucky slaves who enlisted were immediately freed. Later, their families were also freed and allowed to live nearby in a refugee camp. Despite the army's attempts to administrate the camp, many people died of exposure and disease. The army even joined forces with evangelical abolitionists to provide schools at the camp. One such missionary was Reverend John Gregg Fee, who, shortly after his work at the camp, formed an integrated school in Berea that later became Berea College. When all of Kentucky's slaves were freed in 1865, Camp Nelson served as an issuing station for emancipation papers, and the next year the site was designated the **Camp Nelson National Cemetery**. If you drive another 2 miles south of the supply depot site, you can visit the actual cemetery, where some 4,000 Civil War soldiers are buried.

To go any farther east, you have to get across the Kentucky River, and there is no bridge. From Nicholasville take Union Mills Road (Highway 169) down to the river's edge and wait for the ferry. In 1785 the Virginia Assembly granted the **Valley View Ferry** a "perpetual and irrevocable franchise." Let me emphasize the word *perpetual*. More than 200 years later, the little boat is still carrying anyone and anything that needs to cross between Madison and Jessamine Counties at the mouth of Tates Creek. This ferry is Kentucky's oldest recorded business continuously in operation. Originally, workhorses pulled the ferry across; later a motor was connected to the ferry's paddle wheel and the boat was guided between fixed cables. Now a motorized ferryboat can carry three cars at a time. Recently the governments of Jessamine, Madison, and Fayette Counties decided to purchase and jointly operate this sole functioning ferry on the Kentucky River. Operating hours are Monday through Friday from 6:00 A.M. to 8:00 P.M., Saturday from 8:00 A.M. to 6:00 P.M., and Sunday from 9:00 A.M. to 6:00 P.M., except when it is closed due to high or turbulent water. There is no charge to use the ferry, but it's a good idea to check the running status in a advance by calling (859) 258–3611. Press "2" and the (pound) sign after the first traffic message.

Camp Nelson

A group of local citizens have created a foundation to restore and preserve Camp Nelson. You can view the progress of restoration of the Oliver Perry House, an 1855 house that was appropriated for military use during the Civil War. The group also sponsors numerous reenactments and living history events at Camp Nelson throughout the year. For more information, call (859) 887–4351 or (859) 885–4500.

When you arrive on the east bank, keep driving and you'll soon be in **Richmond,** home of Eastern Kentucky University and very much a university town, full of restaurants, bars, hotels, and shops. For the stargazer, the **Hummel Planetarium** on Kit Carson Drive on campus is totally cosmic. This is the twelfth largest planetarium in the nation, and it feels even larger as you crane your neck in the dark dome to catch a view of the galaxy from 9.3 billion miles away from Earth. Shows are Thursday through Saturday evenings and Saturday and Sunday afternoons. Call (859) 622–1547. To get there from I–75, take exit 87 to Kit Carson Drive.

The **White Hall State Historic Site** is accessible from I–75 (exit 90) or directly from Richmond. Take Highway 421/25 and follow the signs to the restored home of one of Kentucky's best-loved big mouths and influential abolitionists, Cassius Marcellus Clay, the "Lion of White Hall." The White Hall building is well fortified in part because Clay's ideological and political opponents were not beyond attempts at physically sabotaging the basement press where he produced his radical paper, *The True American*. After a failed political career, Clay served under President Lincoln as minister to the court of Czar Alexander II in St. Petersburg, Russia, then retired and lived bankrupt at White Hall until his death in 1903. The building is open from April to Labor Day daily and from Labor Day to October, Wednesday to Sunday, 9:00 A.M. to 5:30 P.M. Call (606) 623–9178. Admission is charged.

Berea is a nationally well-known folk arts-and-crafts center located just south of Richmond in southern Madison County off I–75. Stop by the Welcome Center, 201 North Broadway, Berea 40403, for brochures about all the crafts businesses. You can also call (859) 986–2540 or

Native Americans in Kentucky

*Y*ou've probably heard that Native Americans did not have permanent habitations in Kentucky because it was a commonly owned hunting ground. Not true. Thirty-five hundred acres in southeastern Clark County were occupied, farmed, kept clear, and hunted by Shawnee. Archaeologists are in search of the Shawnee village called Eskip-pakithiki, meaning "blue lick place" because of salt-sulfur springs in or near the present-day town of Oil Springs. This relatively permanent settlement was established around 1718 and was occupied by as many as 200 families, according to legend and to a 1736 census taken by French Canadians. By 1754 the village was probably abandoned as the Shawnee moved north across the Ohio River, where many other Shawnee lived. Later, the structures burned and the cornfields returned to a wooded state. Some historians believe that the name Kentucky came from an Iroquois name for this particular area, kenta, *which means level, and* aki, *which indicates location, or "place of level land."*

(800) 598–5263. You'll find more than thirty cra[ ]
makers, potters, leather makers, blacksmiths, stained
weavers, spoon makers, basket weavers, quilters, and
whose studios and salesrooms are open to the public. A[ ]
the big outdoor fairs at the Indian Fort Theatre sponsored
tucky Guild of Artists and Craftsmen.

The following are samples of the many crafts studios you can v..it: Warren May is the state's best-known dulcimer maker. Dulcimers are graceful, Appalachian, wooden stringed instruments played flat on the lap, usually to accompany vocals, often in a minor key. This is an instrument many Americans had probably never heard of before Jean Ritchie. The **Warren A. May's Woodworking Shop** (110 Center Street, Berea 40403; 859–986–9293) is open Monday through Saturday. At **Churchill Weavers** (Lorraine Court at Highway 25; 859–986–3127), you can walk through the loomhouse and see master weavers hard at work creating shawls, throws, and blankets.

An elegant place for fine regional foods and downtown lodging is the **Boone Tavern Hotel and Dining Room** (859–986–9358), owned and run by Berea College. There's even a dress code for evening meals (if you fellows forget your jacket, they'll loan you one). It's open daily for all meals. Berea College is a highly acclaimed liberal arts college that serves talented, low-income students from southern Appalachia. Students pay no tuition but work ten to fifteen hours a week at any of 138 college-owned businesses, which include the Boone Tavern and studios for pottery, weaving, woodworking, broom making, and other crafts. The student-made crafts are sold at the **Log House Sales Room** on Jackson Street. After you've surveyed the student-made crafts on the first floor, head upstairs to the **Wallace Nutting Museum,** where you'll find fine reproductions of seventeeth and eighteeth century furniture. The Log House Sales Room's phone number is (859) 985–3226.

Five generations of Cornelisons have kept **Bybee Pottery** (859–369–5350) thriving since at least 1845, making it the oldest existing pottery west of the Alleghenies. If you're from this region, you've probably seen Bybee's pots. The wheel-thrown, slip-cast (molded), and jiggered stoneware pots are pretty clunky and chip easily, but they are based on traditional designs. The hilarious droop of the studio building itself reflects the age of the pottery. The clays used in all of Bybee's pieces (more than 125,000 annually) come from a small, remarkably pure clay mine less than 2 miles away. Visitors are welcome to mosey around the entire work area. To get there from Richmond, take Highway 52 east for 9 miles. The Bybee salesroom and workshop are open on weekdays

⌐ 8:00 A.M. to noon and from 12:30 to 3:30 P.M. You'll find the best selection if you go early on the day when the kilm is unloaded—Monday, Friday, and sometimes Wednesday.

Fort Boonesboro State Park is on the beaten path and self-explanatory. From I–75 take exit 95 on Highway 627 and follow the signs. The reconstructed fort is at the site of Kentucky's second settlement, established in 1775 by Boone and Richard Henderson when they worked as surveyors for the Transylvania Company. Interpreters at the park dress in period clothing and demonstrate pioneer crafts, such as making lye soap. The park also offers a campground, swimming pool, beach, and more. Hours from April to Labor Day are 9:00 A.M. to 5:30 P.M. Labor Day through October 31, the fort is open only Wednesday through Sunday from 10:00 A.M. to 4:00 P.M. and it is closed November through March. Call (859) 527–3131.

Gardeners, especially herb enthusiasts, may like the ***Olde Rock Barn Gift Shop and Farm House Herbs,*** located in an old limestone building 5 miles south of Winchester on Highway 627. Seasonally, there's a tremendous variety of herbs and perennials, with plant stakes, fountains, wind chimes, and furniture sold year-round. The whole complex is open from 10:00 A.M. to 5:00 P.M. Monday through Saturday. Call (888) 795–0403.

If you continue north on Highway 627 toward ***Winchester,*** you may want to veer to the left (west) 3¹/₂ miles after crossing the bridge onto Old Stone Church Road and see the lovely little church by the same name. This was supposedly the first church established west of the Appalachian Mountains. It still has an active congregation, but they don't mind visitors as long as you don't leave trash.

True Blue

Seventy-five of Kentucky's 120 counties are completely dry (of alcohol sales, that is), and in 15 counties, the largest town is wet and the rest of the county is dry.

In 1925 the ***Leeds Theatre,*** at 37 North Main Street, Winchester 40391, was probably the most popular place in Winchester because it had one of the town's first air-conditioning systems. The theater operated as a movie house until 1986, when it closed in a dilapidated condition. A citizens group, the Winchester Council for the Arts, raised enough money to give the place a facelift, and in 1990 it re-opened as the ***Leeds Center for the Arts.*** Along with local productions, this reborn entertainment palace features national arts performances from dance to jazz concerts. Write the center at P. O. Box 836, Winchester 40392, or call (859) 744–6437 for information on upcoming performances.

CENTRAL KENTUCKY

True Blue

John Travolta, Lee Majors, and Jim Varney are among the actors who once performed summer stock at Pioneer Playhouse in Danville.

Outside art, naive art, and folk art are made by people who have had little or no exposure to art history or theory, but who make nonfunctional art objects based on their own experience of local tradition. "Folk art" can be a slippery category, but it's an area of art that has received a lot of attention in the past couple of decades. Larry Hackley began seeking out folk artists in the region many years ago, and his *Hackley Gallery of Folk Art,* at 28 North Main Street, Winchester 40391, exhibits a curious range of work, from brightly painted wood sculptures to walking sticks carved to resemble the devil and Elvis. Call (859) 745–4571.

Though the telephone has radically altered our society and world, it is seldom commemorated. Winchester's *Pioneer Telephone Museum* is one of a kind. The collection of antique phones, phone booths, switchboards, and memorabilia was long housed in a phone company maintenance building. In 2000 the whole collection was moved to Winchester's new *Bluegrass Heritage Museum,* at 217 South Main Street, Winchester 40391. The museum, created by a combination of citizen activism and city/county support, is located in a building that served as the Guerrant Clinic from 1927 to 1971. Dr. Guerrant's offices were located in the building until 1989. The museum focuses on local and regional history, including agriculture, transportation, and Native American and pioneer heritage, according to curator Nancy Turner. At press time, hours were not finalized, so call (859) 745–7936 for more information.

The clinic building was donated by Wallace and Lana Guerrant, who operate *Mountain Mission Bed and Breakfast* in what was the nurses' home for the clinic. Call (859) 745–1284 for more information.

If you are driving near the *Mount Sterling* Plaza on the bypass, stop at Arby's. Please don't eat. Just get out of the car and look for a rather abrupt grassy knob. That's not a Maya Lin earth sculpture, but the *Gaitskill Mound,* an Adena burial mound dating to between 800 B.C. and A.D. 700.

Although they're not of the same magnitude, this area boasts two other cultural artifacts, instances of a nearly extinct type of American entertainment: the drive-in theater. The *Sky-Vue Drive-In* (859–744–6663) is situated about halfway between Lexington and Winchester near the intersection of Highways 60 and 1678, and the *Judy Drive-In* (859–498–1960) is north of Mount Sterling in Judy on Highway 11. Both are open from Memorial Day to Labor Day, with feature films beginning nightly at sundown. Call for admission prices and other information.

In downtown Mount Sterling there is another artifact from the 1950s. *Berryman's Tasty Treat,* open since 1951 on East Main Street, is a full-fledged vintage take-out dairy freeze famous for its chili hot dogs. Berryman's is open from 8:30 A.M. to 11:00 P.M. Monday through Saturday and from 9:00 A.M. to 11:00 P.M. Sunday. It closes for the winter in mid-November. Its annual reopening in early March is a sign to area residents that spring has arrived. For information, call (859) 498–6830.

For more area information, stop by the Mount Sterling Chamber of Commerce, 51 North Maysville Street, Mount Sterling 40353, in the old *Bell House* building, circa 1815, previously a hat shop and county jail. Ask about October Court Days, a big trading festival reminiscent of earlier times when each county held court once a month in a central location so the more remote farmers didn't have to come to town more often. During this three-day extravaganza, approximately 100,000 people crowd into the town of 5,400.

Just uphill from the Bell House at the corner of Broadway and High Street is the *Ascension Episcopal Church,* a beautiful little church with walnut paneling, exquisite carved wood, exposed beams, and stained-glass windows thought to be the first to cross the mountains (by oxcart!). The doors are open during the day so visitors can drool at the 1877 gem.

Just up the street at 321 Maysville Street, Mount Sterling 40353, is the *Trimble House Bed and Breakfast,* owned by Jim and June Hyska. The

A Shave and a Haircut—Wood Shaving, That Is

"*W*hen I start working, I might as well climb into the wood—that's how intimate it gets," says woodworker **Connie Carlton** of Lawrenceburg. Connie looks for the perfect tree in the woods, cuts it before the sap runs, splits long sections of the trunk lengthwise with a sledge and froe, and shapes the wood on a vise-bench of ancient design called a "shaving horse" amid a tiny sea of curled wood shavings. (The place smells like heaven.) The results are long, smooth, shapely pitchforks, rakes, barrel staves, woodworking tools, and the like. He also makes sorghum molasses and gives haircuts. If you want to buy fine, functional wooden tools or get a hairdo by a man with a steady hand, from Highway 127 take Highway 62 west about 2 miles and turn left on Rice Road. His is the first house on the left. Be sure to call ahead (502–839–6478).

plantation-style house (circa 1872) is graced with antiques, a swimming pool, and a Jacuzzi. A full Southern breakfast is always served. Call (859) 498–6561 for reservations. If you're a history buff, make arrangements to tour *Morgan Station,* the site of the last Indian raid in Kentucky. Daniel Boone's cousin, Ralph Morgan, built the big stone house east of Mount Sterling at 3751 Harpers Ridge Road. The owner, Danny Montgomery, is often willing to show visitors around. Call first at (859) 498–2011.

Mount Sterling boasts a fine woodworker, *Paul Williams,* whose special interest is in making stringed instruments out of native Kentucky hardwoods—dulcimers, Celtic harps, arch-top jazz guitars, acoustic guitars, vertical and lap harps, and mandolins. Although Martin and Gibson brands have made mahogany and rosewood the standard guitar

Kentucky's Re-Covered Bridges

*A*lmost any time of the year is a good time to take the winding road KY 1262 off Highway 60 between Georgetown and Frankfort to the small community of Switzer. There, at the center of a small country park, the **Switzer Covered Bridge** spans Elkhorn Creek. It's a picture postcard scene, this wooden beauty with sawtooth entrances, flanked by trees, and atop stone foundations on each side of the creek.

Switzer looks like a part of the landscape, and it has been since 1855. But if you had made that winding drive, as I did, in March 1997, you would know that Switzer's presence is nothing short of a miracle.

In March of that year, the worst flooding in more than a century hit central Kentucky. The waters of the Elkhorn swelled and pushed downstream with enough force to lift the Switzer Bridge right off its foundation. Had it not been for a modern concrete span just down the creek, Switzer would have been washed away into oblivion. Instead, it

hit the concrete bridge and crumpled into the creek like a folded cardboard box. There were more than a few teary-eyed central Kentuckians standing on the banks in the days after the flood.

But Switzer, one of just 13 covered bridges remaining in a state that once boasted 400, was too precious to be lost. Through a community and state effort, the bridge was lifted, removed, and, ultimately, rebuilt, with new materials added to what could be salvaged. The bridge that spans Switzer today is not exactly the same as it was, but it's close enough.

Switzer isn't the only central Kentucky covered bridge to be "re-covered" in recent years. **Colville Covered Bridge,** which crosses Hinkston Creek near Millersburg, was damaged by flooding in 1999. This bridge, too, was removed and repaired, and was scheduled to be open to traffic again sometime in 2001. To get to Colville, take Highway 1893 west off Highway 68, go about 3.1 miles, then turn right at an unmarked road lined by stone walls.

woods, maple, walnut, and ash can also sound and look beautiful. Be sure to call ahead (859–498–7175).

Mount Sterling is sweet-tooth heaven. Make a molasses run (but not as slowly as molasses itself runs) to *Townsend's Sorghum Mill,* on Main Street (also Highway 460) in Jeffersonville, south of Mount Sterling. Go any time of year because they always have pure sorghum syrup (and occasionally maple syrup) on hand, but in September and October you can watch them process cane. The Townsend family has been raising cane for 150 years. Although they use tractors to do the real work, at festivals they bring out the mule team to turn the old-fashioned cane break. Call Judy and Danny Townsend at (859) 498–4142, or plan to come by after 4:00 P.M.

The ultimate dessert is chocolate, real food for real people. If you are a chocoholic, you might be in mortal danger upon entering *Ruth Hunt Candies.* The aroma of liquid chocolate, sweet cream, and roasting nuts will cause light-headedness in even the strong of heart. Everything is handmade and very fresh. Just like in the old days, you can ask the clerk for ¼ pound of pulled cream candy, ½ pound of caramel and bittersweet chocolate balls, and a handful of hot cinnamon suckers, and they'll reach into the big, colorful bins for the goods.

This operation is small and friendly enough that Larry Kezele, the owner, may have time to show you the whole production process. Ruth Tharpe Hunt started the business in 1921 after her bridge buddies encouraged her to go public with her candy making. The Blue Monday Sweet Bar is a dark chocolate with pulled cream in the center and is perhaps the most famous of the company's products. The candy bar was named by a traveling minister who was eating Sunday dinner at the Hunts' and claimed that he needed candy to get through those blue Mondays. Look for Larry and his staff dressed like Blue Mondays in parades. The company, located at 426 West Main Street, Mount Sterling 40353, is open Monday through Saturday from 9:00 A.M. to 5:30 P.M. and Sunday from 1:00 to 5:30 P.M. Call (859) 498–0676 if you need more information . . . or if you are jonesing and need an order FedExed now.

City Lights

More than 95 percent of the bourbon whiskey made in America is made in Kentucky, and most of it comes from this area. *Wild Turkey Distilleries* (of Boulevard Distillers and Importers, Inc.) is a place to get a fascinating bourbon education. From Lawrenceburg take Highway 62 east of town until it splits with Highway 1510. Bear right, go downhill, and watch for the Visitors Information Center on the right. (Note the high train trestle spanning the Kentucky River. Young's High Bridge is a single-span, deck-over cantilever 281 feet high and 1,659 feet long, the last of its kind.)

Kentucky towns bear an international array of names. Kentucky has a Moscow, Athens, Cairo, Dublin, London, Manila, Paris, and Warsaw.

The Wild Turkey Distillery has been operating continuously since the mid-1860s, except during Prohibition, when nearly all distilleries were shut down. During World War II this facility made only surgical alcohol. Federal law states that for whiskey to be called straight bourbon, it must be manufactured in the United States, of at least 51 percent corn, and stored at 125 proof or less for at least two years in new, charred, white-oak barrels. Char caramelizes the wood, which gives the bourbon its rich color and flavor. The corn is ground, cooked, and cooled. The distillers add rye for starch, then barley malt, which converts the starch to sugar (unlike moonshiners, who simply dump cane sugar in the corn mash). Yeast is added, and when the fermented mash is steamed from below, whiskey vapor rises to the top where it is condensed into liquid form. The whiskey is distilled again, put in barrels, and aged from four to twelve years. It's tasted at every stage, and meticulous production records are kept for every batch. Free tours are available Monday through Friday at 9:00 and 10:30 A.M., and at 12:30 and 2:30 P.M. The distillery runs twenty-four-hour days every day except Sunday, when liquor is not made anywhere in the United States. Call (502) 839–4544.

From Lawrenceburg take Highway 127 north into **Frankfort,** the state capital. At the corner of Capital and Second Streets is an ornate Queen Anne–style house with gingerbread trim, the official **Frankfort Visitor Center** (502– 875–TOUR). Because the city's layout is confusing, a map is good headache prevention.

Directly across Capitol Avenue from the visitors center is **Rebecca-Ruth Candy, Inc.,** at 112 East Second Street, Frankfort 40601. Chocolate and candy addicts will love the tour of one of Kentucky's oldest houses of sweet repute. In 1919 Rebecca Gooch and Ruth (Hanly) Booe quit teaching and went into business making candy. Ruth's grandson, Charles Booe, carries on the tradition today.

Tour the production area to see pipes running full of liquid Dutch chocolate and churning vats of sugar and thick cream. Some candies are made completely by hand on the original 1919 marble slab. Rebecca-Ruth sells literally hundreds of varieties, including delicate mints, crunchy chocolate turtles, fudge galore, and variations on the theme of the bourbon ball. Hours are Monday through Saturday 8:00 A.M. to 5:30 P.M. Tours are given Monday through Thursday from January through October. Call (502) 223–7475 or (800) 444–3766 for a tour schedule or a free catalog.

Go down St. Clair Mall and over the singing bridge, a blue bridge with a steel grid roadway that welcomes cars to Frankfort with a high-pitched hum. Look for **Rick's White Light Diner,** 114 Bridge Street, Frankfort, 40601 (502–227–4889), an irresistible little hamburger joint that's been doing regular business since 1927. The signs painted on the wall by the door read COURTEOUS SERVICE and, my favorite, LADIES INVITED. Sit on one of the spinning stools at the counter and try one of chef Rick Paul's unusual burgers, such as the garlic burger or the super-hot Cajun cheeseburger. Finish the feast with a strong espresso and perhaps a good-natured argument with Chef Paul, whose strength of opinion is rivaled only by the strength of his spices. The diner is open for lunch during the week unless Rick is away on a catering assignment. Call him at his catering service at (502) 696–9138 for information Monday through Saturday.

True Blue

The first successful transplant of a human hand was performed in Louisville, Kentucky, in 1999.

The **Kentucky History Center** is the definitive high-tech repository of documents, photos, and all manner of important archival material concerning the history of our commonwealth. View such things as Daniel Boone's original survey note, in his handwriting. For years the Kentucky Historical Society had dreamed of having a permanent, state-of-the-art facility for research and education, and this impressive 167,000-square-foot facility was the dream-come-true and then some. The center is in downtown Frankfort, next to the railroad tracks on the corner of Broadway and Ann Street. History Center hours are 10:00 A.M. to 5:00 P.M. Tuesday, Wednesday, Friday, and Saturday; 10:00 A.M. to 8:00 P.M. Thursday; and 1:00 to 5:00 P.M. Sunday. Admission is free. Call (877) 444–7867 for information about changing exhibits and special events at the center.

Just across and down a block on Broadway you'll find numerous interesting shops. There are several antiques malls with everything from antique linens to cannonballs. **Poor Richard's Books,** at 223 West Broadway, Frankfort 40601, carries a mix of new and used tomes (including some hand-printed at Larkspur Press in Owen County). Call (502) 223–8018. A few doors away is **Completely Kentucky,** at 237 West Broadway, Frankfort 40601, which, as its name implies, carries products made in the Bluegrass state. Call (502) 223–5240. Outside of Berea, stores that specialize in regional crafts and other indigenous products are surprisingly few, and Completely Kentucky has variety in both items and price range. From wonderful and affordable cherry kitchen tools and foods to fine raku pottery and handmade jewelry to whimsical metal yard "critters," you're sure to find something of interest.

One of Frankfort's newest attractions is actually old—a resurrected bit of Civil War history (and in-town forest) called **Leslie Morris Park on Fort Hill.** There were two Civil War earthwork forts on the hill, Fort Boone and New Redoubt. In 1864 Confederate general John Hunt Morgan's raiders attacked Fort Boone, but local citizens successfully defended the city. You can take a self-guided walking tour (begin at the Fort Hill visitors center in the Old Capitol Annex, 100 Broadway, Frankfort 40601). It's a moderately strenuous trek up Old Military Road, but the reward is a chance to see the walls of Fort Boone and earthworks of New Redoubt, as well as a commanding view of downtown Frankfort.

Through all of its varied projects, **Shooting Star Nursery** is accomplishing the goals of educating people about preserving the world's biodiversity and of promoting renaturalization in Kentucky and elsewhere. The nursery itself supplies more than 3,000 species of nursery-propagated (from seeds, cuttings, and divisions) native plants for gardening, landscaping, and restoring damaged lands such as strip mines and tired farmland. The nursery's botanists spend lots of energy doing consultation for those involved in ecological restoration. Ask about their "septic wetland" design, which is basically a 7-by-20-foot pit filled with 18 inches of gravel, water, and water-loving wild plants. The "brown" wastewater from a house goes in one end, and clean, safe water comes out the other after the plants do the filtering work with their roots. This system can even be made to work on a bed of rock.

Visit the nursery to shop for container and bare-root plants and seeds. To get there from Frankfort, take Highway 127 north out of town to the Frankfort/Owenton exit and turn left; go 10 miles, just past the road's intersection with Highway 2919, to Bates Road. Shooting Star is 1/2 mile in on the left. Nursery hours are Thursday, Friday, and Sunday from 1:00 to 5:00 P.M. and Saturday from 9:00 A.M. to 5:00 P.M. from April through June; Saturday only July through October. Otherwise, appointments to visit are welcome. Call (502) 223–1679 or (502) 223–2906, or write them at 444 Bates Road, Frankfort 40601, to receive a catalog or information about upcoming "Ecological Restoration and Stewardship" workshops.

About 8 miles north of Frankfort is **Canoe Kentucky** (7265 Peaks Mill Road, Frankfort 40601; 502–227–4492 or 800–K–CANOE–1), home base for Ed Councill, canoeist and Elkhorn Creek conservation activist extraordinaire. Canoe Kentucky offers a variety of excursions on a dozen Kentucky waterways, but it is the one in his own backyard, Elkhorn Creek, that is most dear to his heart. Take an excursion and you'll soon understand why. This long and winding waterway—which flows for more than 100 miles through parts of six counties—played an important role in the settlement of the bluegrass area. Poet Walt Whitman, whose soldier brother was encamped in Kentucky in 1863, wrote of "the vale of the Elkhorn." Whether your interest is historic sites, fishing (some sections are great for catching bass), picnicking, or just a quiet-at-your-own-pace getaway, Councill can suggest a good paddle route. Canoe Kentucky even offers moonlight excursions for groups. ("We found that these weren't as much fun when it was a group of people who didn't know each other," Councill explained.) If you want to learn all about the Elkhorn, its history, its wildlife, and the need to protect it in light of rapidly encroaching development, or if you want to try a more unusual aspect of canoeing, such as winter canoeing, Ed Councill's the one to go up (or down) the creek with. Prices vary depending on length and type of excursion. An unguided, 6-mile (2½-hour) excursion costs $26 per person; two people to a canoe. A guide on the trip would cost $50 more per group.

From Frankfort go west on I–64 or Highway 60 to Shelbyville. In 1825 Julia Tevis founded **Science Hill,** a girls' school at 525 Washington Street in downtown **Shelbyville,** because she believed young women needed an education in math and science, not just needlepoint and etiquette. During its 114-year operation, Science Hill was known as one of the best preparatory schools in the country. Etiquette, however, never lost its essential place. A former student remembers this story about Miss Julia Poynter, the last principal of the school: The mother of a "town boy" had a party in her home. One of the students thanked the hostess by saying, "I enjoyed myself thoroughly." Miss Julia reprimanded the girl, saying, "You do not go to a party to enjoy yourself, you go to enjoy others. Tell your hostess that you enjoyed her party."

Today the fully restored Science Hill complex houses six boutiques, the Wakefield-Scearce Galleries, and a restaurant, the **Georgia Room** of Science Hill Inn. In keeping with the nineteenth-century atmosphere, the restaurant serves fine American food with a heavy Kentucky accent. Lunch is served daily, except Monday, from 11:30 A.M. to 2:30 P.M.; dinner is served Friday and Saturday from 5:30 to 8:30 P.M.

Call (502) 633–2825. ***Wakefield-Scearce Galleries*** (502–633–4382) are full of elegant English (plus a touch of Oriental, American, and European) furniture, silver, china, rugs, paintings, and other decorative objects. Much of the furniture is antique, and the reproductions are beautifully made. The quality is high, as are the prices. Whether or not you can afford the decor, these museum-like galleries provide room after room of visual and tactile delight. Hours are 9:00 A.M. to 5:00 P.M. Monday through Saturday.

A few blocks west of Science Hill, at 707 Washington Street, Shelbyville 40065, follow the bagpipe music to Wendy Fay and Sally Nicol's store, ***The Scotland Yard,*** Kentucky's only all-Scottish extravaganza. In the center room is a chart listing family names and their respective tartan plaids. If your last name is Douglas or Stewart or (Lord help you) Colquhoun or Farquharson, you will be able to find ties, skirts, and scarves in all possible weave variations on your tartan. All 490 tartans are represented, in addition to family crests and clan car badges, kilt outfits, bagpipe supplies, maps, jewelry, music, and a room full of very British foods. Hours are 10:00 A.M. to 5:00 P.M. Monday through Saturday. Call (502) 633–0116 or (800) 636–0116.

There are several other charming shops along Washington Street. ***Snowberry Hill,*** at 702 Washington, Shelbyville 40065, carries candles and other decorative items. Call (502) 647–9106. In the same building is ***The Needle Nest,*** with supplies for needlepoint and tapestry. Call the Needle Nest at (502) 633–4701.

Follow Highway 60 (or, if you're in a hurry, take I-64 West) to ***Louisville,*** largest city in the state and home of the world-famous ***Kentucky Derby.*** The greatest two minutes in sports are also part of the greatest twenty-four hours in fashion. For a week before the Derby, everyone and everything is dressed to the nines—houses are repainted, yards are relandscaped, hair is coiffed, and bodies are clothed in the latest styles, no matter the cost or the weather. For Kentuckians the Derby marks the beginning of early summer and, therefore, the first day that it's acceptable for women to shed their dark winter garb and wear white again. Fashion sometimes follows need and sometimes it leads. Several years ago we had a bitter cold, rainy Derby Day, but the dresses were already purchased, and hats were garnished. Women simply wore thermal underwear under sleeveless gowns, and men, for once, were happy to keep on their coats and ties.

The Kentucky Derby is run the first Saturday in May at Churchill Downs Race Track on Central Avenue (502–636–4400). The gates open at 8:00 A.M., and you can join the party on the Infield or wander the paddock area for $40—standing room only or bring-your-own chair or blanket. Racing begins at 11:30 A.M., but the Run for the Roses isn't until 6:04 P.M. (There's not a rosebush on the grounds, by the way.) Dress however you want, and keep your eyes peeled for celebrities. Churchill Downs also hosts thoroughbred racing during a Spring Meet, which runs from the end of April to the beginning of July, and a Fall Meet, from late October through late November.

If you're planning to be seen at the Derby and want to be on the cutting edge of fashion, you may want to check out the annual pre-Derby fashion show held in mid-April at the **Kentucky Derby Museum** on the grounds of Churchill Downs. Celebs and local media personalities model the latest in hats and clothes, setting a precedent for the masses. Any time of year the Kentucky Derby Museum is an interesting stop. Naturally, the exhibits feature the Derby's history, but there are others concerning the whole thoroughbred industry. Hours are 9:00 A.M. to 5:00 P.M. Monday through Saturday, noon to 5:00 P.M. Sunday. Also on-site is the Finish Line Gift Shop and The Derby Cafe. Call (502) 637–1111.

Far from the madding crowd, but not far from Churchill Downs, are several peaceful sites. The most surprising is just inside the I–264 loop between Poplar Level Road and Newburg Road: the **Beargrass Creek State Nature Preserve** (502–458–1328). The best way to get there is to turn onto Illinois Avenue off Trevilian Way (behind the Louisville Tennis Center), then park in the lot next to the **Louisville Nature Center,** where you'll find informative exhibits and a friendly staff. There's a bird blind viewing area behind the building. Trails in the preserve are well defined, though not marked, so pick up a map at the center. No dogs or bicycles are allowed. The preserve encompasses forty-one acres and has a remarkably diverse community of flora and fauna. Because it's smack-dab in the middle of the city, it is constantly in use for environmental education. So if you placed all your bets badly at the track, here's a balm. This lovely spot is open daily from sunrise to sunset, and there's usually someone at the nature center from 8:30 A.M. to 4:30 P.M.

The park is named after Beargrass Creek, which empties into the Ohio River just above the famous **Falls of the Ohio,** a rocky series of rapids over a 3-mile descent, which stopped early travelers on their way south. Beargrass Creek proved to be a place to rest and to develop a strategy for getting around the falls. In 1778 George Rogers Clark set up a military and civilian camp nearby, on Corn Island. Floods on the island caused the settlers to move to the mainland (somewhere between what are now Twelfth and Rowan Streets), where they started building the city of Louisville. Since the installation of the Portland Canal and the McAlpine Dam (easily seen from town near the North-western Parkway and Twenty-seventh Street), the Falls of the Ohio is an exposed coral reef, a fossil bed over 350 million years in age. Some 600 fossils species can be seen; 400 species have never been seen anywhere else. To get a good look at the fossils, cross the river into Clarksville, Indiana, park at Riverside Park, and walk near where the Fourteenth Street railroad bridge and five dam gates meet the shore. From I–65 take exit 0 and follow the signs. There is an interpretive center (812–280–9970) open Monday through Saturday from 9:00 A.M. to 5:00 P.M. and Sunday from 1:00 to 5:00 P.M. Admission is $2.00.

The *Portland Museum* (502–776–7678), features exhibits illustrating 200 years of the city's river history. One of the most enthralling items is an old newsreel of the great 1937 Ohio River Flood. A few exhibits are located in the Beech Grove antebellum home. Admission is $4.00; hours are Tuesday through Friday from 10:00 A.M. to 4:30 P.M. From I–64 take the Twenty-second Street exit and go to 2308 Portland Avenue, Louisville 40212. Staff at the museum is limited, so it's a good idea to call ahead to make sure they'll be open.

Jefferson County has restored and opened to the public a grand-style Greek Revival brick house, circa 1835, known as the *Farnsley-Moreman House.* With an extremely high front portico that haughtily faces the river, the house represents a showy attitude prevalent in prosperous river cities in the nineteenth century. In the 1860s this house sat at the center of what was the largest farm in the county at the time. If you visit, Riverside (as the property is now known), you'll see period antique furnishings and historically authentic kitchen gardens in addition to exhibits reflecting life on the river as far back as 4,000 years. (It is considered the best view of the Ohio River in Louisville.) Call (502) 935–6809 for information on special events. Normal hours are Tuesday through Saturday from 10:00 A.M. to 4:30 P.M., Sunday from 1:00 to 4:30 P.M. To get there, head west on Gene Snyder Freeway (you can access this from I–64 and I–65), and stay on the "greenbelt," as it's called, until you reach Lower River Road. Then just follow the signs. The house is at the intersection of Lower River and Moorman Roads. Riverboat excursions aboard the *Spirit of Jefferson* stern-wheeler depart from the nearby Greenwood Road boat dock, just 4 miles away. Tickets are $9.00. Call (502) 574–2355 for times.

Speaking of Jefferson, in 1810 John and Lucy Fry Speed had a Federal-style mansion built that was based on a design by old Thomas himself. *Farmington* has octagonal rooms, hidden stairs, and orderly gardens. Abraham Lincoln visited this home of his friend, Joshua Speed, for six weeks in 1841 during a temporary break in his relationship with Mary Todd, his future wife.

Originally the house was in the center of a 552-acre hemp plantation. Now it's on eighteen acres, all of which are carefully restored and maintained in keeping with its early-nineteenth-century history. You can visit it Tuesday through Saturday from 10:00 A.M. to 4:30 P.M., Sunday from 1:30 to 3:30 P.M. The address is 3033 Bardstown Road, Louisville 40205. Call (502) 452–9920 for more information.

Another spectacular Federal-style structure, which has been exquisitely restored, is the 1900 Ferguson Mansion, 1310 South Third Street, Louisville 40208, now home to the **Filson Club Historical Society** (502–635–5083). The society has a nationally renowned genealogy library (which costs $5.00 to use) and extensive manuscript, photography, and museum collections (which can be viewed for free). Stop by between 9:00 A.M. and 5:00 P.M. Monday through Friday or 9:00 a.m. to noon Saturday.

True Blue

Louisville is second only to Boston in number of registered historic sites.

Next to Beargrass Creek Park is the **Louisville Zoological Garden,** at 100 Trevilian Way, home to more than 1,300 animals. The zoo has an exhibit of birds of prey and a HerpAquarium, which features a simulated rain forest. It is open daily, year-round. Admission is $7.95 for adults, $5.95 for children. Call (502) 459–2181 for current hours.

From the zoo take Newburg Road to Eastern Parkway, and go west to Third Street; turn right and you're on the University of Louisville campus. The **Speed Art Museum** at 2035 South Third Street, Louisville 40208 (502–634–7000) is a small but outstanding museum not to be missed at any cost. The permanent collection includes works from all periods, including some distinguished medieval, Renaissance, and Dutch masterpieces, and a broad representation of contemporary art. The museum also maintains a stimulating schedule of traveling exhibitions. Hours are 10:30 A.M. to 4:00 P.M. Tuesday, Wednesday, and Friday; 10:30 A.M. to 8:00 P.M. Thursday; 10:30 A.M. to 5:00 P.M. Saturday; and noon to 5:00 P.M. Sunday. During the summer, more culture is in store at the corner of Fourth and Magnolia Streets in Central Park. The **Kentucky Shakespeare Festival** performs free, high-quality, live Shakespeare productions in June and July. Curtain time is 8:00 P.M. Tuesday through Sunday. Call (502) 583–8738 for current schedules.

Indoor theater is always happening in this town. Consult the *Louisville*

True Blue

Courier Journal for performances by the myriad little theaters, and check the schedule at *Actors Theatre,* 316 West Main Street, Louisville 40202. In addition to producing a surprising variety of plays all year (except during July and August), Actors has become nationally known for the Humana Festival of New American Plays. Shows in the festival are booked early, so get the schedule and make reservations by calling (502) 584–1205 or (800) 428–5849. There's a restaurant downstairs at Actors Theatre.

True Blue

In 1893 a pair of Louisville sisters penned the kindergarten greeting song, "Good Morning to You," which later became the most-sung song in the world rewritten as "Happy Birthday to You."

Main Street is art street in Louisville. The glass structure with the big whimsical sculpture is the *Kentucky Center for the Arts* at 609 West Main Street, Louisville 40202. The center hosts a little of everything, including the Louisville Opera, ballet, orchestra, theater for all ages, and a series of national and regional performers. Call (502) 584–7777. A few doors down, the *Kentucky Art and Craft Gallery* (502–589–0102) features the work of some of the state's finest craftspeople. The *Zephyr Gallery,* at 610 East Market Street, Louisville 40202 (502–585–5646), is another place worth exploring. This art cooperative never fails to hang imaginative shows.

The next stop is for kids. The *Louisville Science Center,* 727 West Main Street, Louisville 40202, is a big, colorful, hands-on place orchestrated for discovery. The selling point for adults is the IMAX theater, a four-story screen surrounded by speakers; the experience blows your confidence in logic to pieces. "It's just a movie," you tell yourself as you clutch the nearest person's arm to keep from falling. Call the museum at (502) 561–6100 for show times and admission charges.

Fascinating Facade

*O*ne of Louisville's most fascinating house tours isn't really a house; it's just the front of a house. Like a piece of a movie set, the front of the Charles Heigold House sits forlornly in Thruston Park, off River Road east of downtown Louisville. If this were a movie, it would be a historical drama, set in the mid-1800s, when Heigold, a German immigrant and stonemason, decided to carve his political feelings in stone—on the front of his house. "The Union Forever, All Hail To This Union, Let It Never Desolve It" is among the sayings and figures elaborately carved into the facade in exuberant fashion. The rest of the house was razed when the street on which it originally stood became part of the city landfill. Luckily, city officials decided to save this face for visitors and future residents to ponder and enjoy.

In case you didn't notice, there's a 120-foot baseball bat at Main and Eighth Streets. The erect bat is a beacon for the **Louisville Slugger Museum** (502–588–7228). Baseball fans of all ages will love the museum and tour of the world's largest manufacturing plant of baseball bats. (Over one million are made there annually.) There's a full-size dugout, a replica of Orioles Park, a replica of a northern white ash forest, and exhibits tracing the history of the game and its most famous brand of bat. Despite being called the Louisville Slugger, for twenty-two years the bats were actually made across the Ohio River in southern Indiana. In 1996 the manufacturing plant returned to Louisville. Museum hours are Monday through Saturday, 9:00 A.M. to 5:00 P.M. Admission is $6.00.

Since there are so many restaurants of every kind in town, let's just consider breakfast and dessert. If having breakfast at **Lynn's Paradise Cafe** (984 Barret Avenue, Louisville 40204; 502–583–3447) doesn't get your day off to a smiling start, you might as well just give it up and head back to bed. Owner Lynn Winter's taste in decor is certainly eye-opening—there's an 8-foot red coffeepot out front and all manner of knickknacks inside—but there's nothing silly about her efforts in the kitchen. This place serves great breakfast burritos, chunky French toast topped with fruit and whipped cream, fabulous cheese home fries, and all sorts of other inventive approaches to "home cooking." Lynn's is open 7:00 A.M.

Tattoos—While You Wait (Is There Any Other Way?)

A little-known cultural reference library of sorts is found in the halls of **Tattoo Charlie's,** *a dermagraphic extravaganza. Tattoo art has come a long way since bones and charcoal or needles in a cork. For the uninitiated, you can watch consenting clients being decorated by a certified tattoo technician wielding an electric needle that looks and sounds like a dentist's drill. Prices range from $25 for a single music note, for example, to more than $3,000 for a series of full-color illustrations. Even if you aren't personally interested in a tattoo, check out the tattoo design gallery and museum featuring photos, tattoo machines, and other*

memorabilia. Owner and tattoo master Charlie Wheeler has lined the walls with possible patterns. Then there are hundreds of photographs and slides of customers displaying actual tattoos, no matter where they are. Charlie has a motorcycle seat in his booth where you can relax and watch the show or, perhaps, try out your new tattoo in the correct posture. Tattoo Charlie's is located at 1845 Berry Boulevard, Louisville 40215, on the south side of town; the easiest way to get there is to take Highway 31 south and turn east on Seventh Street Road, then veer onto Berry Boulevard. No appointment necessary. Call (502) 366–9635 for hours.

to 10:00 P.M. Tuesday through Saturday, so if you like t[...]
also get lunch or dinner.

The prize for the most unusual business combin[...]
dessert is the **Quonset Hut Concrete Statuary Gard[...]**
at the Overlook. You can eat ice cream or frozen yog[...]
for concrete birdbaths, statues, pots, urns, or garden [...]
reasonable prices. Recently the Quonset Hut folks also sta[...]
and selling high-quality hammocks that you can try out. Or you can
simply gaze down from the top of Phoenix Hill onto the Louisville skyline. This is a good place for a first date. Take Broadway east to Baxter
Avenue, then turn left (north) to Hull Street; turn left (west) to the top
of the overlook and you're there. Hours are 4:00 to 10:00 P.M. Monday
through Friday, 9:00 A.M. to 10:00 P.M. Saturday, and 1:00 to 10:00 P.M.
Sunday. Call (502) 584–0814.

Kizito Cookies (502–456–2891) wins a prize for the most unusual
method of dessert distribution. Elizabeth Kizito started her business by
carrying baskets of scrumptious chocolate cookies through the downtown streets on her head during lunch hours. She is from Uganda, where
it's commonplace for folks to keep their hands free by means of this bal-
ancing act, but in Louisville, she's become famous for it. These days she
has a retail store at 1398 Bardstown Road, Louisville 40204, where you
can buy coffee, cookies, and muffins while looking over a colorful selection of African earrings or small carvings from Kenya and Uganda.
Hours are 7:00 A.M. to 5:00 P.M. Tuesday through Friday, 9:00 A.M. to 5:00
P.M. Saturday.

Run, Rooster, Run!

*I*f you're going toward Bardstown
from the west on Highway 245, not
stopping at **Rooster Run General**
Store *(502–348–8753) is like being
in Memphis and skipping Graceland.
The store, formerly called Evans Beverage Depot, was the only place in
Nelson County in the late 1960s that
sold alcohol. One day a man had too
many drinks, and his wife showed
up with fire in her eyes, stood in the
Depot door, and snarled his name.*

*When the drunk man sped obediently
to her side, someone remarked, "Well,
would you look at that old rooster
run." Such is the history of town
names in our state. I still wonder
whether the name had anything
to do with the fact that the next town
over is called Hen Peck. Whatever the
truth may be, Joe Evans put the place
on the map by selling over a million
Rooster Run caps to truck drivers
and celebrities alike.*

*School for
Danville was
hed in 1823 with
three pupils. It was the
first state-supported school
of its kind in the nation.
Today, a large number of its
graduates go on to attend
college or technical school
and join the work force.*

More wonderful African-oriented skills are featured at **Kente International** (1954 Bonnycastle Avenue, Louisville 40205 502–459–4595), a gallery/store that carries a line of imported goods from South America, Pakistan, India, and Africa. You'll fall in love with the colorful clothing and tapestries and the striking jewelry and sculpture. The owner, Musa Uthman, is a percussionist extraordinaire and, not surprisingly, sells handmade drums from Africa and India, plus a few made in the United States by Native Americans. The most popular is the beautiful Djamba drum from Senegal; it's hand-carved from a local hardwood, and it has a goatskin head that is tuned with ropes. Musa teaches basic techniques and rhythms during drum workshops, which he gives by appointment on Sunday and just after hours. The store is open from 10:00 A.M. to 6:00 P.M. Monday through Saturday.

If you're looking for fragments of almost anything imaginable, pay a visit to **Joe Ley Antiques** at 615 East Market Street, Louisville 40202. Joe Ley's place is two acres under one roof full—and I mean full—of antique treasures. For architects and home-restoration folks, this is an endless toy shop. Stained glass, chandeliers, mantels, carousel horses, stuffed moose, fine silver—you name it, it's here. Hours are Tuesday through Saturday from 8:30 A.M. to 5:00 P.M. Call (502) 583–4014. Want more? Head down to **Architectural Salvage** at 618 East Broadway, Louisville 40202, for more of the same. This place is crammed full of mantels, hardware, stained glass, real doors, wrought iron, and on and on. Call (502) 589–0670 if you care to ask specifics. I recommend the browsing method myself. Are you obsessed with kitsch items from the 1950s and '60s? Got a chrome toaster collection? Try the **Swan Street Antique Mall** (502–584–6255) at 947 East Breckinridge Street, Louisville 40202. Or for the whole gamut, stop by the **Louisville Antique Mall** (502–635–2852), in a nineteenth-century cotton mill at 900 Goss Avenue, Louisville 40202.

If you want to stay in town but escape briefly, escape to **Cherokee Park,** off Eastern Parkway east of downtown, for bicycling, jogging, and picnicking. (You can rent bikes at **Highland Cycle** nearby at 1737 Bardstown Road, Louisville 40205; 502–458–7832.) Or take Third Street south to **Iroquois Park** and admire a nearly 200-year-old forest. Louisville has some of the most beautiful public parks found anywhere, thanks to foresight on the part of city leaders. In 1891 Louisville hired Frederick Law Olmsted to design and construct the city's park system.

Olmsted is known as the father of landscape architecture; his other credits include New York's Central Park, Biltmore Gardens, and the 1893 Chicago World's Fair. When Olmsted retired in 1895, his stepson, John C. Olmsted, completed the Louisville plan. In all, the Olmsteds created sixteen Louisville parks between 1891 and 1935. Although a 1974 tornado took its toll, citizens rallied in the late 1980s to conserve and, where necessary, restore the parks' beauty.

To explore the world in all its infinite detail is a lifelong process demanding your every sense. But not every sense is challenged equally by those of us who have the use of all human senses. The blind can access nearly any information that seeing people can if they have the tools, and some of their senses, like touch and hearing, are sharpened by intensive use. The **American Printing House for the Blind,** established in 1858, is the world's largest and oldest publisher and manufacturer of education aids for visually impaired people. The printing house has recently opened a museum of rare artifacts relating to the history of technology developed for the blind—from the tactile language of Braille to the audio recording of almost any text that exists in the world. This museum is one of the most important and unique sites in Louisville. Hours are Monday through Friday from 8:30 A.M. to 4:30 P.M. For more information call (800) 223–1839. The printing house and museum is located at 1839 Frankfort Avenue, 40206.

To explore Louisville by yourself is one kind of experience. To be guided on a bus tour by self-proclaimed "tourologists" Mike and Joe Bush is another kind of experience altogether. Try **Joe and Mike's Pretty Good Tours** and find out why this "internationally unknown" tour of Louisville is getting so popular. Call (502) 459–1247 for information and scheduling.

Who Really Invented the Steamboat?

*P*ay your respects to John Fitch, the unhappy inventor of the steamboat in 1791. Then listen to the earth rumble when Robert Fulton turns over in his grave—wherever he's buried, may he rest in some peace. John Fitch was not born in Bardstown, but he died here after a lifetime of work on steam navigation and a lifetime of struggle with inventor James Rumsey, who, like Fulton, claimed to have been the first to apply it successfully. After failing to get sponsors, comparable to today's lusted-after research grants, Fitch came to Nelson County, built steamboat models, and tested them in local streams. **John Fitch's grave** in the square is marked by a small steamboat replica.

Abbeys and Art

hat was once an abused tract of tired farmland is now ***Bernheim Forest Arboretum and Nature Center,*** a 10,000-acre native forest protected since 1928. Available in this legacy of the "Knobs" are hiking, picnicking, limited fishing, unlimited daydreaming, and a self-education in the nature center's museum or in the arboretum, where an enormous variety of ornamental plants are grown in meticulously labeled, manicured beds. I used to skip high school in the spring to make an annual pilgrimage here, armed with my bicycle and a sketch pad. The forest is open from 7:00 A.M. to sunset daily. Call (502) 543–2451 for information. Bernheim Forest is right next to the intersection of I–65 (exit 112) and Highway 245.

While traveling, Mark Twain was asked by the luggage inspector if he had anything besides clothing in his suitcase. Twain said no, but I guess he looked suspicious because the man opened his case anyhow and found a fifth of bourbon whiskey. "I thought you had only clothes!" the man roared. "Ahh," Twain answered, "but that's my nightcap." Twain's drink of choice had to be bourbon, and it had to be from the limestone hills of Kentucky, which provide the water that gives Jim Beam and other regional bourbons a distinctive flavor that makes them the best in the world. For a crash course in whiskey mash, take a free tour of the ***Jim Beam American Outpost and Museum*** (502–543–9877) on Highway 245, a mile east of Bernheim Forest. Hours are 9:00 A.M. to 4:30 P.M. Monday through Saturday, 1:00 to 4:00 P.M. Sunday.

Bardstown is dense with well-advertised historically significant treasures, such as ***My Old Kentucky Home State Park*** and house of John Rowan. Rowan invited his cousin from Pittsburgh, Stephen Foster, to visit in 1852, and shortly afterward, Foster wrote the tune that is now our official state song. The mansion and gardens are open from 9:00 A.M. to 5:00 P.M. daily year-round. From early June through Labor Day, the famous musical, *The Stephen Foster Story,* is performed outdoors. You can't miss the signs. Call (800) 323–7803 for more information.

Near the park on Highway 49 is ***Heaven Hill Distilleries,*** touted as the largest family-owned distillery in the country. The free tour includes a lesson in bourbon making and a visit to the bottling operation. This distillery makes "Heaven Hill," "Elijah Craig," and "Evan Williams." Open Monday through Friday; tours are at 10:30 A.M. and 2:30 P.M. Call (502) 348–3921.

Most Kentuckians do know about ***Wickland,*** the finest example of

Georgian architecture in the country and "the only home in America where three governors have lived," but there's a story about this place that opens the mind to a new way to trace history. Charles Wickliffe, a rags-to-riches figure, built the place in 1815 for his bride, Margaret Crepps. Charles was a Kentucky governor, and his son, Robert, became Louisiana's last pre–Civil War governor. Their daughter, Julia Tevis, married William Beckham, and they lived in Wickland with their ten children, one of whom, John Crepps Wickliffe Beckham, also became governor of Kentucky. That makes three governors in the family. The Beckhams were second-generation nouveaux riches with Deep South connections and a penchant for lavish Southern-style living, which included owning slaves. When the Civil War broke out, they were harassed, so the family fled from Wickland to Canada.

As is true for many women during many eras, Julia left her record of the times in the form of a quilt. Her stunning, full-size Baby Blocks quilt is made entirely of silk and velvet pieces from family ball dresses and gowns. Not designed for wear-and-tear, the quilt showed that even after the "recent unpleasantness," Julia had a place in her life for nonfunctional beauty; it also showed that ball dresses weren't needed any more—posh days were over. Wickland's fourteen rooms are fully furnished with exquisite antiques. The museum offers guided tours year-round, but hours may vary. Admission is $4.00. To get there, go about 1 mile east of Court Square on Highway 62. For more information, write Wickland, P.O. Box 314, Bardstown 40004, or call (502) 348–5428 and talk to resident curator Sara Trigg.

Another old Southern-style mansion that bore big-time political figures into the world is *The Mansion,* 1003 North Third Street, Bardstown 40004, an eight-room bed-and-breakfast. Built in 1851 by Lieutenant Governor William E. Johnson, the house marks the site where the Confederate flag was first raised in the state of Kentucky. Daily tours are conducted at 1:00 and 5:00 P.M. by reservation. Call Mr. or Mrs. Joseph Dennis Downs for lodging reservations at (502) 348–2586.

Arbor Rose Bed and Breakfast is a cream-colored two-story Victorian house at 209 East Stephen Foster Avenue, Bardstown 40004. The 1820 building's most famous features are the wooden mantels in every room that were carved by Alexander Moore, the artisan who did the original finish carpentry at My Old Kentucky Home. However, owners Judy and Derrick Melzer provide other features guests will appreciate, such as a hot tub, breakfast on the garden terrace, and homemade cookies. Call (888) 828–3330 to reserve one of the five guest rooms.

True Blue

Marion County is located at the geographic center of Kentucky.

Two on-the-beaten-path restaurants in town are *Old Talbott Tavern,* the oldest western stagecoach stop in America, circa 1779, which also has bed-and-breakfast lodging in the old inn (502–348–3494), and *My Old Kentucky Dinner Train* (502–348–7500), where you dine in vintage 1940s dining cars pulled by old diesel-electric engines on a two-hour ride to Limestone Springs and back. Both have their merits, but the local, workaday place to eat is the *Hurst Restaurant* (502–348–8929), a small downtown diner facing Courthouse Square. The soups are homemade, and the local talk is always juicy.

At the corner of Highway 62 West, also called Stephen Foster Avenue, and Fifth Street is the *Saint Joseph Proto-Cathedral.* The cathedral, circa 1823, is the oldest west of the Alleghenies and contains a collection of paintings given by the French king Louis Philippe, Francis I, King of the Two Sicilies, and Pope Leo XII. Here's what impresses me: Six solid tree trunks, lathed and plastered, were transformed into the building's huge Corinthian columns. St. Joseph's is open every day. Guided tours are given April through October from 9:00 A.M. to 5:00 P.M. Monday through Friday, Saturday from 9:00 A.M. to 2:30 P.M., and Sunday from 1:00 to 5:00 P.M. You can tour on your own November through March. Admission is free, but donations are encouraged. Call (502) 348–3126.

Behind the cathedral is *Spalding Hall,* circa 1826, a large brick building that was originally part of Saint Joseph College, Seminary, and later Prep School. Two adjoining museums housed here are the *Bardstown Historical Museum* and the *Oscar Getz Museum of Whiskey History,* both free. Displays range from items like Jenny Lind's cape and Jesse James's hat to an original 1854 E. G. Booz bottle, which inspired the word *booze,* and a Carrie Nation exhibit. Hours from May through October are 9:00 A.M. to 5:00 P.M. Monday to Saturday and 1:00 to 5:00 P.M. Sunday. From November through April the museums open at 10:00 A.M. and close at 4:00 P.M., except on Sunday, when they are open from 1:00 to 4:00 P.M.

Think about the basis of homesteading—self-sufficiency. Now apply the concept to the visual arts and you will begin to appreciate Jim and Jeannette Cantrell. The *Bardstown Art Gallery,* downstairs in Spalding Hall, is a fine-art gallery, a framing shop, pottery and painting studios, a hand-set printing press operation, an office, a home, and a small book-sales business, which boasts one of the country's most comprehensive collections of Thomas Merton's writings. That both Cantrells have a love of high quality is apparent in everything from Jim's treatment of light and reflections in his oils to Jeannette's hand-set letterpress gallery announcements. Jeannette curates group and solo shows in addition to displaying Jim's originals in oil, watercolor, pen and ink, and anything else that catches his eclectic eye.

It was by accident that Jeannette became a Merton expert. One of the monks at the nearby abbey asked if she wouldn't mind selling a few of Merton's books to tourists. She started with a few copies of *Seven Storey Mountain,* and now she carries a respectable line of Merton's out-of-print writings, valuable limited editions, related scholarly works, and cassettes of Merton himself reading from his works or just talking about such subjects as Rilke's poetry, silence, art, and beauty. Hours at the Bardstown Art Gallery are officially By Chance or By Appointment, but someone is usually there from 10:00 A.M. to 5:00 P.M. Monday through Saturday and from 1:00 to 5:00 P.M. Sunday. Contact the Cantrells by writing to P.O. Box 417, Bardstown 40004 or calling (502) 348–6488.

To visit Thomas Merton's residence, the ***Abbey of Gethsemani,*** oldest Cistercian monastery in the United States, follow Highway 31E south from Bardstown, veer left at Culvertown onto Highway 247, and watch for TRAPPISTS signs. From the heart of Italy around A.D. 500, Saint Benedict developed a set of rules to help monks in a spiritually based community follow the example of Christ as closely as possible. These Trappist monks

Abbey of Gethsemani

take vows to renounce the capacity to acquire and possess goods, to obey the house rules and the abbot's advice, and to remain celibate. Silence is encouraged but not required. "Enclosure," I've been told, "is enforced not so much to keep laypeople out as to keep the monks in." But these monks do indulge in some wandering. Thomas Merton, quintessential ascetic, aesthete monk from this abbey, was known to go "out" to lecture, to meet with other spiritual people, and occasionally to hear jazz. While visiting the abbey, I met a monk who travels to Owensboro for the barbecue festival. And the organist and composer, Father Chrysogonus, is a musical genius who often travels to Europe for research. No matter what else you think, their life choice is radical.

Economic survival is perhaps the greatest difference between early and modern cloisters. The seventy-six resident monks make and sell fruit-cakes and three kinds of Port Salut Trappist cheese, a pungent, creamy, French-style aged cheese. Everyone takes part in all aspects of the work, from making cheese to doing dishes to answering the phone or laying sewer pipes. The slogan *Ora et Labora* means "prayer and work," but they don't have "all necessary things" on their 2,000-acre farm. They use hired help to raise the beef cattle and to do some construction and maintenance. Health care, for example, is sought in the secular world, including modern services such as weight-loss centers.

Laypeople are welcome to join in parts of life at the abbey. Mass is always open to the public, if you can make it at 5:30 A.M. on weekdays (the monks will have been awake for hours by then), and there are a variety of other prayer services and vespers throughout the day. Sunday Mass is at 10:30 A.M. in the main chapel, a long, narrow, modern building where the choir's chant reverberates as if produced in outer space. Gethsemani has a retreat house with thirty rooms that can be reserved for personal or group retreats. Women are welcome only during the first and third full weeks of each month (that's Monday to Monday), and men can make retreats during the second and fourth weeks. Call far in advance at (502) 549–3117. For a group day visit, call (502) 549–4129. For more information or to order cheese, write Abbey of Gethsemani, Trappist 40051.

If you drive south from Bardstown on Highway 31E, you will arrive in the tiny town of *New Haven.* Downtown on Main Street the old train depot now houses the *Kentucky Railway Museum,* where you can hop a train to Boston—that's Bawston, Kentucky—11 miles away on the old Louisville & Nashville Railroad's former Lebanon Branch. Members of the museum completely restored an L&N steam locomotive (No. 152) and the streamlined No. 32 of the former Monon, made in the late 1940s. When these babies pump by, you feel your heart making reply.

From March through December trips run between 10:00 A.M. a.
P.M. on weekends, when the museum and gift shop are also open. 1
summer there are excursions daily, except Monday. For exact fa.
times, and dates, contact the Kentucky Railway Museum, P.O. Box 24t.
New Haven 40051-0240, or call (502) 549-5470 or (800) 272-0152.

To visit one of the state's most famous and picturesque whiskey distilleries, take Highway 52 east from New Haven, or Highway 49 south from
Bardstown, to Loretto; then take Highway 52 east until you see the sign
on the left for *Maker's Mark Distillery.* Like the process, the facility is
old. In 1953 Bill Samuels Sr. bought the shabby country distillery where
folks were accustomed to filling their own jugs straight from casks of
whiskey in the Quart House. Now Maker's Mark is known around the
world for its super-smooth bourbon (nicknamed "Kentucky cham-
pagne"). The distillery is open year-round, except on Saturday in January and February. Free forty-minute tours are given between 10:30 A.M.
and 3:30 P.M. Monday through Saturday and from 1:30 to 3:30 P.M. on
Sunday. For more information, call (270) 865-2881.

In Loretto take Highway 49 north, then veer right at a fork in the road
onto Highway 152. You'll soon see the sign for *Loretto Motherhouse.*
The Sisters of Loretto, founded in central Kentucky in 1812, was one of
the first American religious communities of women. The sisters moved
here in 1824 from Little Loretto at nearby St. Charles. Near the entrance
of the grounds is the restored cabin, circa 1808, of Father Charles Ner-
inckx, founder of the order. Going toward the cemetery you'll see one of
the country's first outdoor Stations of the Seven Dolors, installed in
1911. On the east side of the drive, you'll see *Knobs Haven Retreat,* a
center at which folks can reserve space for taking a serious, personal
retreat. For rates and further information, contact Elaine Prevallet, S.L.,
Director, Knobs Haven, Nerinx 40049, or call (270) 865-2621.

Next to the main church and convent, circa 1860–1863, you'll notice a
group of abstract sculptures in various media. This is the work of
Jeanne Dueber, S.L., nun and artist in residence at Loretto. Her studio
is in *Rhodes Hall Art Gallery,* at the north end of the driveway. Her
work is amazing in its variety and feeling, and her exploration of form
is almost religious. Large, refined abstract sculptures in wood, resin,
metal, and paper fill the big rooms. A large willow, struck by lightning,
has been transformed into a powerful piece called *Tempest,* in which
Dueber strategically added heads and arms of a man and a woman in
such a way that they seem to be sliding away from each other while
reaching toward each other. Many pieces are playful, like a series on
Pelé, the soccer star, or an academic charcoal drawing of a heavy,

drooping nude woman entitled *Homage to Gravity*. Pieces about Prometheus, ecstasy, companionship, and yoga positions accompany overtly religious work such as crucifixes for churches. If she's working in the first-floor studio and isn't too busy, tell her what you think. You can visit the gallery daily from 9:00 A.M. to 5:00 P.M. To buy a piece, just put your money in the slotted box by the stairs—a self-service fine-art gallery! Contact Jeanne Dueber, Rhodes Hall, Nerinx 40040, or call (270) 865–5811.

For local lodging head south on Highway 49 into **Lebanon** and check into the **Myrtledene Bed and Breakfast** at 370 North Spalding Avenue, Lebanon 40033. The house is an 1833 formal brick affair with a Colonial

Rhodes Hall Art Gallery

columned portico. Famous Confederate raider General John Hunt Morgan used Myrtledene for headquarters in 1862, and a year later, when he returned with the intention of destroying Lebanon, it was from here that he waved the white flag of truce. During his stay, Morgan rode his horse into the front door of Myrtledene and up the front steps; the hoofprints survived well into the twentieth century. A room with full breakfast costs $85 a night. Call (270) 692-2223 or (800) 391-1721 for reservations. By the way, Union soldiers from the 1862 Battle of Perryville are buried in *Lebanon's National Cemetery.*

Since Lebanon is out of the way, you might be happy to know that the little town boasts a classy eating establishment at 157 West Main Street, Lebanon 40033, called *Henning's Restaurant* (270-692-6843). In addition to occupying a handsomely restored building in the historic district, the restaurant offers homemade soups, entrees, breads, and desserts, recommended by the locals.

Although there were once more than 400 covered bridges in Kentucky, there are now only 13. The *Mount Zion Bridge* (referred in some quarters as the Beech Fork or Mooresville Bridge), in the northwest corner of Washington County, is the only remaining example of two-span Burr Arch construction, and, at 102 feet, is the longest in the state. It was almost lost recently before the county restabilized the piers, and it may yet be moved to a more accessible location. For now, the easiest way to see it is to get off the Blue Grass Parkway at exit 34 and go south on Highway 55; at Mooresville take Highway 458 north and watch for the bridge on the left spanning the Beech Fork Creek. The bridge is closed to traffic, but you can walk through it.

Get back to Highway 55 and go north less than a mile; turn south on Highway 529 and bear left at the next T in the road. From the Bluegrass Parkway take exit 42 onto Route 555 and turn left; go about 15 miles to the first light and turn right onto Highway 150. Watch for the sign advertising *Glenmar Plantation Bed and Breakfast.* This museum-like, 1785 vintage brick country home, possibly the oldest brick home in Kentucky, is about as cozy a mansion as one could hope for. There are twenty rooms, six bathrooms, and eight fireplaces (Tolstoy would be right at home). In the plantation tradition, Glenmar is a working, 300-acre farm, sporting llamas, buffalo, and other exotic animals and a large pumpkin patch. Guests can look forward to a hearty country breakfast served by candlelight in the morning. In the summer or whenever the inn is full, the host, Kenny Mandell, brings in live entertainment for guests, everything from musicians to dancers to magicians. Write to 2444 Valley Hill Road, Springfield 40069, or call (859) 284-7791 or (800) 828-3330.

Like nearby *Hodgenville* (covered in the South-Central Kentucky chapter), central Washington County is a repository of sites and stories connected to Abraham Lincoln. Abe's parents, Thomas Lincoln and Nancy Hanks, were from this area, and several of their family buildings are restored or replicated. For details go by the **Lincoln Homestead State Park** at the intersection of Highways 438 and 528, just 5 miles north of Springfield off Highway 150. An 18-hole golf course has been built on old Mordecai Lincoln's land, and I'll bet he's rolling over violently in his grave. The park also has several log structures, such as the original Berry Home, where Nancy Hanks lived when she and Thomas were courting. While the golf course is open year-round, the museum is seasonal; it's open May to September from 8:00 A.M. to 6:00 P.M. and on weekends in October. Ask at the park for a map of the Lincoln Heritage Trail. For more information, call (859) 336–7461.

In downtown *Springfield* notice the **Washington County Courthouse** on Main Street (859–336–5425). Built in 1816, it is the oldest courthouse still in use in Kentucky. Records in the files, including the marriage certificate of Abraham Lincoln's parents, date back to 1792. If court isn't in session, look at copies of this and other documents hanging on the walls. It's open from 8:30 A.M. to 4:30 P.M. Monday through Friday and from 9:00 A.M. to noon Saturday.

In 1822 Father Samuel Wilson, a Dominican priest in Springfield, asked young women of the parish to dedicate their lives to Christian education. One of those who answered the call was Maria Sansbury. A year later she and eight other women opened St. Magdalen Academy in a converted building on the banks of Cartwright Creek. As Mother Angela, Maria is considered the founder of the first order of Dominican Sisters in the United States. In 1891 their school became Saint Catharine Academy, and in 1920 the sisters established a teacher's college. The academy has long been closed, but the college survives today as Saint Catharine College, a two-year liberal arts institution. The **Saint Catharine Motherhouse** (859–336–9303), 2 miles west of town on Highway 150, is under renovation, but visitors are welcome. Not too far away on Highway 52, about ½ mile off Highway 150, is the **Saint Rose Proto-Priory.** Founded in 1806, this was the first Catholic educational institution west of the Alleghenies. Students included Jefferson Davis, who would become the president of the Confederacy. Tours of the priory are by appointment; call (859) 336–3121.

Susie's Restaurant (859–336–7975), near the courthouse, is the quintessential small-town cafe, with tables full of hot "country cooking" and the air filled with the latest local news. It's open 5:00 A.M. to 2:00 P.M. daily.

Five miles north of Springfield on Highway 55 is the *Valley Hill Store,* which owner Rosemary Bailey describes as a "born-again country store." Built in the 1880s, the building was the community post office until 1906. Today, the feel of the old country store is kept alive via tea kettle (always on) and variety (always an interesting mix of primitive antiques and local crafts). Folks from all fifty states have stopped by to see what's on hand and to sign up for Rosemary's informative newsletter, *The Pineapple Press.* (If you'd like a copy, send a self-addressed stamped envelope to 65 Valley Hill Road, Springfield 40069.) The store is usually open from 10:00 A.M. to 5:00 P.M. Wednesday through Sunday or by appointment (call 859–336–0255).

MORE GOOD LODGING IN CENTRAL KENTUCKY

Ask about lower-priced weekend specials and other special rates.

BARDSTOWN

Beautiful Dreamer Bed & Breakfast, 440 East Stephen Foster Avenue, 40004 (502) 348–4004 or (800) 811–8312. A new home built in classic Federal style, across from My Old Kentucky Home. $79 to $99 per night.

Hampton Inn Bardstown, 985 Chambers Boulevard, 40004; (502) 349–0100 or (800) HAMPTON. Newer motel with pool. About $65 per night.

Jailer's Inn, 111 West Stephen Foster Avenue, 40004; (502) 348–5551 or (800) 948–5551. Renovated 1819 historic limestone jailhouse, with Jacuzzi suites and one humorously decorated "cell room." $65 to $95 per night. Tours are also offered for $2.50.

BEREA

Berea's Shady Lane, 123 Mount Vernon Road, 40403; (859) 986–9851. Southern Colonial mansion. Full English breakfast.

The Doctor's Inn, 617 Chestnut Street, 40403; (859) 986–3042. Luxurious B&B accommodations in an elegant Colonial-style mansion. About $135 per night.

DANVILLE

Magnolia Inn, 230 East Lexington Avenue, 40422; (800) 794–1291. A charming Victorian home in the heart of Danville. Suite available. $100 to $200.

Old Crow Inn, 471 Stanford Avenue, 40422; (606) 236–1808. Bed-and-breakfast in "Kentucky's oldest stone manor house." On the premises are a working arts studio and walking trails.

Twin Hollies, 406 Maple Avenue, 40422; (606) 236–8954. An antebellum house updated with whirlpool baths; in a quiet historic neighborhood. Rates are about $75.

FRANKFORT

Capitol Manor House, 119 West Todd, 40601; (502) 227–4297. B&B in an 1850 home.

Graystone Manor, 229 Shelby Street, 40601; (502) 226–6196. A limestone home built in 1905 for a U.S. senator. Even the cereal is homemade.

GEORGETOWN

Jordan Farm, 4091 Newtown Pike, 40324; (502) 863–1944 (evening) or (502) 868–9002 (day). Bed-and-breakfast in a carriage house on thoroughbred horse farm. It has a fishing lake!

Pineapple Inn, in town at 645 North Broadway, 40324; (502) 868–5453. Bed-and-breakfast in an 1876 historic house with period antiques.

HARRODSBURG

Bauer Haus, downtown at 362 North College Street, 40330; (859) 734–6289. Bed-and-breakfast in an 1880 Victorian home. Full breakfast is included.

Baxter House B&B, 1677 Lexington Road, 40330; 2 miles east of town at the road's junction with Highway 1343; (859) 734–4877 or (888) 809–4457. Theme rooms in a large country home with unusual pets. Kids are allowed (the owners have some), and bonfires and wagon rides will be offered. Rates are between $89 and $109.

Canaan Land Farm B&B, 2 miles east of Shakertown on Highway 68; (859) 734–3984. Seven rooms and a log cabin, at a small farm with goats and sheep. $75 to $115.

LEXINGTON

Camberley Club Hotel at Gratz Park, 120 West Second Street, 40507; (606) 231–1777 or (800) 555–8000. A historic downtown hotel complete with a ghost or two. Rates are about $129.

Cherry Knoll Inn, 3875 Lemons Mill Road, 40511; (859) 253–9800 or (800) 804–0617. A handsome 1850s mansion in a country setting. Dinner served. About $100 per night.

Homewood, 5301 Bethel Road, 40511; (859) 255–2814. Two rooms and a corporate apartment in a new house on a 300-acre farm. $75 to $100.

Silver Springs Farm, 3710 Leestown Pike, 40511; (859) 255–1784. Bed-and-breakfast in Federal-style house on a farm, formerly a pre-Prohibition distillery. Two rooms or a cottage for people, and a barn and paddock for horses. $99 and up.

Swann's Nest at Cygnet Farm, 3463 Rosalie Lane, 40510; (859) 226–0095. Distinctively appointed suites and rooms on a thoroughbred farm near Keeneland Race Course.

LOUISVILLE

Camberley Brown Hotel, Fourth Street and Broadway; (502) 583–1234 or (800) 555–8000. A 1920s landmark with an excellent restaurant. $99 and up.

Galt House, Fourth Avenue at River Road; (502) 589–5200. Overlooking the Ohio River. Rooms are about $115.

Old Louisville Inn, 1359 South Third Street, 40208; (502) 635–1574. An elegant eleven-room Victorian guest house; great breakfast popovers. About $95.

Seelbach Hilton, 500 South Fourth Avenue, 40202; (502) 585–3200 or (800) 333–3399. A luxurious Beaux Arts showplace in the heart of downtown. Rooms $99 and up.

MOUNT STERLING
Days Inn, I–64, exit 110; (606) 498–4680 or (800) 325–2525. About $60 per night.

NEW HAVEN
Sherwood Inn, 138 South Main Street, 40051 (502) 549–3386. Bed-and-breakfast in a restored railroad hotel next to the Kentucky Railway Museum. About $50 per night.

NICHOLASVILLE
Cedar Haven Farm, 2380 Bethel Road, 40356; (859) 858–3849. B&B on a working farm. Full country breakfast.

O'Neal Log Cabin, 1626 Delaney Ferry Road, 40356; (859) 223–4730. B&B in an 1820 log cabin. Continental breakfast.

Sandusky House, 1626 Delaney Ferry Road, 40356; (859) 223–4730. B&B in an 1850 Greek Revival House. Full breakfast.

PARIS
Rosedale, 1917 Cypress Street, 40361; (800) 644–1862. Bed-and-breakfast in the restored 1862 home of Union brigadier general John Croxton.

RICHMOND
Barnes Mill Bed and Breakfast, 1268 Barnes Mill Road, 40475; (859) 623–5509. 1916 Victorian home. Homemade bread served at breakfast.

The Bennett House,
419 West Main
Street, 40475;
(859) 623–7876.
Romanesque-style house,
on the National Register of
Historic Places. Restoration
ongoing.

SHELBYVILLE

The Wallace House,
613 Washington, 40065;
(502) 633–2006. B&B in a
historic 1805 house that
was one of Kentucky's first
Masonic Lodges.

SPRINGFIELD

Maple Hill Manor Bed and
Breakfast, 2¹/₂ miles east
out of Springfield on Highway 150 (Perryville Road);
(859) 336–3075.
An antebellum Greek
Revival mansion, circa
1851, restored with
Jacuzzis and porch grills
with every room.

VERSAILLES

Bluegrass Bed and
Breakfast Reservation
Service; (859) 873–3208.
Information about private
bed-and-breakfasts and
cottages in the Versailles
and Lexington area that do
not advertise.

B&B at Sills Inn,
270 Montgomery Avenue,
40383; (800) 526–9801.
Large restored Victorian
home with numerous
Jacuzzis. Gourmet break-
fast is featured.

Inn at Morgan Bed &
Breakfast, 135 Morgan
Street, 40383;
(800) 972–1026. A romantic
Victorian getaway featuring
a heart-shaped Jacuzzi
for two.

Rose Hill Inn,
233 Rose Hill Avenue, 40383;
(800) 307–0460. An 1820s
official landmark home
within walking
distance of town. Four
rooms and one cottage
are available.

WINCHESTER

Holiday Inn Winchester,
Mount Sterling Road at
I-64, exit 96A;
(859) 744–9111 or
(800) HOLIDAY. About $60
per night.

Windswept Farm,
5952 Old Boonesboro
Road, 40391;
(859) 745–1245. Country
B&B in a Greek Revival
house.

MORE FUN PLACES TO EAT IN CENTRAL KENTUCKY

BARDSTOWN

Dagwood's, 204 North
Third Street, 40004;
(502) 348–4029. A varied
menu for lunch and dinner
in a casual setting.

Kurtz Restaurant,
418 East Stephen Foster
Avenue, 40004;
(502) 348–8964. Always a
soup/sandwich/pie special
for lunch; country and
regional cooking for dinner.

BEREA

Hometown Cafeteria, I–75,
exit 76; (606) 986–7086.
Popular for its home cooking—enjoy real mashed
potatoes and straight-
from-the-oven pie.

HARRODSBURG

Cafe Benjamin, 133 South
Main Street, 40330;
(859) 734–0025.
All-American fare served
in a recently renovated
historic building. Open
daily for lunch and dinner.

Old Happy Days Diner,
112 East Lexington Street,
40330; (859) 734–4607.
Barbecue and homemade
pies. Closed Sunday.

LEXINGTON

a la lucie, 159 North Limestone, 40507; (downtown);
(859) 252–5277. Possibly
the best restaurant in Lexington. Excellent, creative
nouvelle cuisine in a glam-
orous and tightly packed
space. Reservations are
recommended.

Ed and Fred's Desert Moon,
164 Southeastern Avenue,
40508; (859) 231–1161.
A self-conscious, eclectic
blending of Southwestern
and nouvelle cuisine.

Pacific Pearl Asian American Bistro, 1050 Chinoe Road, 40502; (deep in the suburbs, so call for directions); (859) 266–1611. Unusual Asian dishes New Age style, and more martinis than you can shake a shaker at.

Parkette Drive-In, 1216 New Circle Road Northeast, 40505; (859) 254–8723. Drive-through? No, a real drive-in, with sign, service, and menu much the same as when it opened in 1952.

Ramsey's Diner, Woodland and High Streets in downtown Lexington, (859) 259–2708; 4053 Tates Creek Road, 40517; (859) 271–2638; and 1660 Bryan Station Road, 40505; (859) 299–9669. Down-to-earth menu of "classy comfort food"—even brussels sprouts and crawfish.

LOUISVILLE

The Mayan Gypsy, 813 East Market, 40206; (502) 583–3300. Authentic Mexican dishes from the Mayan culture of the Yucatan. Malanga root fritter, pumpkin-seed-and-egg tamale, and mole like you've never tasted.

Mazzoni's Oyster Cafe, 2804 Taylorsville Road, 40205; (502) 451–4436. Originator of the rolled oyster in 1884.

Vincenzo's, 150 South Fifth Street, 40202; (502) 580–1350. Fine Italian cuisine by Agostino Gabriele. Six-time winner of the "Best of Louisville" designation.

MIDWAY

Bistro La Belle, 117 East Main Street, 40347; (859) 846–4233. Lunch weekdays, dinner Wednesday through Saturday, and Sunday brunch.

NEW HAVEN

Sherwood Inn, 138 South Main Street, 40051; (502) 549–3386. Dinner served Wednesday through Saturday.

WINCHESTER

Hall's on the River, From I–75 take the Athens-Boonesboro Road exit and drive south toward the river; (859) 527–6620. Hall's is also famous for seafood entrees and take-home foods like beer cheese.

Jazzman Cafe, 1100 Interstate Drive, 40391; (606) 744–6425. Barbecue and other delicious soul food.

Eastern Kentucky

ost of North America is inhabited by a wild soup of dissenters' descendants, but what makes eastern Kentucky different is the mountains.

The Appalachian Mountains are a long, beautiful line of steep, nearly impregnable rock that has always tended to keep outsiders out and insiders in. Although the Appalachian culture initially strikes outsiders as foreign, visiting can have the strong allure of a homecoming, in part because your roots may be in European cultures that are better preserved here than anywhere else in the big melting pot. The isolation also has caused eastern Kentuckians to live close to the land, close to one another, and to survive self-sufficiently. As you meet people, listen to the language of this region, the beautiful phrases loaded with humor, knowledge of quirky human nature, and sensitivity to the cycles of the natural world.

There are opportunities in this region to expose yourself to very fine traditional craftsmanship by meeting individual artists or craftspeople and by visiting craft cooperatives where knowledge and tools are being shared with those who want to take the baton. Music and dance, for which mountaineers have always been admired, have developed in fascinating ways and play an important role in the life of this region. Festivals and community dances, which are always open to visitors, are good events to attend if you want to get an authentic taste of the music here. In addition to music, the mountains themselves can soothe the soul.

I have a wonderful recent memory of traveling through the mountains at the end of a long, hot day and stopping on a bridge where a "passel" of people had gathered. Below, by the side of a wide brook, a small revival was in progress. Babies were being passed from lap to lap, and people of all ages were sitting in folding chairs by the little stage, clapping and singing. A sweet hymn in an irresistible minor key rising just above the constant tumble of the water calmed me and opened my eyes to the changing mountains, rosy in the last light of the setting sun. Even in the heat of summer, a mist gathers in the folds and hollows of the land and baptizes everyone equally, even passersby.

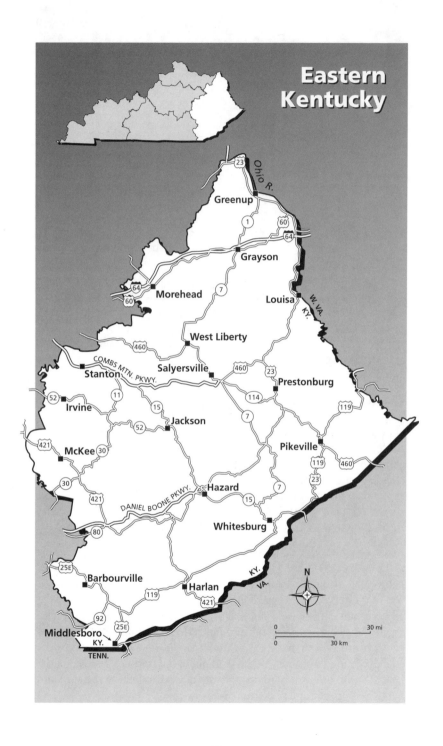

Through the Gap

D r. Thomas Walker was hired by Virginia's Loyal Land Company to go west in search of fertile settling land. In 1750, when Walker found the only natural route west, a divide he named Cumberland Gap, he built a small cabin to claim the territory, mapped the route, and went home. You can visit a replica of Walker's crude cabin at the **Dr. Thomas Walker State Historic Site** on Highway 459 off Highway 25E just southeast of Barbourville (606–546–4400). Though Walker and his group missed reaching the bluegrass region by just a few days of traveling, they did succeed in blazing a trail through the mountains for more than 300,000 pioneers to roll toward a new life in the West.

The 20,000 acres of **Cumberland Gap National Historic Park,** off Highway 25E south of Middlesboro, include the 800-foot natural break in the Cumberland Mountains through which Native Americans and, later, Daniel Boone and other settlers entered Kentucky. Go to **Pinnacle Overlook** and you can see three states, as well as the twin tunnels that go 4,600 feet through the mountain to connect Kentucky and Tennessee. Seventeen years in the making, the tunnels finally opened in 1996, replacing a stretch of Highway 25E so treacherous that it was known as Massacre Mountain. Near the overlook is **Fort McCook,** which was built by Confederate troops to guard the passage.

Bad Branch State Nature Preserve, *near Whitesburg; (502) 573–2886*

Carter Caves State Resort Park, *Olive Hill; (606) 286–4411 or (800) 325–0059*

Furnace Mountain *(must write for information to the Abbess, Box 545, Clay City 40312)*

Lilley Cornett Woods, *Skyline; (606) 633–5828*

Little Shepherd Trail *(in the Kingdom Come State Park), Cumberland; (606) 589–2479*

Lost Squadron Museum, *Bell County Airport, Middlesboro; (606) 248–1149*

Mine Portal Number 31, *Lynch; (606) 589–5812*

Mountain Homeplace, *Paintsville; (606) 297–1850*

Red River Gorge *(contact Natural Bridge State Resort Park), Slade; (606) 663–2214*

Seedtime on the Cumberland, *music festival in early June at Appalshop, Whitesburg; (606) 633–0108*

More than 55 miles of hiking trails wind through the park, but one of the most interesting is the **Ridge Trail** on Brush Mountain, which runs the entire length of the park from the Pinnacle Overlook to a site on the far eastern side of the park called White Rocks, where, on a clear day, you can actually see the Great Smoky Mountains. Early pioneer records note that the 600-foot-high white limestone rock face was an important landmark. Other great hiking destinations include an area called **Indian Rocks,** where native people

True Blue

Between 1750 and 1783, some 12,000 settlers had entered Kentucky through the Cumberland Gap.

used to fashion flint tools (there are still remnants of their work), and the **Goose Nest Sink,** a massive sinkhole created when part of a cave ceiling collapsed. Civil War sentries viewed the valley from this spot, where now you can look down into the canopies of 100-foot-high trees. The Sand Cave is an extraordinarily beautiful and humbling space, a wide cave with a one-and-a-half-acre sand floor next to a 100-foot-high waterfall. One popular stop on the trail is the **Hensley Settlement,** a restored cluster of farms and houses inhabited from 1903 until 1951. To drive, take the Brownies Creek Road from Cubbage, or take a shuttle from the visitors center in Middlesboro. For all park information, stop by the center during business hours, or call (606) 248–2817. Write to the Cumberland Gap National Historic Park for campsite reservations and so forth at P.O. Box 1848, Middlesboro 40965.

Well-researched historic tours by private guides Tom and Barbara Shattuck of the **Wilderness Road Tours** are available daily. Make reservations by writing them at 408 Arlin Hills, Middlesboro 40965, or calling (606) 248–2626. The two-and-a-half-hour Cumberland Gap Area tour, which is given from an air-conditioned van and costs $15, can begin from a number of regular starting points in the area or from wherever you're staying locally. The guides have distilled the area's dramatic history down into memorable narratives, while the countryside speaks eloquently for itself as you watch it flow by your window.

Middlesboro is just north of the gap, outside the national park, in a circular basin that was probably formed between 30 million and 300 million years ago by a large meteor that disintegrated or was blown back into space upon impact. Another possibility is that the depression was formed by the collapse of an underground cavern, since no meteor fragments have been found.

Coal fragments, chunks, and seams, on the other hand, are everywhere and at the heart of the recent history of the area. The **Bell County Chamber of Commerce** on North Twentieth Street is housed in a building faced with 40 tons of bituminous coal. Next door is **The Coal House Museum,** a little open-air collection of mining artifacts—old mine train cars, headlamps, drill bits, and photos. Ask about the **Cumberland Mountain Fall Festival,** which is held annually in Middlesboro during late October as a celebration of the area's English heritage. The event that will knock your socks off is the Official Kentucky State Banjo Playing Championship. Call (800) 988–1075.

Follow North Twentieth Street to the top of the hill, turn left on Edgewood, right onto Arthur Heights, and left when the road comes to the edge of the cliff. The second house on the left is the ***Ridge Runner Bed and Breakfast,*** a twenty-room grand Victorian home built in the early 1890s especially for John B. Cary, the secretary-treasurer of Middlesboro Town Company, the English company that developed the Cumberland Gap area. (In the early 1900s the U.S. Post Office Americanized the official spelling of the town's name from the English *-ough* to *-oro,* but you still see both spellings in use.) The street is named after Alexander Arthur, Middlesboro's founder. The Ridge Runner has four rooms available for between $65 and $71 per night. A tornado that narrowly missed the house in the late 1980s managed to clear the trees from the front hillside, leaving an open view of the town below. Irma Gall and Sue Richards, the two women who own and run the place, are involved in a fascinating community center/clinic/mission in Stinking Creek, Knox County. Ask them about the history of the center and their continuing work there—great stories. Call (606) 248– 4299 for reservations.

Miracle Mountain Crafts is an education and a hidden treasure. Go north of Middlesboro about 5 miles on Highway 25E; just north of a bridge and just south of the road's junction with Highway 188 is a small house on the right sitting by itself. James Miracle (pronounced MY-ra-cle) is in his wood shop all day, every day but Sunday. He loves his work, and he'll take time to talk. Since 1967, when the Smithsonian discovered the handy Miracle family, James has been busy making expressive wooden animals, chairs, dulcimers, and myriad toys, the most popular of which is the "limberjack," a jointed puppet that dances when you bounce it on a thin board tucked under your leg. Split oak for chair bottoms, yellow poplar for small animals—all come from his farm. When an out-of-state customer called to order the biggest dough bowl James could make, he cranked out a massive 28-by-43-by-10-inch yellow poplar bowl, big enough to satisfy even amazon bakers. To place an order, write James Miracle, Route 2, Box 151, Middlesboro 40965. To visit, call (606) 248–2971, or just surprise him.

With genius and fine craftsmanship in mind, stop by the Bell County Airport, located just 2 blocks off Cumberland Avenue on the west side of Middlesboro, where Bob Cardin and his crew of mechanics are doing a full Lockheed P-38F Lightning restoration at the ***Lost Squadron Museum.*** "Glacier Girl," a World War II fighter plane, was the fourth in a formation of six Lightnings that made forced landings on a remote glacier in Greenland on July 15, 1942, because they ran out of fuel. For fifty years the planes were buried deeper and deeper under glacial snow and ice until Pat Epps, the owner of Epps Aviation at Atlanta's DeKalb-Peachtree Airport; Richard Taylor, an Atlanta architect; and a group of technical specialists formed the Greenland Expedition Society in order to find and retrieve a plane. The story of the expedition is amazing. Over a three-year period, the crew located the planes, then dug through 268 feet of glacier with a huge hole-melting device designed just for this project, then carefully removed the plane, part by part, and flew it to a hangar in Middlesboro. Supported by a Middlesboro businessman, corporate sponsors, aviation groups, and numerous volunteers and interested individuals around the country, the restoration began in October 1992. It's been a long, slow process, but the plane is expected to be completed in 2001. The plan is to fly the original mission route to England, after which "Glacier Girl" will visit air shows and be on display at the museum. Visitors are welcome to watch the work in progress weekdays from 8:00 A.M. to 5:00 P.M. Admission is free. When the plane is done, there still will be only six P-38Fs flying in the world. Call the museum at (606) 248–1149, or check on the progress online at www.thelostsquadron.com.

True Blue

Middlesboro is home of the oldest municipal golf course in the nation.

Between Middlesboro and Pineville is the **Kentucky Ridge State Forest,** which includes **Pine Mountain State Resort Park.** Both have entrances off Highway 25E. Follow signs to the Herndon J. Evans Lodge at the top of the mountain, where you can get trail maps and park information, or call (606) 337–3066. At the park's nature center, notice what looks like a petrified tree trunk by the entrance. The trunk was found at a strip mine in northwest Bell County. The tree, which may be 300 million years old, grew in a swampy area and was buried in flood sediments, which caused it to rot. Over the course of a few million years, sand percolated through the cavity and hardened, making a fossilized sandstone cast of the tree.

One of the most special trails in the whole state park system is the **Hemlock Garden Trail,** which goes through a 782-acre area protected by the Nature Preserves system. The Hemlock Garden is a ravine featuring massive hemlocks, tulip poplars, beech trees, and a beautiful mountain brook. On the southwestern boundary of the park, it can be reached on the **Laurel Cove Trail** or the **Rock Hotel Trail.** Linger as long as you are able. After all, how often are you in the presence of living beings more than 200 years old?

During the last weekend in May, the **Mountain Laurel Festival** is held to celebrate the blooming of the much-loved mountain flower. The whole event is held in the Laurel Cove Amphitheater, a beautiful natural stage that seats more than 3,000 people, and culminates in the crowning of a Mountain Laurel Queen. The **Great American Dulcimer**

Festival is also held outdoors during the third or fourth weekend of September. This is a wonderful, small festival during which dulcimer makers sell, demonstrate, and teach in booths during the day. At night spectators wrap up in quilts under the stars and watch some of the best performers play on a stage behind a reflective pond. Styles range from traditional to classical, pop, big band, and country rock, all played on lap or hammered dulcimers.

Eighteen miles southwest of Pineville via Highway 190 in Frakes is the **Henderson Settlement,** a United Methodist ministry started in 1925 as a school and community outreach center. Now Henderson Settlement is a multipurpose community service facility and the only Methodist mission in the country with an agricultural development program— 1,300 acres of land, livestock, orchards, gardens, and a big community greenhouse. The old high school houses a library, offices, and a weaving room where people can learn and pursue the craft. Weavings and other locally made crafts are sold in **Log House Craft Shop** (606–337–5823), open Monday through Friday from 8:00 A.M. to 4:30 P.M. Visitors are welcome to tour the place or to come for an extended stay for a retreat or work camp. Call ahead for reservations at (606) 337–3613.

The Red Bird Mission in Beverly is another similar United Methodist mission complex with a school, hospital, community outreach program, work camps, and a craft shop. From Pineville follow Highway 66 north for 26 miles. From the Daniel Boone Parkway, take exit 34 and go south on Highway 66 into town. Directly across the street from the mission hospital is **Red Bird Mission Crafts,** in operation since 1921. The area craftspeople represented there are especially skilled at making hickory bark furniture, exquisite willow baskets, and hand-woven rugs. Hours are 9:00 A.M. to 4:00 P.M. Monday through Friday. You can reach the craft shop at (606) 598–2709.

> ### True Blue
>
> *Among the country music stars from eastern Kentucky are Billy Ray Cyrus from Greenup County, the Judds from Ashland, Tom T. Hall from Carter County, Keith Whitley from Elliot County, Lorretta Lynn and Crystal Gayle from Johnson County, and Dwight Yoakam from Floyd County.*

Head northeast on Highway 119 to **Harlan,** a little mountain town populated primarily by people of Welsh descent. Natives say that because the Welsh have always been fantastic vocalists, it's no surprise that Harlan's fame is musical. The **Harlan Boys' Choir,** an all-male, award-winning choir, received national acclaim after performing at the inauguration of President George Bush in 1989. What most people don't know is that the choir was an offshoot of a 1945 girls' group called **The Harlan Musettes,** now under the direction of Marilyn Schraeder

(606–573–3577). David Davies (606–573–3559) directs the boys, who range from third grade through high school. The repertoire is classical and the sound exquisite. Stop by the school to catch a rehearsal or call one of the directors for the performance schedule.

Another Harlan original is the *Poke Sallet Festival,* held during the first full weekend in June. The festival affords you plenty of opportunities to eat poke sallet, barbecued chicken, corn pone, and buttermilk—a mountain meal if ever there was one. Poke sallet is a cold salad of very young poke plant leaves (which are bitter and mildly poisonous when the plant is several months older); the leaves are cooked way down, like turnip greens, and have a flavor similar to asparagus. They're said to have healing powers. Call (606) 573–4717 for more information on the festival.

Some people perpetually have fishing on the brain. If that describes you, call the Army Corps of Engineers at (800) 261–5038 to get fishing reports and other information about the two wildlife management areas, *Cranks Creek Lake* and *Martins Fork Lake,* that are just south of Harlan. Both are beautiful spots for just relaxing, too.

If you like to explore on foot, another gorgeous place to spend time in any season is *Stone Mountain,* a 200-acre gorge that is part wilderness and part history lesson. From Harlan take Highway 421 south to Highway 1138 and park in the Herb Smith lot. The long, twisty hike up the hollow of Stone Mountain follows a historic, hundred-year-old wagon road that leads to an amazing tunnel, which was built for wagon-carried freight to be connected with a Virginia railroad. The tunnel was built by punching through the sandstone caprock with hand-operated drills, hammers, and not a little black powder. At the Virginia end of the tunnel, you can see the vast Powell Valley.

Head north of Harlan on Highway 421, straight up the mountain. At the summit of Pine Mountain you'll see a sign for *The Little Shepherd Trail,* a 38-mile gravel trail that runs along the ridge of the 2,800-foot Black Mountain all the way to Whitesburg.

On the other side of Pine Mountain, make a hard right onto Highway 221, go east "a fur piece" (in this case, about 10 miles) and turn onto Highway 510, then immediately into the driveway of the *Pine Mountain Settlement School* (606–558–3571). Here you will find 800 acres of forest and farmland, native woods, and stone buildings. The history of the place begins with an early settler named William Creech, who recognized the need for a school based on what he knew of a settlement school in Hindman. That school was founded by Katherine Pettit, who, in turn, based her ideas on Jane Addams's work in urban settings. From 1913 until 1972 the Pine Mountain Settlement School was a remarkably wholesome and successful school, community center, and medical facility.

After the regular school closed in 1972, the folks at Pine Mountain decided to flow with the real needs of the community, and it became an environmental education center. Good timing—eastern Kentucky was and is suffering massive environmental exploitation in a nation tending toward overconsumption, waste of resources, overpopulation, and a general lack of concern for and understanding of the fragile, crucial cycles of the natural world. The school definitely takes an activist approach. In 2000, the school led a successful effort petitioning the state of Kentucky to declare 5,226 acres unsuitable for surface mining. The acreage includes the school, its viewshed, and a water source area on the south face of Pine Mountain. To introduce the petition, school representatives used the words of founder William Creech Sr., just as he wrote them in 1915: "I don't look after wealth for them. I look after the prosperity of our nation. I want all young-uns taught to serve the livin God. Of course, they won't do that, but they can have good and evil laid before them and they can choose which they will. I have heart and cravin that our people may grow better. I have deeded my land to the Pine Mountain Settlement School to be used for school purposes as long as the Constitution of the United States stands. Hopin it may make a bright and intelligent people after I'm dead and gone." For more information, write Pine Mountain Settlement School, 36 Highway 510, Bledsoe 40810. Visitors are welcome to tour the fascinating campus daily from 8:00 A.M. to 8:00 P.M.

The next major town to the east is *Cumberland.* It's small (population 2,780) but busy. In the beginning, though, it was really small; in 1870 six families settled this spot, and by 1911 Cumberland was incorporated with a population of 185 souls.

In town, follow the signs to the campus of Cumberland's Southeast Community College, then to its *Appalachian Cultural and Fine Arts Center,* at 700 College Road, Cumberland 40823, for more mountain history. Tours of the entire facility, including the three-story atrium space with rotating art exhibits and traditional crafts on display, are free. Most interesting for scholars or casual travelers is the center's amazing photo and oral history archives. Call (606) 589–2145, ext. 2119, for general information or to find out about special events.

Downtown on West Main Street, next to the Rebecca Caudill Public Library (named for the famous children's book author, who was born nearby), is the *Poor Fork Arts and Craft Guild,* a shop that features the craft items made by the guild's seventy-five members. Hours are 10:00

A.M. to 5:00 P.M. Monday through Saturday, but the shop may be closed in January and February. Call (606) 589–5626.

Directly up the mountain from Cumberland off Highway 119 is the **Kingdom Come State Park** (606–589–2479). Here is another access point to the Little Shepherd Trail. The trail and the park are named after John Fox Jr.'s famous novel about Appalachian life, *The Little Shepherd of Kingdom Come*. In 1903 Fox's book was the first American novel to sell over one million copies. This park is known for its incredible vistas and rich mountain woodlands. Two of the most spectacular sites are the Log Rock, a natural rock arch that looks like a log, and Raven Rock, a huge hunk of stone that thrusts some 290 feet into the air and has at its base a capacious sand cave, which is used as an amphitheater for concerts and other performances. Stop by the visitors center for trail maps.

Follow the valley (and the railroad) just 2 miles southeast from Cumberland along Highway 160 to a tiny little town called **Benham,** a place that instead of evolving, was made, every bit constructed intentionally, in 1911 by International Harvester as a company town right "on" the seam of coal that the company was mining. In the preceding decade, company towns had gotten terrible reputations for the sordid conditions of such isolated, temporary communities. Benham, however, was among the company towns built after national attention had been drawn to the situation, and large, profitable companies chose to show off their benevolence by building exceptionally pleasant and civilized "encampments" for their workers. The rows of identical houses were often premade kit-type structures ordered from Sears or Montgomery Ward.

All this social history and more about the mining process is illustrated by excellent displays in the **Kentucky Coal Mining Museum,** at 221 South Main Street, Benham 40807, in the original commissary building. The scale-model coal tipple is wonderful! Admission is $4.00, and hours are Monday through Saturday from 10:00 A.M. to 5:00 P.M. and Sunday from 1:00 to 4:00 P.M. Call (606) 848–1530. Next door is the **Coal Miners Park,** which features a walking track, picnic and shelter area, an old L&N caboose, and the Coal Miner's Wall. You can't miss it. Just watch for the 2-ton lump of coal and the 1940s electric locomotive engine that moved the miners inside the mine. Across the street and up the hill in the old community school building at 100 Central Avenue, Benham 40807, is **The School House Inn** (606–848–3000), a restaurant and an active inn with thirty rooms.

Continue on Highway 160 for 2 more miles to another company town, **Lynch,** built in 1917 by U.S. Steel, Coal, and Coke Company. It's worth the trip to see *Mine Portal Number 31* and the entire walking tour of what was at one time the largest coal camp in the world, where 10,000 people of 38 nationalities lived and worked in more than 1,000 structures. Today you can see the original lamp house, rail depot, firehouse, bath facility, powerhouse, water supply plant, conveyor, coal tipple, and mine portal. For forty years more than 1-million tons of coal per year came out of that very portal. (Part of this mine is still in use.)

Go down another 4 miles to the south and up to 4,145 feet on *Big Black Mountain,* the highest point in Kentucky. There's an old fire tower at the peak. This is one of the few places in the state where it would not be unusual to find a rattlesnake or even a black bear. Bird-watchers should keep their binoculars handy—this mountain supports breeding populations of species that are not usually seen anywhere else in the state, including the solitary vireo, the Canada warbler, and the rose-breasted grosbeak.

If you go back to Cumberland, head east along the gap line and Highway 119 will take you into Letcher County. Right near the county line, on a winding section of road on Pine Mountain, is a general store and post office called the *Oven Fork Mercantile,* which has been restored to look like it might have in the 1930s. It sells a little bit of everything and a lot of candy. Hours are 10:00 A.M. to 5:00 P.M. Monday through Saturday (closed on Wednesday), 1:00 to 5:00 P.M. on Sunday. Call (606) 633–8909.

As you continue to wind along the Cumberland River bottom on Highway 119 for 15 miles, watch for Highway 806. Check out *J. D. Maggard's Cash Store,* an authentic kind of place that's been run by the same family since it was built in 1914. Maggard's provided the location for scenes in the movie *Coal Miner's Daughter,* the story of Loretta Lynn. Call (606) 633–7786.

In just 2 miles, Highway 806 leads to a little community called Eolia. Nestled between Pine and Black Mountains, the two highest in Kentucky, Eolia is said to get its name from the Native American word meaning "valley of the winds." So you'll know what it means when you see the sign for the *Valley of the Winds Art Gallery* (606–633–8652), the studio and sales gallery of a family of artists, Jeff and Sharman Chapman-Crane and their young son, Evan. For sale are original works by all three family members, as well as prints of Jeff's simple, expressive line drawings, which make great note cards. Visitors are welcome but should call first; the gallery is open by chance on most weekdays and many weekends.

Get back on Highway 119 and head east 1 mile to Highway 932 on the right (east) side of the road. Turn and go 1.7 miles to the entrance of the

Bad Branch Nature Preserve (606–633–0362), on the left. This place is so special that I barely have the nerve to include it here, but if you visit, you must promise to treat it with great care, to soak it into your soul, and to support nature preserves here and everywhere in any way that you are able. This gorge, which is rimmed by 100-foot cliffs, is home to a very unique ecosystem of rare plant species and breathtaking wildflowers. The trail leads you through a hemlock and rhododendron kingdom along some of the only clean, pure water you're going to see. At the end is a spectacular, 60-foot waterfall arching over the edge of a sandstone cliff. Open sunrise to sunset daily.

Get back on Highway 119 again and head over Pine Mountain into **Whitesburg.** Downtown, next to the north fork of the Kentucky River, is the Appalshop building, which is open to visitors. ***Appalshop*** is a community-oriented, not-for-profit arts and education center working to preserve traditional culture and history and to encourage conscientious involvement in contemporary arts and social issues. Appalshop is best known for making powerful documentaries about folk-culture figures and about social activism in Appalachia. While visiting, you can ask to watch almost any of Appalshop's videos—for example, *On Our Own Land,* about the history and demise of the broad form deed in Kentucky, or *Chairmaker,* about the life and work of Dewey Thompson, a furniture maker from Sugarloaf Hollow. The Headwaters Television series is a weekly broadcast of these documentaries on public television.

June Appal Recordings, Appalshop's own record label, also has made a

Harry M. Caudill

*B*e sure to stop at one of the high lookout points along Highway 119, where you can get a more abstract sense of the texture and shape of the land. You'll also get a very nonabstract sense of the meaning of "mountaintop removal," a method of strip mining coal by taking off whatever is above it, usually the entire top of a mountain. With this panorama before you, pay mental tribute to one of Letcher County's great native sons, the late Harry M. Caudill: writer, teacher, lawyer, politician, and outspoken activist in Appalachian social and economic issues. His historical writings, including Night Comes to the Cumberlands *and* Theirs Be the Power, *are disturbing and powerful books about the troubled power relations in these mountains. In his storyteller (preserver) mode, Caudill has written a number of honest, intimate portraits of his people in books such as* The Mountain, the Miner and the Lord.

massive cultural contribution by recording Appalachian musicians and storytellers, famous and obscure, ranging from contemporary folk dulcimer artists, such as John McCutcheon, and traditional mountain banjo players, such as Morgan Sexton (who won a National Heritage Award from the National Endowment for the Arts in 1990), to mountain storytellers, including Ray Hicks. Appalshop's Roadside Theatre is a small theater and storytelling troupe that delights and instructs folks all over the region. Appalshop also runs a community radio station, WMMT 88.7 FM, to which you are hereby commanded to tune in while in the area. Like the river, Appalshop's efforts flow out into the whole Kentucky-Virginia area, giving us all an education and a renewed sense of pride and hope. For literature and catalogs write Appalshop, 91 Madison Street, Whitesburg 41858, or call (606) 633–0108. Also, ask about the schedule of live performances held in the theater year-round.

Have a meal downtown at the ***Courthouse Cafe*** (606–633–5859), a charming little restaurant that serves healthy, delicious lunches and dinners made from scratch—baked turkey breast sandwiches, large salads, and ever-changing special meals. Josephine Richardson, one of the owners, acts as dealer for a number of local artists and craftspeople. The quilts, wood carvings, paintings, and photographs she has on display in the restaurant are for sale. Hours are 10:00 A.M. to 8:30 P.M. Monday through Friday (the daily specials are ready at 11:30 A.M.). Read through a copy of the local paper, *The Mountain Eagle*. There's a very democratic section, usually on page B4, called Speak Your Piece, for which you anonymously call an answering machine and the editor prints, verbatim, what you say. The "pieces" range from heated discussions about international issues to layoffs at the coal mines to "I hate my boyfriend's guts, and I hope he knows it."

Other works by area craftspeople are featured in the ***Pine Mountain Crafts Co-op*** in town on Highway 119. Stop by to see demonstrations of work. Admission is free. Hours are Monday through Saturday from 10:00 A.M. to 5:00 P.M. and Sunday from 1:00 to 4:00 P.M. (606) 633–0185.

On the west side of the county in a community called Blackey is an area museum disguised as a general store, the ***C. B. Caudill Store and History Center*** (606– 633–7738). From Whitesburg take Highway 15 north, then turn on Highway 7 south toward Isom. The store is just past Blackey on the right. There are usually a few fellows chatting on the big front porch. The store, which opened in 1933, was for many years owned by Joe Begley, an upbeat, dedicated activist who used his store to unite diverse groups over issues such as the 77th Strip Mining Bill and the area health clinic. "Everyone should be a politician," he said. "Even Christ was a protester, and a strong one at that." But the walls of the store tell some of their own stories. Joe intentionally collected mining artifacts, everything from hats, boots, lights, and tools to scrip, old mine company currency useful only within the mining camps. His unintentional collections are amusing—scan the shelves for things like fifty-year-old tubes of hair-restoration creme. Begley, who died in March 2000, was honored as a man of rare courage who never failed to take a stand on issues facing the people of the mountains. His wife, Gaynell, still runs the store, with assistance from Appalshop.

Also ask at Appalshop about the **Carcassonne Dance.** Once or twice a month at the Carcassonne community center, people get together for a big square dance, the traditional kind with a caller and usually a live "house" band. Mountain squares and contra lines are so unique that even if you're an experienced country dancer, this will be a challenge. Just listen and have fun. From C. B. Caudill Store, stay on Highway 7 for a few hundred yards and turn right on the first road on the right, Elk Creek Road. Follow the pavement to the very top of the mountain.

True Blue

Some of the trees in Lilley Cornett Woods predate the arrival of the Pilgrims in America in 1620.

Back on Highway 7, go west past Blackey and the Caudill Store, turn south on Highway 1103, and follow the signs to the **Lilley Cornett Woods.** Because this is one of the only old-growth forests in the state, it is of great value to ecological researchers and to beauty addicts alike. The wise and eccentric Lilley Cornett purchased this land just after World War I and did not allow any live timber, except for blighted chestnuts, to be cut. His children continued the tradition, and finally, in 1969, the state purchased the land and continues to preserve it. Time is the key. Old-growth forests are characterized by a large number of trees that are more than 200 years old, many of which are of great commercial value.

In order to protect the forest, visitors are not allowed to hike without a guide. The guides, however, are real treats, and they will take you out whenever you arrive. You'll learn more in an hour hiking with these folks than you could in a year reading dendrology books. Come between 9:00 A.M. and 5:00 P.M. From May 15 to August 15 the woods are open daily, and in April, May, September, and October, it is open only on weekends. For more information, contact Superintendent, Lilley Cornett Woods, 91 Lilley Cornett Branch, Allie 41821, or call (606) 633–5828.

On the east end of Letcher County, very near the Virginia border on Highway 119 North, is a town called *Jenkins,* originally a mining camp built by Consolidation Coal Company—note the rows of identical houses. On the east side of town, watch on the left for *Whitaker Music Store,* an old, run-down music store with a surprising collection of old albums, sheet music, books, and a few instruments. The rock 'n' roll albums are funny, but there are some valuable items in Ervin Whitaker's country music collection. The store is open from 9:00 A.M. to 5:00 P.M. Monday through Saturday.

Jenkins, like Lynch and Benham, was built as a company town. You'll notice the telltale signs: rows of nearly identical frame houses clustered in a tight grid. This town was once part of the Rockefeller family holdings. To get a real sense of this history, stop by the former train depot that now houses the *David A. Zeeger Coal-Railroad Museum.* Myriad little objects pertaining to the everyday life and work of the miners (non-Rockefellers) in this town are on display, including scrip, the only legal, nonmoney form of currency you're likely to see in America outside of video arcades and subways. Open on weekdays. Call (606) 832–4676 for information.

Leaving Jenkins to the east on Highway 119, you'll soon be entering Pike County, the largest county in the state. South of Pikeville, in the center of the county on Highway 1789, is *Fishtrap Lake,* a large lake known for its largemouth bass, bluegill, and crappie. Directly south of Fishtrap Lake on the state border with Virginia is the *Breaks Interstate Park,* where the Russell Fork River, a tributary of the Big Sandy, has done its darndest to imitate the Grand Canyon. For more than 5 miles, the river canyon has high jagged walls, some exceeding 1,600 feet in height. It is the largest canyon east of the Mississippi River. It is believed to have been formed primarily during the late Paleozoic era, some 250 million years ago. Unlike the Grand Canyon, this gorge is lush and tree covered. There are more than 12 miles of hiking trails, and the park has four fantastic overlooks, one of which is at the Rhododendron Lodge and Restaurant. Contact Breaks Interstate Park, P.O. Box 100, Breaks, VA 24607, or call (540) 865–4413.

In October *white-water rafting* is possible on the mighty Russell Fork River. Since it drops in elevation 350 feet in a long series of minor waterfalls and rapids, with a few calm pools in between, it is rated among the best rafting rivers in the country. Some of the rapids are Class VI and require both skill and raw nerve to get through. Guided trips are available through Sheltowee Trace Outfitters only in October for between $50 and $125 per person. Call (800) 541–RAFT.

For better or for worse, Pike County is known nationally as the locale of the infamous Hatfield-McCoy feud, a violent interfamily vendetta that began during the Civil War and was sustained almost until the twentieth century. Buried in **Pikeville** in the **Dils Cemetery** are several major figures in the feud from the McCoy side. This cemetery also was the first in eastern Kentucky to be racially integrated. In 1996 a Pikeville College professor began an inventory of the African-American graves; since then, markers have been placed on many that had no headstones. The City of Pikeville has leased the cemetery from Dils family descendants, and it is open year-round during daylight hours. Take Bypass Road to the east side of town; the cemetery is just north of Bypass's split with Highway 1460 on the east side of the road. For more information visit the Pikeville Visitors Center at 101 Huffman Avenue, Pikeville 41501, between 8:30 A.M. and 4:30 P.M., Monday through Friday, or call (800) 844–7453.

At the visitors center you can also find out about the **Pikeville Cut-Thru,** a massive rerouting of highways, railroads, and rivers on the west side of town. After fourteen years of labor, millions of dollars, and a whole lot of blasted and hauled rock and dirt, the cut-through was completed in 1987. You have to see it to believe it. For the best view take Bypass Road to the northwest side of town, turn uphill on Oak Lane, and curve around to Cedar Drive.

Windows into Geologic History

*T*he ostensible reasons for engineering the massive road cut-through near Pikeville, which straightened the course of the Levisa Fork of the Big Sandy River, were to provide more direct road and rail transportation in the area; to reduce the frequency and severity of flooding in the town; and, after the former river channel was filled with rubble, to create over 400 acres of new flat land adjacent to town. An unintentional but spectacular fringe benefit of the road cut was an opportunity for geologists to see a whole series of "exposures," or windows into geologic history, as opposed to the usual fragmentary view gained from smaller cut-throughs or from core samples. In the series of cuts near Pikeville, someone with a trained eye can see a frontal section view of an ancient river delta, the Pocahontas delta system, which ran off the Appalachians about 300 million years ago, during the Mississippian-Pennsylvanian era. A geologist would see a river with channels, levees, and splay deposits flowing into overbank deposits of shale and coal. She would see vertical layers of former channels of the ancient river as they migrated back and forth across the valley, like rococo layers of marzipan in an Italian wedding cake that has been cut into vertically stepping tiers.

Asphalt roads may seem to dominate eastern Kentucky now, but there was a time when railroads were king. Head southeast from Pikeville on Highway 460, which becomes Highway 80, and you'll end up in Elkhorn City. The **Elkhorn City Railroad Museum** on Pine Street offers exhibits of memorabilia from that time, including a caboose, everybody's favorite extinct railcar; switchstands; meters; and so forth. Know what a velocipede is? Find out. Admission is free, but tours are given by appointment. For details, call (606) 432–1391.

Big Sandy Country

few miles west of Paintsville off Highway 40, you can visit **Mountain HomePlace** (800–542–5790 or 606–297–1850) and get a sense of what farm life in the mountains was like in the mid-1800s. Set up as a living-history farm, the complex includes a home, crib barns, horse-powered gristmill, chicken house, blacksmith shop, and small school, as well as costumed interpreters going about the activities of daily life—tending gardens, feeding stock, hewing logs, making shingles, processing sugar cane, and even preparing and eating their daily supper. Mountain HomePlace is open Wednesday through Saturday from 9:00 A.M. to 5:00 P.M., Sunday from 1:00 to 6:00 P.M. Admission is $6.00 for adults, $4.00 for children. There's a wonderful gift shop with items made by local craftspeople.

In downtown Paintsville you can tour one result of coal mining, the **John C. C. Mayo Museum,** a large, ornate house built by the local baron between 1905 and 1912 for a "mere" $250,000. The house is currently home to Our Lady of the Mountains, a Catholic elementary school, so hours are by appointment only. Call (606) 789–3661. Next door to the museum/school is the **Mayo Methodist Church,** also built by Mayo. (Local legend has it that there was once an underground tunnel connecting the two buildings.) The church's prized Pilcher organ was a gift from Mayo's friend Andrew Carnegie.

Johnson County's history involves some outstanding women. Country music stars Crystal Gayle and Loretta Lynn are both Johnson County natives. Loretta Lynn was born and raised in a beautiful setting in **Butcher Hollow,** near Van Lear. From Paintsville take Highway 302 south and follow the signs to the board-and-batten cabin where she lived. The place was rebuilt for the filming of the 1980 movie *Coal Miner's Daughter,* a biography of the singer's difficult but triumphant life. Remnants of an orchard make the place feel authentic. Stop by Webb's Grocery (606–789–3397), owned by Loretta Lynn's brother Herman

True Blue

Webb, if you want to take a tour. They're given year-round, most every day.

Just west of Butcher Hollow on Highway 302, in Van Lear's tiny downtown in the former Consolidated Coal Company office building, is the **Van Lear Historical Society Miners' Museum.** If you haven't yet seen a real-life mining camp, check out the model of a typical company town in the museum. Hours are 9:00 A.M. to 3:00 P.M. Monday through Saturday from March through November, or by appointment. Call (606) 789–0068. Admission is free. To get there, take U.S. 23 south to Highway 302, then go east on Highway 78 or Miller's Creek Road.

Another legendary woman is Jenny Wiley, an early settler of the Big Sandy area who survived a remarkably tragic capture by Shawnee Indians and, after nine months of captivity, during which time she gave birth, subsequently escaped. She died at seventy-one and is buried in a cemetery 5 miles south of Paintsville on Highway 321 near the site of **Harmon Station,** the first white settlement in eastern Kentucky. Mathias Harmon was one of the hunter–Indian fighters now known as "Long Hunters" because of the length of their sojourns in the wilderness. In 1750 he and his companions built a fortlike log hunting lodge on this site; in the late 1780s they built a more permanent blockhouse.

The trail that Wiley and the Native Americans followed was once well worn and cleared, but it had disappeared into the undergrowth until recently. The 185-mile **Jenny Wiley Trail** has been restored and is now marked for hikers. You can access the trail from Greenbo Lake, Carter Caves, and Jenny Wiley state parks. If you want to hike the whole thing, you can start in South Portsmouth (Greenup County) and travel south. The best way to see eastern Kentucky is on foot, and this trail roughly traces the Pottsville escarpment and runs the gamut of sites; you see lush gorges, open farmland, strip mines, mountain towns, and miles and miles of woods. For a free copy of *Kentucky Trails Guide,* write to the Kentucky Department of Travel, Dept. WWW, P.O. Box 2011, Frankfort 40602, or call (800) 225–8747.

For more information on the Jenny Wiley Trail and other local outdoor activities, contact the **Jenny Wiley State Resort Park** (800–325–0142 or 606–886–2711) between Paintsville and Prestonsburg on Highway 3, just east of Highway 23/460 on Dewey Lake, a clear lake famous for its white bass run in April. In the park you can tour one of the last one-room schoolhouses to close in Kentucky. The park has the usual array of overnight lodging in the park lodge, in cabins, or at campsites. It may be a little cheesy, but it's also breathtaking to ride the sky lift out over the wooded hollows.

The *Jenny Wiley Summer Music Theatre* presents one very colorful, musical version of the legendary Jenny Wiley story in addition to three Broadway musicals, which have included *Hello, Dolly* and *The Sound of Music*. You can take in a different performance every night for four nights in a row. The outdoor performances are at the Jenny Wiley State Resort Park in an amphitheater open from late May through late August, Tuesday through Sunday; the house opens at 7:30 P.M., with curtain at 8:15 P.M. Call (606) 886–9274 for more information.

Prestonsburg is also home to the *Mountain Arts Center,* a beautiful 47,000-square-foot entertainment complex that opened in late 1996. This center, with recording studio, classrooms, and a 1,000-seat performance hall, began as the dream of a retired music teacher, Billie Jean Osborne. Osborne, who is from Betsy Layne (country singer Dwight Yoakam grew up a few houses away), envisioned a theater where eastern Kentucky audiences could enjoy top entertainment. Refusing to take no for an answer, she spurred a coalition of state and local officials to make her theater a reality. The center features top entertainers in all genres—from country and gospel to classical music—along with regular performances by the Kentucky Opry, Osborne's own country music showcase. Performance times vary; call (888) 622–2787 for ticket information.

The Civil War in Prestonsburg

*I*n addition to being the site of Daniel Boone's winter camp in 1767–68, Prestonsburg was also the site of two wintertime Civil War engagements. Each May a reenactment is held at the National Historic Landmark. (For more information, call 606–886–1341.) The Battle of Ivy Mountain, which lasted less than an hour and a half, resulted in the Union's capture of Piketown (now Pikeville), where the Confederates had been stationed. The Battle of Middle Creek, in January 1862, occurred along the creek between Paintsville and Prestonsburg. The battle marked the beginning of Union domination of Kentucky and was a major accomplishment for the Union commander, James Abram Garfield, who became the twentieth President of the United States and died months later from injuries sustained by an assassin's bullet.

The Mountain Arts Center is on a section of Highway 23 that has been designated *Kentucky's Country Music Highway.* Along a stretch running from Ashland to Letcher County, through seven counties, signs honor a dozen country and bluegrass music stars who came from the region, from Billy Ray Cyrus (Greenup County) and the Judds (Boyd County) to Patty Loveless (Pike County).

The recently restored **Samuel May House** in North Prestonsburg is now open for tours by appointment (606–437–2724 or 606–889–0704). Built in 1817 as the main residence on a 300-acre farm, it is now the oldest standing brick house in the whole Big Sandy Valley. The house was built in the classic Federal style.

The David community, which is about 6 miles southwest of Prestonsburg on Highway 404, has two surprises in store for you. One is a small crafts shop called **David Appalachian Crafts,** which features quality traditional mountain crafts like split oak baskets, wood carvings, and quilts. Hours are 9:00 A.M. to 4:00 P.M. Monday through Saturday. Tuesday through Friday there are usually craftspeople at work at the shop. Write them at P.O. Box 2, Highway 404, David 41616, or call (606) 886–2377.

Also in town is the **David School,** a nonsectarian, not-for-profit, wonderful school committed to educating local high school dropouts from low-income families. In 1972 Dan Greene founded the school in an old mining camp with hopes of helping kids who were functionally illiterate. Now, more than 95 percent of the David School students have finished their high school education, and there's always a waiting list. Other schools around the state and nation are looking to Greene's program as a model. If you are inspired, stop by.

Due south of the David School is a longer-lived educational institution built upon similar hopes, **Alice Lloyd College** (606–368–2101). Take Highway 7 south, then Highway 899 southwest into Pippa Passes, in Knott County. The school's founder, Alice Lloyd, was a Radcliffe graduate who contracted spinal meningitis at the age of forty and moved with her mother to the mountains of Kentucky to die in an abandoned missionary house. Despite her illness, she typed letters with her left hand to businesspeople and friends in Boston, asking for help in establishing a school. It was opened in 1917 on the hillsides of Caney Creek Valley, where it stands today.

Alice Lloyd, who lived until 1962, gave her students a free education, but there was one string attached—she requested that after graduation the students return to eastern Kentucky to work and live. Almost 4,000 graduates have become teachers in the region, and more than 1,000 have become mountain doctors and other professionals. Visitors are welcome to tour the beautiful campus all year.

Just a few miles away on Highway 550, slightly south of Highway 80, is **Hindman** and, strung along Troublesome Creek, the **Hindman Settlement School** (606–785–5475), yet another educational facility that long has been a social and cultural gold mine. The school was founded in 1902 on the folk school plan and operated successfully for many years, but like other settlement schools, it closed and has had to serve the community in new ways. Today it hosts some of the best workshops in the state on traditional dance and mountain crafts and culture. Visitors can tour the campus free, Monday through Friday between 8:00 A.M. and 5:00 P.M. You'll see a film about Jean Ritchie, the nationally acclaimed folk musician and composer from the nearby town of Viper.

If it's a Wednesday or a Friday when you happen to be in Hindman, stop by the school's **Marie Stewart Crafts Shop** for fresh-baked goods. Actually, you can stop by the restored hundred-year-old cabin on Highway 160 anytime between 9:00 A.M. and 4:30 P.M. to see a wide range of traditional regional crafts. The shop is a co-op, and all of its members are juried. You may be lucky and be there on a day when the craftspeople are giving demonstrations. For more information call (606) 785–5475.

You're in store for more regional crafts and an architectural museum of sorts at the **Pioneer Village,** due south of Hindman. Take Highway 160 south to Carr Fork Lake, then take Highway 15 south just a little farther into Red Fox and watch the east side of the road for the long driveway to the village. This group of cabins was moved to this location in Rainbow Hollow when the Carr Fork Dam was built. Some of the log structures date as far back as the 1780s. Presently the cabins are standing, but the logs are not chinked (filled in between with mud, rock, straw, etc.). The craft shop, which pays for the cabins' maintenance, features all local handmade crafts by more than 200 craftspeople and sold on consignment. Ask to see the corn-husk dolls made by folk singer Jean Ritchie's sisters, Kitty, Mallie, and Jewel. Hours are Monday through Saturday from 10:00 A.M. to 6:00 P.M., Sunday from 1:00 to 6:00 P.M. Call (606) 642–3650.

Water-based relaxation, camping, picnicking, swimming, and all sorts of fishing are available April through December at **Carr Creek State Park** and the 750-acre lake, **Carr Folk Lake,** created by the dam that caused the cabins at Pioneer Village to be moved. The lake has been well stocked with crappie and largemouth bass. Water from this lake eventually ends up in the Kentucky River. Call (502) 642–4050.

True Blue

Nearby **Hazard** is a booming little riverside town at the end of the Daniel Boone Parkway. Because it sits on and near some of the widest, richest seams of coal in the area, coal is at the heart of almost everything here, a fact made loud and clear during the third weekend of September when Hazard hosts the **Black Gold Festival.** In town, spend a little time at the **Bobby Davis Museum** (234 Walnut Street, Hazard 41701; 606–439–4325) next door to the visitors information center (606–439–2659). This free museum is a visual history book of the area from the nineteenth century through World War II. Hours are 8:30 A.M. to 4:30 P.M. Monday through Friday.

Let me be devious and point out a more modern artifact of history. Go north of town on Highway 15 and turn onto Dawahare Drive and into the Holiday Inn parking lot. The ground under the west wing of the building is sinking, so the building is collapsing as if it had been in an earthquake. It wasn't. The east part of the inn is built on natural, solid rock while the west disaster was built on "fill," rock and dirt added to fill the area—a process some engineers believe can be done on reclaimed mine sites.

An architectural treat is in store just north of Hazard in Buckhorn on Highway 28, which is off Highway 15 North. The Log Cathedral, now functioning as the **Buckhorn Lake Area Church,** is an unusually large and beautiful log structure built in 1907 as part of the Witherspoon College campus. Harvey S. Murdoch of the Society of Soul Winners helped found a Christian elementary and high school and called it a college in order to give the students extra status. The massive logs are white oak, cut from the surrounding woods. Inside, the space is lovely and impressive. The gem in the crown of the cathedral is a Hook and Hasting pipe organ, which has been restored and sounds great. Sun streaming through the old amber glass windows bathes the oak sanctuary (and you) in a warm and beautiful golden glow. To experience it, stop by the parsonage next door. If the pastor's not home, try the little store across the road, where caretakers also have a key. You're also invited to come for services, held on Sunday at 11:00 A.M. If you'd like to make an appointment to tour the church, call (606) 398–7382.

To see the region on foot, try some hiking trails in the **Buckhorn Lake State Resort Park** (606–398–7510), 20 miles northwest of Hazard. Take Highway 15 North, then Highway 28 to the west and watch for signs. There's a lodge with a dining room overlooking the lake, campgrounds, and a marina where you can slip your canoe into the 1,250-acre **Buckhorn Lake.**

Like the mountain schools in the area, *Frontier Nursing Service* in Hyden off Highway 421 (southwest of Hazard in Leslie County) is an institution committed to promoting health and growth, but in this case its main concern is with the physical body. Mary Breckinridge started Frontier Nursing as a school in 1925. Her original students and the generations of nurses to follow have made strong impressions on the minds of everyone who has encountered them riding on horseback to remote hollows and mountain towns to deliver babies and administer health care. Folks at Frontier Nursing have revised their charter and are also involved in child care, general education, and regional economics. The grounds are lovely, and the history of the service is inspirational. Make sure to go in the tiny chapel, which has a fifteenth-century Flemish stained-glass window, and to see the Wendover Big House, a log home built in 1925 for the founder. Eight rooms for rent in the house are the only lodging in the county. The rate of $65 per night includes breakfast. For information, call (606) 672–2317.

Frontier Nursing Service, in Hyden, is the oldest American school of nurse-midwifery in existence.

The Gorgeous Gorge

The *Red River Gorge* in the Daniel Boone National Forest is one of the most beautiful and best-loved wilderness areas in Kentucky. Actually, the area was quite obscure until its existence was threatened in the late 1960s by a proposed 5,000-acre impoundment on the Red River's north fork. Intense controversy raged until 1975, when the plan was nixed. All the publicity caused the park to be badly overused by visitors who weren't ecologically sensitive. Today the park has been reorganized; large areas are strictly protected, and visitor education is an important part of forest management.

The gorge was formed by erosion and weathering, in much the same way that the Grand Canyon was carved out by the Colorado River. The north fork of the Red River cut through the area more than 340 million years ago and left behind some fantastic geologic phenomena in limestone, conglomerate sandstone, and siltstone, all of which are tucked under a layer of shale. The most outstanding of these phenomena are the eighty natural rock arches, a number surpassed in the United States only by Arches National Park in Utah.

The Daniel Boone National Forest is 60 miles east of Lexington on the Bert T. Combs Mountain Parkway. A good place to begin exploring the Red River Gorge, at the northern end of the forest, is *Natural Bridge*

State Resort Park (800–325–1710 or 606– 663–2214), a full-fledged state park with a big lodge, cottages, camping, a pool, recreation areas, and a variety of hiking trails leading to a spectacular natural stone bridge. This park is not very isolated, but it can serve as a point of reference for outings to more remote places. From I–64 take the Bert T. Combs Mountain Parkway southeast, get off at the **Slade** Interchange onto Highway 11, and follow signs to the park.

On the way in or out, you should have a meal at **Miguel's Pizza** (606– 663–1975), a little building with a beautifully carved wooden front door on the left near the park entrance. Miguel Ventura's parents, who live next door, grow an enormous and wonderful garden. Order a veggie pizza, and you'll be likely to find it laced with whatever's in season—heavenly. If you're a climber, take note that this is the only store in the area that sells

Natural Stone Bridge

a good variety of climbing supplies. Miguel's is open Wednesday through Sunday from March 1 through Thanksgiving.

Just on the west side of Miguel's you will notice the **Kentucky Reptile Zoo** (606–663–9160). After all, how many places do you pass that look like a faux Swiss chalet with a painting of a man astride an alligator on it? Despite its oddball facade (it's a converted restaurant building), the Kentucky Reptile Zoo is actually a very well-run and educational reptile center. And its founder, Jim Harrison (the man depicted astride the alligator), is well respected in venom research circles. He is a leading supplier of snake venom for medical research and also is helping a university in Brazil breed rattlesnakes whose venom may be used to help hold human skin together after surgery. In addition to seeing several dozen kinds of snakes (including pythons and black mambas) and three alligators, your visit will include an informational demonstration by Harrison or a staff member, and possibly a demonstration of venom extraction. From Memorial Day through Labor Day, the zoo is open

If I w... *for th...* *the st...* *have t...* *Count...* *little, n.o.-even-on-the-map community north of Hyden just off Highway 257. Runners-up in the area would include Devil's Jump Branch, Confluence, Cutshin, Thousandsticks, Yeaddis, Smilax, Yerkes, and Krypton (watch out, Superman!).*

There's a Morel to This Story

*E*astern Kentucky communities have festivals celebrating all kinds of foods, from Gingerbread Days in Hindman in September to the Kentucky Apple Festival in Paintsville in early October. There's even a Poke Sallet Festival, honoring a local green, in Harlan in June. But the most exotic eastern Kentucky food festival has to be the **Mountain Mushroom Festival** in Irvine in late April. Up to 20,000 people show up in this town of 2,800 with mushrooms on the mind—grilled, fried, baked, and en casserole mushrooms, that is. For many years, folks in Estill County have gone to the woods to hunt for the morels, or wild mush-

rooms, that pop up in poplar thickets and apple orchards in the spring. Locally, these delicacies are called landfish for their somewhat fishy taste. The annual festival includes a hunt to see who can find the biggest morel, a mushroom cook-off, and even a Fungus Run. Call the Estill County Chamber of Commerce at (606) 723–2554 for the current year's festival dates. If you're planning to do any mushroom gathering on your own, make sure you know what the edible variety looks like. (Check out the poster hanging in the Irvine City Council chambers.) You don't want to take home a poisonous variety.

..aily from 11:00 A.M. to 6:00 P.M. In September, October, and March through May, it's open only on weekends. Closed December through February. Admission is $4.00.

There is a designated driving loop through the area beginning in Nada, 1¹/₂ miles west of the Slade Interchange on Highway 15. Take Highway 77 north through the **Nada Tunnel,** a 10-foot-wide, 13-foot-tall, 800-foot-long tunnel cut by hand in 1877 to give small-gauge trains access to the big timber in the area. Stay on Highway 77 and it will run into Highway 715, which runs parallel to the river. At Pine Ridge, Highway 715 connects with Highway 15 again, which leads back to Natural Bridge. Ask for a map in the lodge at Natural Bridge.

Big timber is the subject of a small museum in the recently restored **Gladie Creek Cabin,** which you'll pass on this loop drive. This was the 1884 cabin of John Ledford, who bought and logged more than 4,000 acres here. The U.S. Forest Service recently rebuilt the cabin and filled it with historic objects that refer to the early years of the logging industry in eastern Kentucky, including log branding irons, tools, models of old equipment, and photographs.

Gladie Creek Historical Site also serves as the visitors center for the north end of the Daniel Boone National Forest. This is another good place to get trail maps, weather reports, and general advice about hiking or anything else concerning the National Forest. Hours are 8:00 A.M. to 4:30 P.M. Monday through Friday and vary on weekends. Call the Stanton Ranger District (606–663–2852) for information. Aside from the driving loop, another way to reach Gladie Creek is from the north. Take Highway 77 south to Highway 715; go east for about 11 miles and watch the right side of the road.

The absolute best way to be in the Red River Gorge is to be hiking, crawling, if you must, for driving does not do the woods justice. You must sweat, propel yourself by your own energy, drink when you're thirsty, eat when you're hungry (or can't wait any longer for the granola bar), feel the leaves brush against your legs, feel the sunshine on your shoulders when you come to an opening in the forest canopy, hear and see the animals, and so taste the life of the mountains. More than 165 miles of foot trails in the Daniel Boone Forest offer ample opportunity to be here the right way. Get maps from the Hemlock Lodge at Natural Bridge, at Gladie, or anywhere you see a ranger. Hike as many trails as you're able.

Ask at the lodge, or anywhere you see a ranger, about the **Clifty Wilderness** area, a 13,300-acre area that adjoins the Red River Gorge. Hiking,

camping, canoeing, horseback riding, and fishing—thes
ways to spend time here, where there are some 170 speci
more than 750 flowering plants, several of which are
gered. Call (606) 663–2852 for maps and information.

I will concede that canoeing is as good as hiking for seeing the wᴏᴏᴅ
Nothing beats gliding silently through the forest, unless maybe it's
crashing dramatically through some wild white water. Either way, if you
want to canoe the Red River and didn't bring a boat, contact *Canoe
Kentucky* at (800) K–CANOE–1 for information about trips. From
October through May you can hire a guide or self-guide in its boats
through Class I, II, or III rapids. Rates are between $35 and $45.

The *Sheltowee Trace* (Trail #100) is the only backpacking trail that traverses the entire length of the
Daniel Boone National Forest. It goes 257 miles
through nine counties, beginning in Rowan
County in the north and ending in Tennessee,
where it connects with the John Muir Trail (named
for the father of the Sierra Club), which connects
to the great Appalachian Trail. If you're planning a
backpacking trip, check with a ranger. The Shel-
towee Trace is marked with a white diamond or turtle-shaped blaze. The
word *sheltowee* is Shawnee for "big turtle," Daniel Boone's Native American name when he was captured and adopted by Shawnee chief Blackfish.

> **True Blue**
>
> *There are about 175
> species of native and intro-
> duced tree varieties that
> grow wild in Kentucky,
> including 17 species of oak.*

For a taste of the area's social and cultural history, stop by the *Wolfe
County Historical Museum* on Main Street in downtown Campton.
From the Mountain Parkway take exit 43, go downtown, and watch for the
signs. It's only open on Sunday from 2:00 to 4:00 P.M.

The *Pioneer Weapons Hunting Area* is a 7,480-acre area in the
National Forest, north of the gorge, which is designated for hunting
deer, turkey, grouse, and squirrel, but you must use only primitive
weapons—black-powder muzzle loaders, bows and arrows, blow guns,
spears, rubber bands, whatever. Before you hunt, be sure to call the forest supervisor (606–784–6428) so that you understand the regulations.

A good place to eat in Frenchburg is *Peck's Place,* on Highway 460.
Nannie and Steve Peck dish up delicious home-cooked plate lunches
Monday through Friday. Call (606) 768–3851 for more information.

If you turn toward the north from the Corner Restaurant on Highway
36, take the first street to the right, follow it to the end, and you'll see a
trail going up the hillside. This trail leads to *Donathan Rock,* a great

ige rock teetering near the edge of a cliff from which you get a perfect aerial view of Frenchburg below. Park in town and walk over. Traveling a mile farther north on Highway 36 brings you to the *Roe Wells School.* Watch carefully for it on the left—the sign is small. The schoolhouse is a typical, quaint, one-room country school. Look in the windows; the old desks and books, chalkboard, and even a few messages from the teacher remain. It would make a perfect movie set. If you want to go inside, make an appointment by calling (606) 768–3323.

Leaving Frenchburg in the southeasterly direction, there are several surprises in store for you. Take Highway 460 east for 7½ miles and look on the right side of the road for *Barton's Foods,* Manufacturer of Relish, Sorghum, and Jellies. Charlotte Roe is glad to show visitors around the operation. Your nose will tell you what's cooking at the moment. One day it's a hot chowchow relish; the next, it's cinnamon and pear preserves (which tastes like apple pie); and the next it's old mill molasses, Delano Roe's magnum opus. Barton's is best known for Moonshine

Look Out, Stonehenge

*F*rom Frenchburg, which is in the heart of the National Forest near the Pioneer Weapons Hunting Area, take Highway 36 north, then Highway 1274 east for 2.2 miles to the first paved road on the right (south), marked only by a small brown sign denoting **Spratt Stoneworks.** Turn and bear left onto a gravel road, then left again until you find yourself at the third fork in the road. Go to the brick house on the hill and ask for Verne Spratt, the old man who owns the land where there are a number of curious and very well-preserved stoneworks and earthen constructions. The Kentucky Heritage Council gave Spratt a grant to preserve the site and to develop a trail.

The large stone effigy or geometrical construction is thought to be a serpent mound, but this has not been proven archaeologically. It's a strange series of stone walls completely blanketed in moss. To the southeast is a group of about two dozen small stone mounds, some linear, some round or ovate. Because the land surrounding these constructions is not arable, it's unlikely that these were built by white farmers. They are probably prehistoric; a number of stone mounds found in this region have been dated to the Middle and Late Woodland periods. Spratt is likely to tell you stories about how John Swift's hidden silver mines are nearby. He can point out eighteenth-century graffiti on the rocks and will read to you from Swift's diary, which names rock formations that seem to correspond with some on his farm. To visit the site, you must call Spratt ahead at (606) 768–6619, preferably in the evening. This is guaranteed to be a strange adventure, something that will pique your curiosity forever.

Strange As It Sounds

*E*astern Kentuckians have their own way of saying things, and as you travel this part of the state you'll not only notice a distinctive accent, but you'll also encounter some fascinating local expressions. For example, man or woman, don't be surprised if you're called "honey" by total strangers of both sexes. A ghost is a "haint"; "loaded for bear" means angry or looking for a fight; and a "passel" is one way to indicate a large quantity. If someone tells you to "quit lollygaggin' around," it means to stop delaying or taking so long; and there are a passel of other local expressions. One day a friend from Hazard and I were having lunch at a local restaurant when an acquaintance of hers came in. In the course of conversation, I mentioned that I wasn't from the area. "Oh, honey, I knew that," he said. "You talk way too plain to be from around here."

Jelly, which contains just 10 percent Georgia Moon. Many of the delectables are available for sale. Hours are 8:00 A.M. to 4:30 P.M. Monday through Friday. Call (606) 768–3750.

A ¹/₂ mile east of Barton's is another surprise and treat, the **Swamp Valley Store and Museum** (606–768–3250). The humor around here runs thick, but it's all deeply rooted in local history. Clayton Wells, the jovial owner, was a pack rat from his youth, and now it has paid off. He kept every little thing of his and his family's, and other folks', too. In the past twenty years or so, Clayton has restored and moved a whole slew of historic buildings onto the property near his country store. He filled each one with appropriate artifacts, and—voila!—a museum. What makes the place outstanding (and funny) are his accompanying stories: "My people always told about . . ."

The main museum house, for example, was the home of John Poplin, Clayton's great-great-grandfather, a slave driver who brought slaves from Sand Gap, Virginia, to Lexington, Kentucky. Other buildings include an old metal silo called Photo Silo, which could be a twist on the little drive-in photo-developing units that sit in mall parking lots, but it's not. Inside are school photos of every child in Menifee County for fifty years. Clayton and his friends also record music here and sell square-dance tapes for $10. They're pretty good. Other buildings include the E-Z Rest Casket Shop, which is full of authentic, family tools for blacksmithing, shoe repair, stone masonry, and casket making; the Doctors Museum, which is chock-full of the tools and oddities that local country docs used to carry; and the Cheese Shop, supplied with everything necessary to make cheese, except milk. There's more, but you have to visit Swamp Valley to appreciate it. It's worth the drive. Even folksy National Public Radio personality Garrison Keillor stopped by once to do a little historical research. Keillor wanted to verify the record-breaking length of marriage of Lynn Boyd Wells and Alydia Rupe Wells, Clayton's oldest uncle and aunt. They were married something like eighty-two years! Amen.

The old **Botts School building** stands about 200 yards away from Swamp Valley. Although it's now a community building, you can still feel its age; it was a one-room schoolhouse since before the time Menifee County was a county. If it catches your fancy and you want to see inside, ask Clayton Wells of Swamp Valley Store or stop by the Botts General Store that's directly across the street. Either way, you'll get some stories.

One of the most special surprises in this immediate area is **Furnace Mountain, Inc.,** a spiritual community founded in 1986 by Zen master Seung Sahn. The community owns 500 acres of beautiful woodland near Clay City in Powell County, where visitors are welcome to hike or join in daily meditation practices. The main function of Furnace Mountain is to host a variety of retreats, primarily traditional three- to ninety-day Zen Buddhist retreats. Retreats are also conducted in other disciplines such as twelve-step programs, Christian meditation, and clinical pastoral education.

Kwan Se Um San Ji Sah, which means "Perceive World Sound High Ground Temple," is indeed a place that sits beautifully on high ground and affects the way one perceives the world, due to its exquisite blend of eastern Kentucky craftsmanship with Far Eastern aesthetics. This timber-frame temple has the classic tapering vertical lines and uplifting roofline of Oriental architecture and the materials of the mountains— recycled Douglas fir siding, a cherry wood floor, and deep sky-blue ceramic roof tiles. For more information, write c/o the Abbess, P.O. Box 545, Clay City 40312, leave a message at (606) 723–4329, or check out the center online at furnacement@kih.net.

A nice area for hiking and birdwatching is **Pilot Knob State Nature Preserve,** located off Highway 15 near Cave City. The preserve includes one of the tallest "knobs," or large hills, in the area—a 730-footer from which Daniel Boone supposedly looked out over the Bluegrass region for the first time. There are so many Daniel Boone exaggerations made in Kentucky, that one is always a little suspect of such claims, but it is nonetheless a good spot for modern explorers to gaze upon a lovely vista. Open most days.

In downtown Clay City on Main Street there is a free museum devoted to the area's work history. Artifacts at the **Red River Historical Museum** include lots of tools from the railroad and the area's iron and logging industries. Also, there's a huge rock with supposedly ancient carvings. Hours May through October are Saturday and Sunday from 1:00 to 5:00 P.M. (606) 663–4000.

You can get your bluegrass music inside and out at **Meadowgreen Park Bluegrass Music Hall.** This hundred-acre park with music hall is home base for the Kentucky Friends of Bluegrass Mountain Club, an organization whose goal is to preserve the musical heritage of the Appalachian Mountains. There are indoor shows October through April and large outdoor festivals in spring and fall. For more information, write Meadowgreen Park Bluegrass Music Hall, 465 Forge Mill Road, Clay City 40312, or call (606) 663–9008.

You are still in beautiful country when you travel to the south side of the Red River Gorge. From Natural Bridge head south on Highway 11 through Zachariah and Zoe (my name town and the site of my worst bicycle wreck) to **Beattyville,** a friendly little mountain town with the best-named restaurant in the world, **The Purple Cow,** on Main Street. Eat any meal

> ### True Blue
>
> *Kentucky's Red River Gorge area has the largest concentration of rock shelters and arches east of the Rockies.*

there any day of the week, just for the fun of it. The weekend after the third Monday in October, Beattyville is host to the world's only **Woolly Worm Festival,** devoted to the humblest of all meteorologists. Call (606) 464–2888 for festival information.

From Beattyville take Highway 11 south and turn east on Highway 30 to Booneville, home of **Morris Fork Crafts.** The shop offers traditional mountain items including quilts, baskets, toys, and wooden items. Hours are usually Monday through Friday from 9:00 A.M. to 3:00 P.M. Saturday hours are by appointment. Call (606) 398–2194.

Continue on Highway 30 east and you'll come to **Jackson.** This town was originally known as Breathitt, but in 1845 it was renamed to honor President Andrew Jackson, who died that year. The **Breathitt County Museum** (336 Broadway, Jackson 41339; 606–666–4159), which has exhibits on logging and coal mining along with Civil War artifacts. The photo collection of life in the area during the 1940s is especially impressive. It's free and open Monday through Friday from 8:00 A.M. to 4:00 P.M.

About 9 miles south of Jackson on Highway 15, and some 500 miles from the nearest ocean, is a **Scuba Center.** Why, you may ask? It's because of Raymond Hudon's interest in the sport. He rents and sells equipment out of his home and sometimes gives lessons in his swimming pool. Local divers do take the plunge in some local lakes, including Buckhorn and Dale Hollow. The center is open by appointment only; for information, call (606) 666–4354.

From Highway 15 south veer off to the southeast on Highway 476 to **Robinson Forest,** a large research and educational forest owned and managed by the University of Kentucky. Visitors can take a self-guided hike along a nature trail and see a wide variety of flora and fauna typical of this area. The forest is a unique example of an old-growth forest ecosystem on the Cumberland Plateau. This property has been threatened in recent years by the university, which has been toying with the idea of allowing coal mining. After seeing the gorgeous forest, you will want to write some fan mail. As the Buddhists say, "Just do it." A climb up the Camp Robinson Lookout Tower is worth the effort. To get to the tower, take Highway 426 way into the forest and turn left on Clemons

The Wild-Bird Charmer

*B*eattyville's two most important claims to fame are, first, that it is the place where all three forks—north, middle, and south—converge to form the Kentucky River, and second, that Beattyville has been the lifelong home of Nevyle Shackelford, Kentucky's (and my) most loved syndicated nature and mountain culture columnist, and his wife, Gladys, gardener and cook extraordinaire. Some of my earliest childhood memories were of "Uncle" Nevyle's amazing feats, like growing apples and pears on the same tree and charming wild birds. Since his fame was as a writer, let me quote him from a 1972 excerpt from his column, Outdoor Lore:

One of the easiest of all wild songbirds to tame, the chickadee comes readily to winter bird feeders and, with a little patience and a handful of sunflower seeds or walnut kernels, can be coaxed to feed from the hand. And once its confidence is gained, it will remember from year to year and keep coming back to provide delightful companionship for its benefactor.

One winter, often to the consternation of visitors dropping by, I had a small flock of chickadees that would fly in at my call and eat from my hand. When I was wayfaring outside these birds would accompany me on my little journeys, buzzing my head, and often alighting on my head and shoulders. Actually, they became so tame that I could reach up and lift them from their perches like picking apples from a twig. Observing this, some of my visitors considered me some sort of a wizard with hidden powers extraordinary. While a bit flattering, this was far from true. The trick was, the chickadees associated me with food and nothing more.

Road to the tower trail. The forest is open daily, year-round. Call (606) 666–5034 for more information.

Iron Country

f these United States can be called a body, Kentucky can be called its heart.

These words are from the first stanza of "Kentucky Is My Land," a poem by the late poet laureate of Kentucky, Jesse Stuart, a wholesome, hopeful writer whose work was deeply rooted in his eastern Kentucky homeland. Because W-Hollow was Stuart's home and source of inspiration, more than 700 acres have been made into a pastoral museum and maintained as Stuart knew it—cattle graze in some pastures and young forests are being allowed to grow to maturity. The ***Jesse Stuart State Nature Preserve*** lies between Highways 1 and 2 just west of Greenup, off Highway 23. Visitors can walk the hills and fields Stuart walked and visit Op's Cabin, the old white clapboard house where he did some of his writing. For those who know his work, the fictional Laurel Ridge is Seaton Ridge. His home borders the preserve but is private property. The Kentucky State Nature Preserves Commission (502–564–2886) maintains the nature preserve and the Jesse Stuart Foundation, a nonprofit organization devoted to preserving and sharing Stuart's work. To order books, write the foundation at P.O. Box 391, Ashland 41114, or call (606) 329–5232.

Continue south on Highway 1 to ***Greenbo Lake State Resort Park,*** where the lodge is named after Jesse Stuart and even includes a read-

Breathitt County's Ice Man

*P*aul Griffith, a retired highway department maintenance analyst, has created his own winter wonderland in his yard on Highway 30, near Shoulderblade, about 8 miles west of Jackson. When the first real cold spell hits, Griffith goes into action. He turns on an elaborate system of hoses that spray water from five ponds over trees and other frames. The results are strange and glistening cascading ice formations that draw the delighted attention of passing motorists and school bus passengers. Griffith says he just enjoys looking at his icy creations. "They're beautiful," he explains. "It just relaxes me to sit and look out the window at them." But he doesn't get so relaxed that he isn't planning ahead: He's still trying to figure out a way to add color to his creations (adding food color to the water didn't work; he thinks that tinted spotlights might).

ing room where you can enjoy his novels, short stories, and poems. The last weekend in September the park hosts a Jesse Stuart Weekend, during which speakers lecture on the life and works of Stuart, a guided tour of W-Hollow is given by family members, films are shown, and exhibits are open. Otherwise, the lake is marvelous for fishing, the dining room is popular, and camping is available. The 24-mile-long Michael Tygart Trail connects the park with the Jenny Wiley National Recreation Trail. Call (606) 473–7324 for more information about the park or the festival.

Nine miles south of the park, at the intersection of Highways 1 and 3111, is the *Oldtown Covered Bridge,* spanning the Little Sandy River near the site of a Shawnee village. The 194-foot-long, two-span, Burr-type bridge was built in 1880 and has not been restored. *Bennett's Mill Bridge* is 1 foot longer, twenty-five years older, and has one less span than the Oldtown Bridge, and it's functional. It was built in 1855 for access to Bennett's Grist Mill on Tygart Creek. What is amazing is that the original frame and footings are intact. This bridge is on Highway 7, just west of the Greenup County Locks and Dam. (Warning: Grays Branch Road, the direct route from the dam, is a rough, dirt logging road.)

The county seat, *Greenup,* is a very interesting little river town at the confluence of the Little Sandy and Ohio Rivers. Though it's suffered through some terrible floods (the 1937 flood destroyed its hundred-year-old courthouse), there are still some old places worth seeing. Stop by the Greenup Library at 614 Main Street (606–473–6514) and get a free map of *Greenup's walking tour.*

Follow the Ohio River south on Highway 23 into *Ashland,* the largest city in Kentucky east of Lexington and headquarters for Ashland Oil and Armco Steel (not to mention that it's the hometown of country

Poetry in Motion—Relocated to Eastern Kentucky

*I*t has been 150 years since large numbers of elk ranged freely in these mountains. In fact, every elk was entirely extirpated from Kentucky until now. Every year for the next decade, 200 elk will be released into the wild with the hope that in two decades their population will increase to more than 8,300. This program may be the largest relocation of game animals in modern times. Initially the elk will be released in Perry, Knott, and Breathitt Counties in wildlife refuge lands inside the Robinson Forest and in the Cyprus Amax Wildlife Management Area.

music stars Naomi and Wynonna Judd and Wynonna's movie-star sis, Ashley). Downtown you'll notice a surprising number of large, ornate houses built by early industrialists during the last half of the nineteenth century. My favorite is at 1600 Central Avenue. The highest peaks of the roof sport two cast-iron dragons, reminiscent of French faitages or the figures on ancient Macedonian tombs, meant to ward off evil spirits. It was originally built at the corner of Winchester Avenue and Seventeenth Street but was hauled intact to the present site some twenty years later by a team of mules. The dragons did their job.

Another awesome building is the Mayo Manor, circa 1917, at the corner of Bath and Sixteenth Streets, which now houses the **Kentucky Highlands Museum.** Even without the museum items, the mansion would be worth touring. Make sure to climb the grand staircase to the third floor, where there is a large panel of handsome stained glass in the ceiling. The museum is organized by subject and period, and exhibits range from Adena, Fort Ancient, and Hopewell Indian cultures to rail, steam, and industrial histories, the evolution of radio, a World War II room, an impressive antique clothing collection, and a special exhibit on the third floor that usually is worth a visit in itself. Hours are 10:00 A.M. to 4:00 P.M. Tuesday through Saturday. Admission is $3.00. Call (606) 329–8888 for special programs and more information.

Not far from the museum in downtown Ashland is **Central Park,** a forty-seven-acre area set aside when Ashland was laid out in the 1850s. It contains a number of ancient Native American mounds that have been restored to their original proportions. They were found to contain human bones and pottery and other artifacts that correspond with the Adena period (800 B.C. to A.D. 800). The mounds and historic houses are part of a 2-mile walking tour of downtown Ashland. Stop by the visitors center at 1509 Winchester Avenue, Ashland 41101, for a free map

Lower Shawneetown

*T*hough no one knows the exact spot, somewhere in Greenup County is the site of Kentucky's very first white settlement . . . before Fort Harrod. (And I do hate to admit this, since Harrodsburg is my hometown and the generally recognized title holder.) Sometime prior to 1753

French fur traders and Shawnee Indians settled across the Scioto River at a place referred to in records as Lower Shawneetown. However, all traces of the settlement disappeared before 1800. So, there's some work here for archaeologists in need of a project.

between 9:00 A.M. and 5:00 P.M. Monday through Friday. Call (800) 377–6249.

For more contemporary local human artifacts, try the **Ashland Area Art Gallery** (1516 Winchester Avenue, Ashland 41101; 606–329–1826). The gallery changes exhibits monthly and features regional work in the Artists Market. Hours are 10:00 A.M. to 4:00 P.M. Monday through Saturday.

Architecture buffs, brace yourselves. The **Paramount Arts Center** (1300 Winchester Avenue, Ashland 41101; 606–324–3175) is out of this world. Art deco has never been better, and the people of Ashland cared enough to give this place an enormous facelift (but what a face!). If you're in town on a night when a cultural event is scheduled, go, no matter what's playing. It books everything from Marcel Marceau to the Sistine Chapel Choir to Ray Charles. Or you can just tour the building between 9:00 A.M. and 4:00 P.M. Monday through Friday. Whether you've ever been to Ashland before or not, you may have already seen the Paramount Center in Billy Ray Cyrus's "Achy Breaky Heart" video. Billy Ray was born in nearby Flatwoods, Kentucky.

In the early 1920s Paramount-Famous Lasky Corporation planned to build a chain of "talking picture" theaters like the Paramount across the nation to showcase Paramount Studios films. After a few theaters were built, the Depression hit and truncated the plan. In 1931 this joint was built for $400,000. The ceiling is painted with the famous art deco pseudo-Moravian sunburst surrounded by leaping gazelles. On the red walls are murals of sixteenth-century theatrical figures. The seats are done in plush red velvet. Ornamental pewter and brass are everywhere, even in the bathrooms. Opulent is the word.

About 10 miles from Ashland on Highway 23N is **Russell,** home to numerous antiques shops and restaurants. Not to be missed, however, is **Rail City Hardware** (606–836–3121)—part general hardware store, part railroad museum. Owners Sharon and Bill Lanham collect miniature trains as a hobby and have two tracks set up right in the store. Over the years, other people in the area have brought in items from the C&O railroad, which ran through the town. So in addition to the usual hardware goods for sale, at Rail City you also can see a fascinating collection of (not-for-sale) railroad lanterns, oil cans, even pot-bellied stoves. The store is right in the center of town on Highway 244, and it is open Monday through Saturday from 8:30 A.M. to 5:00 P.M.

More opulence is in store for you at **Irish Acres Antiques,** a seemingly endless gallery filled with very fine American, European, and Asian antiques of all periods. The furniture will leave you wide-eyed, but don't fail to notice the significant details—glassware, silver, and ceramics. To get there, take I–64 west, get off at the exit, turn right, and follow signs for 12 miles to Irish Acr 10:00 A.M. to 5:00 P.M. Tuesday through Saturday. Call (60€ This is a sister store to the Irish Acres Antiques in Nonesuc the same family and run with the same pizzazz.

Excessive haute couture making you queasy? One good antidote is going fishing. Try the *Yatesville Lake,* south of Louisa on Highway 3. Its famous for its largemouth bass. (There's a marina, if you have your boat.) For land lubbers there's an interesting reconstructed wetlands area on a high bluff near the entrance to the Yatesville Lake Wildlife Management Area. Camping is available in the park.

Two pig-iron furnace ruins near Ashland are accessible to the public. One is the *Clinton Furnace,* built by the Poage brothers in 1833. Take Highway 60 south, turn left (east) on Highway 538, and left again on Shopes Creek Road to the furnace ruins. The other, *Princess Furnace,* was put into operation in 1864. From town take Highway 60 south, then Highway 5 north; watch for a rough stone structure near the road.

A Pig-Iron Primer

*T*he furnace ruins in the Ashland area were all once part of a much larger community of pig-iron operations. Because the sites are usually in bad condition and none of them are part of guided tours, let me explain how they worked. It was a clumsy process, but these furnaces produced tons and tons of rough pig iron that were refined into steel, wrought iron, and ingot iron. The Civil War was fought with bullets and cannonballs from these humble industries. The earliest furnaces of the late eighteenth century produced approximately 3 tons of iron from 9 tons of ore— today's steel furnaces need only about half an hour to produce the same amount of steel the old furnaces could produce in a year.

Enormous stones were quarried from the nearby mountains and used to build the furnaces by the sides of hills. A bridge was built to the top of the chimney, where they dumped the "charge," which consisted of iron ore, also mined locally; limestone, which acts as a fluxing agent; and charcoal, for heat. The charcoal, in turn, was made by burning prime hardwood down to lumps of black, porous carbon. When all this was dumped into the top of the furnace, pig iron and slag came out the bottom and cooled in ditches. When you visit these old furnaces, climb inside, if possible, and look up the stack; often they taper beautifully to a small round opening at the top. In my opinion, the art of stone-masonry of this quality is dead. It's important to know what's possible.

..ie furnace tour continues west of Ashland in Carter County. Just 2 miles north of Grayson is a little community called **Pactolus**, which also has a run-down furnace right by the road. This one was a blast furnace that used hydropower from the Little Sandy River. If your interest is piqued, continue north on Highway 7 to the ruins of the **Iron Hill Furnace,** once the largest charcoal-powered blast furnace in the region. Stay on Highway 7 until it merges with Highway 2, then continue to Highway 1773, turn left (west), and go 4 miles to **Boone Furnace** on Grassy Creek. The blast furnace, built by Sebastian Eifort, started producing iron in 1857.

South of Grayson is the **Mount Savage Furnace,** one of the best preserved and most beautifully made furnaces in the state. If you only want to see one furnace, this is the judge's choice. Take Highway 7 south of Grayson and turn east on Highway 773. The furnace is on the left, about 1 1/2 miles east of Hitchins. The gorgeous stonework was done in 1848 by a Prussian mason named John Fauson.

Carter County is home to **Carter Caves State Resort Park,** one of the most magnificent small parks in this region of the United States. From Grayson take I–64 or Highway 60 west, then go north on Highway 182. In addition to a lodge, camping facilities, a pool, canoe trips, and hiking trails, there are twenty navigated caves, three of which are lighted for tours. Many of the caves are wild and can be seen only if you're excited by the idea of real spelunking. One of the best times to try your hand (and elbows and knees) at caving is during the park's annual Crawlathon in early February, when the best guided tours are given.

Two of the park's most significant parts are **Bat Cave** and **Cascade Caverns,** both of which are State Nature Preserves. Bat Cave is part-time home to one of the nation's largest wintering populations of the Indiana bat, a federally endangered species. The bats hang in tight clusters in cracks and on the ceiling. There are no winter tours of this cave because it is important not to disturb these creatures during the winter; they have stored just enough fat to keep them alive during hibernation, and flying would use up their reserves. Cascade Caverns is not contiguous with the rest of the park. Take Highway 182 south, turn west onto Highway 209, and follow signs. Aboveground, on the north slopes by the caverns, are some rare plants that are usually found much farther north, and there are a number of mountain maple trees, a shrublike tree found here along the stream that flows out of the cave toward **Tygarts Creek,** where the hemlock forest and old yews will take your breath away. During the summer the park offers guided canoe trips. Better yet, when the water is high enough—from late winter through early spring—you can take your own trip beginning anywhere upstream and ending in the park. East of **Olive Hill,** where Highway 1025 goes under I–64, you can launch a canoe and take a gorgeous 12-mile paddle to the park. Though generally innocuous, there may be Class II rapids and dangerous deadfalls along this part of Tygarts Creek, so be careful. For information about any facet of Carter Caves State Resort Park, call (606) 286–4411 or, for lodge reservations, (800) 325–0059.

While driving from Carter Caves to Cascade Caverns, watch for the **Northeastern Kentucky Museum** and gift shop, a decidedly quirky little joint. From late April through October, 9:00 A.M. to 5:00 P.M., seven days a week, you can take a visual crash course in regional history beginning with ancient Native American artifacts through pioneer times, the Civil War, World War II, and into the present. If you're visiting in the winter and want to tour this informative amateur museum, make an appointment with Jim Plummer at (606) 286–6012.

Another look at the Civil War and its effect on Carter County is offered in the form of a summertime outdoor musical called *Someday.* It's a love story with Class II rapids and deadfalls, just like the creek. From mid-June to mid-July, show time is Friday and Saturday at 8:30 P.M. Call (606) 286–4522 for information and tickets. The drama takes place inside **Grayson Lake State Park** (606–474–9727), just south of I–64 if

Mount Savage Furnace

you take exit 172. There's a large man-made lake surrounded by sandstone, a campground, a marina, and lots of fish. The adjacent Grayson Lake Wildlife Management Area is said to be home to bald eagles, among other wildlife, especially birds. Bring your binoculars.

Morehead is a typical university town except that it's plopped right down in the hills of eastern Kentucky. A friend of mine chose to go to Morehead State because he loves to rock climb and sail, two sports one can't pursue in one's free time at most Kentucky colleges. Sailing and all other forms of boating and water play are available at *Cave Run Lake,* an 8,270-acre lake fed by the Licking River. If you're interested in learning about how such massive bodies of water are formed and maintained, arrange a tour of the Corps of Engineers dam and towers. If you want a less technical view, just dive in. Fishing may be the most popular thing to do at Cave Run. In fact, it's becoming known as the "muskie capital of the world." For information on fishing, camping, or anything concerning the lake, call the U.S. Forest Service at (606) 784–65624.

How about seeing Cave Run Lake from an eagle's point of view? Take the Lakeview Ridge Hiking Trail, beginning at the U.S. Forest Service's visitors center (606–784–5624), on Highway 801, where you can also get maps and more information, Monday through Friday, 8:00 A.M. to 4:30 P.M. For about a mile the trail is merged with the Sheltowee Trace, then it goes high above the lake for another 4 miles and ends at Shallow Flats, where there is a wetland interpretive area.

And if you were wondering where all those muskies and other fish come from, tour the *Minor E. Clark Fish Hatchery,* also off Highway 801 between the lake and Highway 60 (you'll see signs). With 111 rearing and brood ponds on more than 300 acres, this is one of the

Glamour Fish

*M*uskellunge, *musky,* Esox masquinongy, *briartooth, water wolf... whatever you call a muskie, you'd better be ready for it when it hits your line. Maybe it's considered a "glamour" fish because it puts up such a fantastic fight. Maybe it's because a muskie can measure up to 50 inches and weigh more than 40 pounds. If it's* *because they taste so great, you may not be able to find out if you hire a fishing guide, who may insist on catch-and-release. Maybe you don't care about eating fish, but you do want to get up close and personal with a long, silver dude with a severe underbite. Call* **Cave Run Muskie Guide Service** *for a good time,* (800) 452–1600, *any time of year.*

largest state-owned, warm-water hatcheries in the United States. Admission is free, and visitors are welcome Monday through Friday from 7:00 A.M. to 3:00 P.M. Call (606) 784–6872 for more information.

At *The Kentucky Folk Art Center* (606–783–2204) in Morehead, you'll find a surprising, delightful, thought-provoking, and ultimately impressive collection of carvings, paintings, assemblages, walking sticks, painted furniture, gourd creatures, and other works by folk artists from across Kentucky. The collection began in one room of the Morehead State University art department and was later moved to a small house on campus. Now an independent and fully accredited, nationally recognized museum, it is housed in a renovated historic building at 102 West First Street, Morehead 40351, near the Highway 60 bypass. By some definitions, folk art comprises objects that are part of everyday life and that somehow reflect the beliefs, social structure, and experiences of the people in a given region; formal training is usually not received outside the culture from which it springs. You'll understand better when you see the collection. You'll also find yourself thinking deeply and laughing your head off—great responses to art of any kind. There's also a museum store, a rare, fun place to buy birthday presents. The Kentucky Folk Art Center is open Monday through Saturday from 8:30 A.M. to 4:30 P.M.

At the Folk Art Center, also ask about scheduling a tour of the *Cora Wilson Stewart Moonlight School.* This humble one-room schoolhouse was where this dedicated teacher started the nation's first adult education night school in 1911 to combat illiteracy. She went on to receive important state and national positions in education. The building is owned by Morehead University and was moved from its original location to First Street, next to the early 1900s train depot that houses the Morehead Tourism offices.

While in Morehead, stop by the *Dixie Grill* (172 East Main Street, Morehead 40351; 606–784–9051) for beans and corn bread. Folks will know you're from out of town if you don't eat it properly: The corn bread should be crumbled into the bowl and eaten right along with the beans.

Morehead's biggest celebration is the *Appalachian Celebration,* a weeklong festival held in late June. Events, which take place on the university campus, include storytelling, displays by local folk artists and craftspeople, and all kinds of wonderful traditional bluegrass, country, and mountain music. Most events are free. Call (606) 783–2204 for a schedule or more information.

Down at the bottom tip of Cave Run Lake, where the Licking River begins to look like a river again, is the town of West Liberty, the Morgan

County seat. Come to town the last weekend in September for the *Morgan County Sorghum Festival.* In the evenings, people around here put on their dancing shoes. During the day someone always sets up a mule-drawn sugar cane mill at the Old Mill Park on the banks of the Licking River, so you can see how sorghum molasses is made the old-fashioned way. Call (606) 743–2300 for more information. If you can't make it during the festival, you can get some good sorghum at *Wyck Smith's farm* (606–725–4660) on Highway 772. You can see his cane mill from the road. The sorghum is boiled down in September, and it is usually sold out by December.

More Good Lodging in Eastern Kentucky

ASHLAND
Ashland Plaza Hotel, Fifteenth and Winchester Streets, 41101; (606) 329–0055. $65 and up.

BEATTYVILLE
Travelwise Motor Inn, Highway 11; (606) 464–2225. $40 and up.

BENHAM
School House Inn, 100 Central Avenue; (606) 848–3000. Country inn in restored school building. $60 to $85.

BLAINE
Gambill Mansion, Highways 201 and 32; (606) 652–3120. Room and suites in a 1923 home with spacious front porch. $100 to $150.

BUCKHORN
Buckhorn Lake State Resort Park, Highway 1833; (606) 398–7510. $42 and up.

CAMPTON
Inn the Woods, P.O. Box 215, Campton 41301; (606) 668–9999. Two rooms; on 1,500 acres that are great for hiking or horseback riding. Gorgeous cliffs and natural arches. No pets. $132 and up.

Torrent Falls, 1435 Highway 11 North, 41301; (606) 668–6441. B&B with three rooms, one suite, one cottage. Hiking trails with cliffs and a 162-foot-high waterfall. $60 and up.

CATLETTSBURG
Levi Hampton House, 2206 Walnut, 41129; (606) 739–8118 or (888) 538–4426. B&B in an 1847 Colonial Revival mansion with four rooms and a suite, all with hot tubs. $75 and up.

HAZARD
Days Inn, 359 Morton Boulevard, 41701; (606) 436–4777. $54 and up.

JACKSON
Jackson Inn, Highway 15; (606) 666–7551. $44 and up.

LEECO
The Old School House, 124 Mount Paran Road, 41301 (south of Natural Bridge); (606) 464–9991. B&B in native stone house built in the 1930s by the Works Progress Administration.

LOUISA
Lakeview Hideaway, Route 3, Box 4125; (800) 813–1868 or (606) 686–1155. Three suites overlooking Yatesville Lake.

MANCHESTER
Blair's Log Home, Daniel Boone Parkway, exit 19 to Highway 80/421 East for 5 miles; (606) 598–2854. Country log cabin with two rooms and hiking areas.

MIDDLESBORO
Best Western Inn, 1623 East Cumberland; (606) 248–5630. $44 and up.

Ridge Runner B&B, 208 Arthur Heights, 40965; (606) 248–4299.

MOREHEAD
Appalachian House,
910 North Willow Drive,
40351; (606) 784–5421.
B&B with two rooms. The
owners make and play dul-
cimers in their on-site
gallery.

Brownwood, Highway 801
South, in Farmers; (606)
784–8799. B&B with one
suite, three cottages, and a
whirlpool.

Holiday Inn, I–64 at Highway 32; (606) 784–7591.
$55 and up.

Mountain Lake Manor, off
Highway 32, 12 miles north
of exit 137 on I–64;
(606) 876–5591 or
(800) 737–7433. Deluxe
rooms or camping; 1,100
acres of mountain land
used for trail riding; large
lake used for fishing and
boating.

PIKEVILLE
Daniel Boone Motor Inn,
Highway 23 North;
(606) 432–0365. $40 and up.

Days Inn, Highway 23
South; (606) 432–0314. $44
and up.

PRESTONSBURG
Holiday Inn, Highway 23
South; (606) 886–0001. $66
and up.

Super 8, Highway 23; (606)
886–3355. $49 and up.

ROGERS
Cliffview Resort,
900 Cliffview Road, 41365;
near Natural Bridge; (606)
668–6550. Furnished
cabins, hiking trails, lake.
$125 and up.

SANDY HOOK
Charlene's Country Inn,
Highways 7 and 32;
(606) 738–6674 or
(606) 738–5712. B&B in
Colonial-style home in
Appalachian foothills with
six rooms, one suite, and a
full buffet-style breakfast.

WHITESBURG
Salvers House, 126 Hayes
Street, 41858; (606)
633–2532. B&B with five
rooms.

**MORE FUN PLACES TO EAT
IN EASTERN KENTUCKY**

ASHLAND
C. R. Thomas Old Place,
1612 Greenup Avenue,
41101; (606) 325–8500.
Gourmet burgers.

Damon's, 500 Winchester
Avenue, 41101; (606)
325–8929. Ribs.

BEATTYVILLE
The Purple Cow, Main
Street, 41311; (606)
464–9222.

BUCKHORN
Buckhorn Lake State
Resort Park, Highway 1833;
(606) 398–7510.

CLAY CITY
Wagon Wheel Restaurant,
20 Black Creek Road,
40312; (606) 663–0658.
Great buffet with skillet-
fried chicken and real
mashed potatoes.

CUMBERLAND GAP, TN
Ye Olde Tea and Coffee
Shop, 529 Colwyn Street,
37724; (423) 869–4844.
Mountain view.

GREENUP
Greenbo Lake State Resort
Park, Highway 1;
(606) 473–7324. Variety of
sandwiches, entrees, and
regional specialties such as
country ham and
fried catfish.

HAZARD
Blake's Road House,
173 Village Lane, 41701;
(606) 436–4409. Steaks,
chicken, and seafood.

Frances' Diner, 449 Chester
Street, 41701; (606)
439–9085. Home cooking.

North Fork Grill, 470 Main
Street, 41701; (606)
436–0769. Daily specials.

MIDDLESBORO
J. Milton's Steakhouse,
Highway 25 East;
(606) 248–0458. Steaks,
chicken, and seafood.

PIKEVILLE
Pine Mountain State Resort Park, Highway 25 East; (606) 337–3066. Varied menu including traditional Kentucky dishes.

PRESTONSBURG
Jenny Wiley State Resort Park, 39 Jenny Wiley Road; (606) 886–2711.

RUSSELL
Fletcher House Cafe, 342 Belfonte Street, 41169; (606) 836–0955. Sandwiches, barbecue, steaks, and seafood.

SLADE
Rose's Restaurant, 1289 Natural Bridge Road, 40376; (606) 663–0588. Pinto beans and corn bread, sandwiches, and a daily special.

Natural Bridge State Resort Park, Highway 11 near Slade; (606) 663–2214.

Northern Kentucky

ike some of its most fascinating inhabitants, northern Kentucky is
a bit eccentric. Places to explore range from exquisite Gothic cathe-
drals and puppet theaters in dense urban areas to anachronistic service
stations and prehistoric museums in sparsely populated rural regions.
Mark Twain once said that when the world came to an end, he wanted to
be in Kentucky because it's always a good twenty years behind. Such mis-
conceptions! Innovation has always been at the heart of this area's
delightful idiosyncrasies. Northern Kentucky boasts architecturally significant bridges, downhill snow skiing, and refreshingly creative farms
that specialize in everything from irises and turkeys to maple syrup. Historic buildings and fine craftspeople round out the picture, making this
relatively small area one of the most diverse in the state.

Heart of the North

ynthiana, a small town on Highway 27 about 30 miles north of Lexington, offers classy overnight lodging at *The Seldon-Renaker Inn,*
24 South Walnut Street, Cynthiana 41031. Go downtown, turn right on
Pleasant Street, then right again onto Walnut Street, and watch for the
sign on the right. The inn is a graceful Victorian house, built as a residence by Seldon Renaker in 1885 and later used as a boardinghouse,
dress shop, tearoom, and doctor's office. Rooms are around $60 per night.
In the morning coffee and doughnuts or coffee cake are available in the
first-floor communal parlor. For reservations, call (859) 234–3752.

Major events such as foundings, wars, and weather catastrophes shape
the history of a community, but so do lots of smaller happenings—the
first phone call, a new wing on the school, or the
passing of a local "character." At the *Cynthi-
ana/Harrison County Museum* on South Walnut Street, you can learn about both kinds of
events and how they affected life in this community. You'll discover that Cynthiana was
chartered as a town on December 10, 1793, and

True Blue
Main Street in Cynthiana, Kentucky, has more cast-iron-front buildings than Chicago.

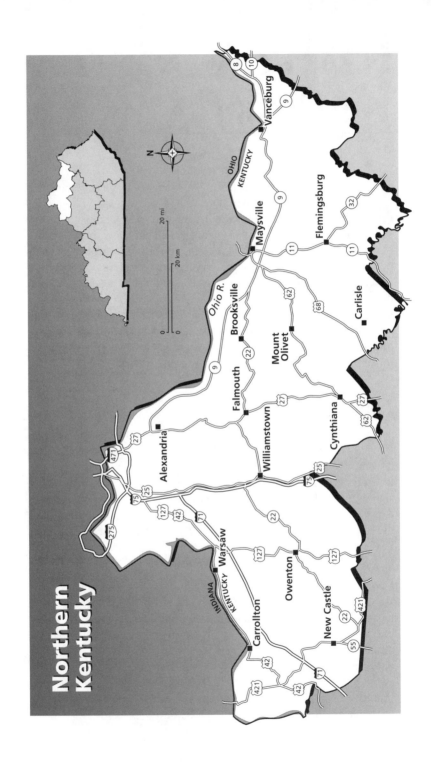

Northern Kentucky

learn about the two Civil War battles, but you also can learn that the first train pulled into town on May 18, 1854; that the first dial telephone call was made at 2:01 a.m. on November 18, 1962; and that the first convenience store opened in 1967. There are all kinds of artifacts, from old photos and Civil War uniforms to bonnets and hula hoops, all donated by local citizens—and nothing is refused. The museum is open Friday and Saturday from 10:00 A.M. to 5:00 P.M. Admission is free. For more information, call Harold Slade, the museum's main "hanger-upper," at (859) 234–5835.

South of downtown on Highway 27, is a little shop with a lot of good things, and a good story as well. *Kentucky Cardinal Cheese Store* traces its roots back to the 1930s, when it was established as the Kentucky Cardinal Dairies. The dairy bought the milk for its cheese from local farmers. In the 1950s a big cheese company from Wisconsin bought the company, later selling it to Webber Farms, Inc., in 1981. But the retail operation came full circle, going back to local, independent operation when Earl McNabb, who ran the distribution center for Webber's, bought it from Webber's in 1983. In 1999 the McNabbs sold the store to current owners Connie and Joe Lemons. Along with cheese, the Lemons offer a selection of jams, jellies, dressings, mustards, and country hams plus crafts— woven baskets, Kentucky Bybee pottery, and woodcrafts the owners make and handpaint themselves. They think of themselves as keepers of an old country store that is adapting to modern times—they recently added a toll-free order line (800–432–4337). If you prefer to shop the old-fashioned way, stop by Monday through Friday from 9:00 A.M. to 6:00 P.M., Saturday from 9:00 A.M. to 5:00 P.M.

The most delectable maple syrup south of the Mason-Dixon line comes from the steep woods of *Sugar Bush Farm,* where the two best kinds of maple, sugar maple *(Acer saccarum)* and black maple *(Acer nigrum),* grow abundantly. Robert Aulick and Paul Haubner have rigged a spider's weblike plastic tubing system that links three groups

Zoë's Top Picks in Northern Kentucky

Big Bone Lick State Park,
Big Bone; (859) 384–3522

Blue Licks Battlefield State Park, Blue Licks; (859) 289–5507

Cathedral Basilica of the Assumption, Covington; (859) 431–2060

Curtis Gates Lloyd Wildlife Refuge, Crittenden; (859) 428–3193

Dinsmore Homestead, Burlington; (859) 586–6117

Mutter Gottes Kirch (Mother of God Church), Covington; (859) 291–2288

National Underground Railroad Museum, Maysville; (859) 564–9411

Newport Aquarium, Newport; (859) 261–7444

Pendleton County's Wool Festival, first weekend of October, Kincaid Lake State Park; (859) 654–3378

Vent Haven Museum (of ventriloquistic figures), Fort Mitchell; (859) 341–0461

of 200 tapped trees and runs the sap downhill to the bottomland near Fork Lick Creek and into old milk tanks. In late winter and early spring, the sap is hauled twice a day to a tobacco barn and pumped into overhead tanks that feed into the wood-fired evaporator. The sap is boiled at about 220 degrees Fahrenheit, and liquid gold flows into the small finishing tanks, where it is admired by the alchemists before they strain and can it for the world's pleasure. Even the state health inspectors like to examine the product. It takes 40 to 50 gallons of sap to make 1 gallon of syrup. Eat it over fresh yogurt or hot pancakes, and you will be feasting like a god.

You can find the Sugar Bush Farm folks every year at several regional festivals, including **Pendleton County's Wool Festival** (859–654–3378), held off Highway 159 next to Kincaid Lake State Park during the first weekend of October. You are also welcome to go directly to the farm to meet these delightful folks in their own setting. To get there from Highway 25, which runs parallel to I–75, go to Williamstown and take Highway 22 east out of town about 5 miles. Turn south on Highway 1054 for about 3 miles and look for a green sign on the right side of the road. Take Green Road all the way to the end. Come in February to see syrup-making in action. Depending on the size of the harvest, there may or may not be any left at other times of the year. The amount varies depending on the weather in the year prior to tapping. A dry summer means less sap. They usually end up with 75 to 175 gallons of maple syrup, boiled down from thousands of gallons of sap. Another of the farm's products is honey, gathered from thirteen hives, and available in pints and quarts. It's best to call ahead (859–654–3433) if you want to come visit.

In **Williamstown** there are several antiques shops to explore. For refreshment after an afternoon of shopping, stop at the **Lucas-Moore Drug Store** (112 North Main Street, Williamstown 41097; 589–824–3349), where there's a small, authentic soda fountain. The drug store has been in business for more than 100 years, and the fountain has been there for perhaps fifty, but the original equipment looks and works as good as new. You can get a reasonably priced sandwich, a soft drink, or a milk shake whipped up in a Hamilton Beach blender and poured from a stainless steel container.

If you really want to get away from it all, spend the night at **Mullins Log Cabin** in Cordova, south of Williamstown via Highway 36. There's no phone, no television, no electricity, not even running water (the old-fashioned privy is out back, about 150 feet from the house). The cabin has become popular for "pioneer weddings," in which some couples even don period clothing and arrive in horse-drawn carriages. Contact owner Judy Mullins at (859) 824–4306 for information about visiting or staying overnight.

Thaxton's Licking River Canoe Rental offers canoe trips on the Main Licking River, the south fork, and the middle fork from April through October. Seeing the countryside by its natural roadways can connect one to the land in a way that driving a car cannot; no road noise, no cursing at your fellow human beings for passing on a hill, nothing between your skin and the living world. Located in Butler just 9 miles north of Falmouth, the outpost is near a bridge on Highway 27 a few hundred yards south of its intersection with Route 177. Call (877) 643–8762 (toll-free) or (859) 472–2000 for more information.

In the 200-year-old town of *Falmouth,* the most notable well-preserved historic building is a handsome two-story log cabin, circa 1790, called the *Alvin Mountjoy House* (203 Chapel Street, Falmouth 41040, which runs parallel to Main Street downtown; 859–654–3165). In addition to the traditional walls of huge poplar logs, pine floors, and big fireplaces built of stone from the nearby Licking River, it is one of the few existing eighteenth-century cabins with basements. The present-day owners, Carol and Nancy Houchen, are glad to show the house. Stop by their store, called Houchens, which is just two doors away. Their daughter, who lives in the Mountjoy cabin, is also willing to let you in, when she is home.

The *Kincaid Regional Theatre* is a small, professional summer theater that features new shows every season. From mid-June through the end of July, you can see Broadway musicals in Falmouth Auditorium. In downtown Falmouth go east on Shelby Street, south on Chapel Street, and look for signs. Curtain time is 8:00 P.M. Thursday through Saturday and 2:30 P.M. Sunday. Dinner packages are available. For reservations or a performance schedule, write KRT, Route 5, P.O. Box 225, Falmouth 41040, or call (859) 654–2636.

Every quilter I know harbors a special kind of gratitude for *The Quilt Box,* one of the largest and most comprehensive quilt shops in the state. When I first laid eyes on Charlotte Willis's marvelous quilt, *Kentucky Pride,* my initial question was, "Where did she find such gorgeous materials?" This shop has them: Natalie Lahner and her daughter Darcy Koenig have made it their mission to carry every quilt-related item imaginable, including more than 2,000 bolts of 100 percent cotton fabric in colors and patterns that will make you drool, along with patterns, notions, books, and finished quilts. They also make custom quilts

True Blue

The Franklin Sousley Monument in Flemingsburg honors one of the World War II veterans who raised the American flag at Iwo Jima.

based on wallpaper, upholstery samples, or unusual designs.

The store is in a restored 150-year-old log structure, which is tastefully married to the Lahners' residence, a reproduction seventeenth-century house. (An addition was completed in 1997.) Kids love seeing the rabbits, chickens, sheep, ducks, miniature horses, or whatever current farm residents are on the loose. The shop hours are from 9:30 A.M. to 5:00 P.M. Monday through Saturday. From I–75 take the Dry Ridge/Owenton (exit 159) and go west on Highway 22. Turn right on Highway 467 or Warsaw Road, go exactly 2.4 miles, and look for the Walnut Springs Farm mailbox and the sign for The Quilt Box. Follow the gravel road 0.4 mile to the second house on the road. Call (859) 824–4007.

The **Country Grill** at 21 Taft Highway in **Dry Ridge** serves consistently good-'n'-good-for-you meals made from fresh ingredients. Hours are 9:00 a.m. to 9:00 P.M. Monday through Thursday; 9:00 A.M. to 10:00 P.M. Friday; 8:00 A.M. to 10:00 P.M. Saturday; and 8:00 A.M. to 9:00 P.M. Sunday. Its phone number is (859) 824–6000. It's a good sign when the parking lot is always full.

A Right Smart Piece

*W*hen asking directions in Kentucky, you need to understand how far "a piece" is. Unfortunately, I can't give you an absolute definition. "Just a little piece" can mean a couple of miles or a few hundred yards, depending on the look in a person's eyes and the tone of the voice. If you don't imply, by your demeanor, that you will believe the directions, the direction-giver may as well lie . . . and might. A body can travel "a little piece" without completely running dry on patience. Private polling tells me "a little piece" is equivalent to "two whoops and a holler." "A far piece" is as far as language permits us to discuss distance and is, in fact, unattainable. "A right smart piece" is pretty far, but you can get there. And, finally, you must be warned about "no piece at all" or it will fool you all your life, because it sounds like you're already there, but it's farther than that. Newspaperman Allen M. Trout defined it this way: "Say you take a chew of tobacco when you start. When you have walked far enough to have chewed and spit all the flavor out, you have come no piece at all." Those who abstain from tobacco use will surely be lost.

Sanity Land

A few miles south of **Owenton** on Highway 127 sits a pink frame house in a yard full of angular alligators and stylized wide-eyed beasts. This is not a cubist zoo, but **Siegel Pottery.** Although Greg Siegel has a reputation for producing clay reptiles and collectible marbles, he also makes a variety of functional pots, but not without some humor. For example, a big, sturdy dinner plate glazed with a long pink spiral surrounded by blue comma-shaped dots is called *Boys and Girl.* Many of the sculptural pieces are decorated with local clays and fired in a wood-burning kiln, which produces a rich, earthy effect. The Siegels work at home, so hours are by chance. Rebekka Siegel is nationally known for her exquisite modern quilts. If you have a serious love for this art, ask to see a few of her favorites, or whatever is in progress. She also teaches seminars in quilt technique and design. You can reach the Siegels at (502) 484–2970.

Also in Monterey is **Larkspur Press,** sponsor of many of the aforementioned literary readings and a fine, fine little press that is Gray Zeitz's pride and joy. Larkspur books, primarily small chapbooks or broadsides by Kentucky writers, are of high quality in form and in content. All productions are done in letterpress from type set by hand and printed on paper that makes you want to touch and linger. Visitors are welcome, but call ahead, because Zeitz keeps odd hours. Write to Larkspur Press at 340 Sawdridge Creek West, Monterey 40359, or call (502) 484–5390.

To get to Port Royal from Monterey, take Highway 355 north. From the Frankfort area go north on Highway 421 a little way, then veer onto Highway 193 and go "a right smart piece." There is nothing to see in **Port Royal** but the land and the people who live by the land. That's all there is to see in many other areas of the state, but I'd like for those who are familiar with writer, teacher, and farmer **Wendell Berry** to take a good look at northern Henry County, where he makes his home. The Kentucky River forms the eastern border of the county. Here the river basin is wide, the flat bottomland soil rich, the steep hills wooded and deserted. This varied terrain insists that it be farmed in various ways. Except in the wide river bottomland, the arable areas are limited to small, odd-shaped patches, which Wendell Berry chooses to farm with a team of draft horses.

One of the truths Berry repeats is that finicky areas like these are not unique to Henry County. The idiosyncrasies of all lands must be intimately and humbly understood before we can live on them as responsible stewards, he contends. We talk of preserving the wilderness, but we don't preserve the farmland from which we feed ourselves. Farmers are, after all, people who use nature directly, not only for themselves, but also for consumers, by proxy. Wherever you live and travel, look at the land and think about the mystery of your dependency on nature and about how you can respond responsibly. Don't try this alone—talk to people and read Wendell Berry's work.

From Port Royal follow Highway 389 north into Carroll County, through the town of English, where there are ramps onto I–71, and into *Carroll-ton.* For such a small town, it has a tremendous amount of visible remnants of its history. This National Historic District encompasses 25 blocks and includes 350 buildings, many of which are more than 200 years old. It's perched right above the confluence of the Kentucky and Ohio Rivers. A self-guided walking tour is about the best way to see the nineteenth-century and Victorian architecture. Start with the museum in the 1880 *Old Stone Jail* on the Courthouse Square. Some of the cells have been restored, and, during the restoration work, hidden contraband was found and is now on display. The jail was actually used to detail prisoners as recently as 1969.

Afterwards, go upstairs, where female inmates were housed, to the Carrollton Visitors' Center (800–325–4290) for maps and more historic information. There is an excellent historic driving-tour booklet available. Hours are 9:00 A.M. to 5:30 P.M. Monday through Friday, noon to 5:00 P.M. Saturday. The jail is closed in winter.

There are several interesting shops in downtown Carrollton, including the *Antique Mall on the Square* and *The Craft Patch.* You can get a sandwich at the *Mustard Seed.*

Downtown Carrollton boasts some unusual places of lodging, one of which is also the place to eat, if you're here with historic interests. The *General William O. Butler Bed & Breakfast* is a Georgian-style house that was home to one of the most prominent families in the founding era of the community. Like all men of the time, William O. Butler had to have versatile skills. He was a statesman, poet, farmer, lawyer, and soldier. His wife, Eliza Todd, came from a prominent Lexington family; she was a relative of Mary Todd Lincoln. The couple built their New Orleans–style brick house in 1825. Innkeepers Dick and Norma Firestone have restored the house and filled it with antiques. The backyard is interesting, too, with its herb gardens, fish pond, "Garden Railroad," and view of the river. At press time, the Firestones were in the process of installing a croquet court. There are two guest rooms, $75 to $95 per night. Call (502) 732-6154.

The *Carrollton Inn* at 218 Main Street is a restored 1812 Colonial inn with ten overnight rooms (starting at $39.50) and a full dining room and lounge. While you eat, try to imagine the flatboatmen stopping here at the tavern. Today it serves Kentucky classics like "hot browns" and freshly churned homemade ice cream. Tempted yet? The phone number is (502) 732–6905.

People from across the nation send or bring their Christmas cards to the little town of Bethlehem, in Henry County, for a special Christmas postmark.

Another historic tour in the area is of the *Butler Turpin House,* a very ornate Greek Revival home built in 1859 and appointed inside with period furnishings and heirlooms of the family. The stone kitchen is especially interesting. The house is located in the *General Butler State Resort Park,* just off I–71 at exit 44 to Highway 227 (signs are prevalent). Guided tours of the Butler Turpin House are given four times daily from March through November.

General Butler State Resort Park has become regionally famous for hosting mountain-bike competitions. Call "Bike Butler" at (502) 484–2998 for a seasonal schedule. There are four major competitions each year—the MudFest in April, "Mud, Sweat, and Tears" in July, an Off-Road Triathlon in August, and the Kentucky Open in September. It's a sport that is almost scarier to watch than to participate in. The park also has a lodge with a restaurant, cottages, and a campground. For information about either the Butler Turpin House or the General Butler State Resort Park, call (502) 732–4384 or (800) 325–0078.

East of Carrollton on Highway 42 is another historic house that is open for tours, the *Masterson House.* Built in 1790, it may be one of the oldest existing brick houses in this region along the banks of the Ohio River anywhere between Pittsburgh, Pennsylvania, and Cairo, Illinois. The bricks were made and fired on-site during construction. The restorers have even planted historic trees started from seedlings gathered from other pioneer homes. Admission is $2.00, and it is open only on weekend afternoons from 1:30 to 4:30 P.M. between Memorial Day and Labor Day. For more information, call Mary Jo Grobmyer at (502) 732–5786 or the Carroll County Visitors Center at (800) 325–4290.

Just upriver a few miles is *Warsaw,* a peaceful one-traffic-light river town in the smallest county in Kentucky. There the *Gallatin County Historical Society* has restored and furnished an 1843 Gothic Revival–style home. Follow I–75 to I–71 west and take the Warsaw exit. In town, turn right by the courthouse (the second-oldest continuously operating courthouse in the state, circa 1837) at the only stoplight and look behind the funeral home for the ***Hawkins-Kirby House.*** To arrange a tour, call local historian Sue M. Bogardus at (859) 567–4591.

You don't have to call anyone to get a fabulous view of Ohio River traffic from an observation tower at the ***Markland Locks and Dam,*** on Highway 42 in Warsaw. It's a great place for a picnic, too. Any questions? Call (859) 567–7661.

Odd Bones

*E*ccentricity saves lives. (How's that for a bumper sticker?) The little-known ***Curtis Gates Lloyd Wildlife Reserve*** (859–428–3193) would not exist if the eccentric Mr. Lloyd had not written a twenty-four-page will that thoroughly outlined the future management plan for his 365-acre farm down to every detail. Before he died in 1923, Lloyd erected an enormous granite monument to himself in the woods. One side reads: CURTIS G. LLOYD BORN 1859—DIED 60 OR MORE YEARS AFTERWARDS. THE EXACT NUMBER OF YEARS, MONTHS AND DAYS THAT HE LIVED NOBODY KNOWS AND NOBODY CARES. The other side says: CURTIS G. LLOYD MONUMENT ERECTED IN 1922 BY HIMSELF FOR HIMSELF DURING HIS LIFE TO GRATIFY HIS OWN VANITY. WHAT FOOLS THESE MORTALS BE! A fool? Not quite. His preserve boasts one of the shamefully few stands of virgin timber in Kentucky. A forest teeming with wildlife and wilderness left to its own beautiful accord—a black walnut, 36 inches in diameter, towers over acres and acres of huge red oaks and poplars. (Please be careful during deer hunting season!) To think that I–75 is within

Speaking Figuratively

*Y*ou know that polite-but-blank stare your children sometimes give you when you're trying to tell them something? Imagine a whole room of it, and you have an idea of what awaits you at **Vent Haven Museum** in Fort Mitchell (33 West Maple Avenue, Fort Mitchell 41011; 859–341–0461). Vent Haven is home to more than 500 ventriloquistic figures (the world's largest known collection), left as a legacy by one William Shakespeare Berger, a Cincinnati businessman and amateur ventriloquist. Assembled between 1947 and Berger's death in 1972 at age ninety-four, his collection includes figures of all shapes, sizes, and heritages, some predating the Civil War; others able to walk, move their noses, spit, and smoke cigarettes. It's a little disconcerting but fascinating, and a tour (by appointment only, May through September) will sure be something to talk about.

earshot . . . From Crittenden follow Highway 25 south a few miles and look for the sign.

Big Bone Lick State Park is probably the only prehistoric graveyard you'll ever lay eyes on. From Florence take Highway 127 south (through Sugartit) and turn west on Highway 338 (Beaver Road) at Beaverlick to the town of Big Bone, then follow signs to the park. Probably during the end of the Ice Age (more than 10,000 years ago), many of the largest mammals on the continent that came to this area to lick the rich veins of salt and sulfur died, leaving their bones scattered around the massive mineral deposit. Some of the bones have been identified as belonging to the huge ground sloths, tapirs, musk oxen, giant bison, and deerlike animals called cervalces, all now extinct. No one knows exactly what the cause of the worldwide destruction of these species was. Some say that glacier expansion drove animals south and created an overly dense population that eventually starved. Others blame an epidemic, unscrupulous primitive hunters, or the hand of a god.

Gobble Gobble

*A*lthough thousands of people on I–75 see the sign on the side of the barn daily, **Tewes Poultry Farm** is off the beaten path in spirit. The Tewes family (pronounced TOO-wis) raises and processes more than 3,000 turkeys annually, and more than 600 chickens every two weeks in addition to keeping some Leghorn hens for eggs. Poultry isn't everything, however. Mary Tewes, the head of the one-hundred-acre farm and omnipresent matron, is the proud mother of eighteen, grandmother of seventy-eight, and great-grandmother of an ever-growing number. After almost half a century on the place, she still makes meals on a big wood cookstove, works alongside the younger generations sorting and washing eggs, tends to customers, and does the hundreds of tasks that are necessary on a "small" farm.

Way before the interstate existed, the Teweses made final payments on their land by selling Easter chicks dipped in pastel-colored food dyes. Today I–75 cuts through the front pasture, a lumberyard sits adjacent to the house, and planes rush overhead to the Greater Cincinnati International Airport. Easter chicks would barely pay the feed bills and aren't considered ethical anymore. Despite the changes, the Teweses carry on a diverse, wholesome operation. Stop to get fresh fryers, big-breasted roasters, turkeys, bacon, eggs, and a vitamin-like dose of friendliness. The birds are dressed on Thursday or Friday, so the birds are fresh for the weekend. Tewes Poultry Farm is just north of Florence. From I–75 take the Buttermilk Pike exit and go into Crescent Springs. Turn left on Anderson Road and look for the farm about a mile on the left. They're always home and you're always welcome, but call ahead anyway at (859) 341–8844.

The salt lick also was used by Native Americans and, after 1729, by pioneers who boiled down the brines to make highly valued salt. Legend has it that early Virginian settlers, who were fascinated with the massive bones, used mastodon ribs for tent poles and vertebrae for stools. Even Thomas Jefferson was intrigued. He reportedly had more than 300 specimens kept in the White House for research, but a servant pounded them into fertilizer. Not all the bones are lost, however; Big Bone Lick State Park's museum houses an incredible collection of vertebrate fossils from the area. Hours vary throughout the year. Call (859) 384–3522 for information.

Are you ready for a lesson in botany? Directly across the road from the state park is *Big Bone Gardens,* a six-acre pleasure garden and sales nursery owned by Mark Lawhorn and Mary Ellen Pesek. There are two big "twin" ponds, a bog area, two little ponds full of decorative aquatic plants that are for sale, and a super-duper campy concrete garden sculpture collection (baby deer and hoboes). Plant prices range from $1.00 to $50.00, and the varieties range from common native waterside grasses to Asian lotus plants. The gardens are open on weekends from early spring through July and by appointment otherwise. Park at the Methodist church across the street (but not during Sunday services, please). For an appointment call (859) 384–1949.

The tiny town of *Rabbit Hash* sits high on the banks of the Ohio River on Highway 20. It's not much of a town now, but it has an amazingly inveterate business, appropriately called the *Rabbit Hash General Store,* that has not boarded up its windows since 1831. That's over 168 years of the screen door slamming on the funny little wooden-frame store. In addition to the usual "convenient store" items, there are locally contributed antiques and crafts. Stop by any day and have a soda.

Kentucky has hundreds of bed-and-breakfast establishments, but this one, the *Willis Graves B&B Inn,* is one of the classiest, inside and out. The 1830s Federal-style brick home was built for Willis Graves, Burlington's county clerk for the first two decades of the nineteenth century. The home has been exquisitely renovated—Flemish bond brick work and Federal mantels are all original. Unlike many B&Bs, the furnishings are appropriate. The inn is only a twelve-minute drive to the airport, so it's a good option for business travelers. Rates begin at $69 per night. Call (888) 226–5096 (toll-free) or (859) 689–5096, or check out the B&B's Web site at www.bbonline. com/ky/willisgraves/. This Web site includes listings of bed-and-breakfasts across Kentucky.

Just 6.5 miles west of the hectic interstate on Highway 18 is a place that recaptures life in a quieter, slower-paced time. *The Dinsmore Homestead* is a living history site designed to show modern folks what daily life was like in the 1840s. The homestead includes a house, furnished with furniture and belongings of the family that owned it for five generations, beginning in 1839. There are numerous special events and workshops throughout the year, from basket making to a heirloom plant sale. There are also hiking trails. The homestead is open for tours from April through mid-December on Wednesday, Saturday and Sunday from 1:00 to 5:00 P.M. Admission is charged. Call (859) 586–6117 for information.

Said to be "the world's smallest house of worship," the *Monte Casino Chapel* (859–344–3309) measures just 6 by 9 feet—no better place for an intimate conversation with God. Just close the door and let fly. The chapel was built in 1810 in a vineyard on a hill just outside of Covington by Benedictine monks. In the late 1960s the chapel was moved to its present site on the campus of Thomas More College. From I–75 take I–275 east and exit on Turkeyfoot Road. Monte Casino Chapel is next to a large pond on the left side of the road.

> ## True Blue
>
> *The only replica of the tomb of Jesus in the United States is in the Garden of Hope in Covington.*

Not said to be the world's smallest house of drama, the *Village Players of Fort Thomas* do, nonetheless, use a very small, intimate, three-quarter stage where plays are performed live, year-round, except during the month of June. Call (859) 781–3583 to get up-to-date scheduling. The theater is located at the corner of Fort Thomas and Highland Avenues in Fort Thomas.

If you take the Buttermilk Pike exit off I–75 and cross to the east side of the interstate, you won't miss the ever-expanding *Oldenberg Brewery and American Museum of Brewing History* complex (859–341–7223). As you tour this operating brewery, you'll also see what is billed as the largest collection of beer and brewing memorabilia ever assembled. (There are nearly one million items on display, so who's to argue?) Beer-can collectors, this is the place for you! Tours of the museum and the brewery are given daily, Monday through Saturday from 10:00 A.M. to 5:00 P.M. and on Sunday from noon to 5:00 P.M. A one-and-a-half-hour tour and taste-test session costs $5.00. The brewery also has an on-site restaurant that is open for lunch and dinner.

Head toward the river, get on Highway 8, follow it west into Constance, and look for the *Anderson Ferry* (859–485–9210), a two-boat operation in business since 1817. Today this is the quickest crossing from Cincinnati, via Ohio's Highway 50, to the airport on I–275, especially when the bridges nearer town are choked by rush-hour traffic. Paul Anderson's two ferries, *Boone 7* and *Boone 8* or *Little Boone,* haul passengers on demand year-round. On the Kentucky landing an old character named Arnold occasionally hangs out and "treats" customers to an endless pseudohistory of the boats and his life. From November through April hours are 6:00 A.M. to 8:00 P.M., and from May through October from 6:00 A.M. to 9:30 P.M. On Saturday it starts running at 7:00 A.M., and on Sunday the start time is 11:00 A.M. The ferry runs about every fifteen minutes. Cars are charged $3.00.

Metro Area

I f *Covington*'s century-old *Cathedral Basilica of the Assumption* at the corner of Twelfth and Madison Streets (859–431–2060) were in a major coastal city or in Europe, people would rave about it. As it is, this remarkable work of French Gothic architecture is little known to the world. The building is closely modeled after Paris's Notre Dame and the Abbey Church of Saint Denis, complete with flying buttresses and fantastic gargoyles perched high on the facade. Glass is everywhere. Eighty-two windows, including two enormous rose windows, glow endlessly with the changing sun. Measuring 24 feet by 67 feet, the hand-blown, stained-glass window in the transept is said to be the largest in the world. The rich color, variety of shapes, and expressive details can leave you staggering and dizzy in the huge chamber. In one chapel are several paintings by Frank Duveneck, a Covington native who became an internationally known portrait and genre painter and sculptor. My favorite is the austere center panel of the Eucharist triptych of Mary Magdalene at the foot of the cross. To the visual strength of the space, add the music of three massive pipe organs, and you will be transported. (The basic building was constructed, beginning in 1894, for the price of $150,000, the cost of many of today's middle-American homes.)

The altar in the Blessed Sacrament Chapel reads BEHOLD THE BREAD OF ANGELS BECOMES THE FOOD OF WAYFARERS, so the faith-inspired beauty of this temple of worship is available to us worldly wanderers. The basilica is open daily from 10:00 A.M. to 4:00 P.M., when greeters are present to answer your questions.

Adjacent to the basilica is the former chancery and the recently opened *Cathedral Museum,* where the cathedral treasures are on display. Gold and silver vessels for worship are decorated with cloisonné enamel and semiprecious stones. The choice of the first Catholic missionary to Kentucky, Father Brodin is included in the collection. Museum and gift shop are open when the cathedral is, except on Monday.

Mutter Gottes Kirch (West Sixth and Montgomery Streets; 859–291–2288) is another of Covington's fabulous churches that is open to visitors. Started in 1870, Mutter Gottes Kirch (translated, Mother of God Church) was built in Italian (rather than French) Renaissance

Cathedral Basilica of the Assumption

True Blue

The film Rain Man, *starring Dustin Hoffman and Tom Cruise, was filmed in the northern Kentucky/ Cincinnati area.*

basilica design. Clock-bearing twin spires over the front facade seem to be held in place by the large apse dome. Inside, the lower panels of the magnificent stained-glass windows depict Old Testament promises while the upper panels depict the corresponding fulfillments. Other inspirational art includes sculpture, some by Covington artist Ferdinand Muer; Stations of the Cross; an 1876 Koehnken and Grimm pipe organ; beautiful floor tile; and large frescoes and murals by Johann Schmitt, who was once Frank Duveneck's teacher and whose work is in the Vatican.

Four galleries with new exhibitions presented nearly every month make the *Northern Kentucky Arts Council Carnegie Arts Center,* at 1028 Scott Boulevard, Covington 41011, a bustling art district in itself. There's also a 750-seat theater, so call (859) 655–8110 when you're in town to find out what live performance you might see.

Go through Covington's Riverside Drive–Licking River Historic District on the east side of town by "the Point" where the Licking River empties into the mighty Ohio. Follow Second Street east until it becomes Shelby Street and wraps around to become Riverside Drive. On the strip of land between the street and the river is the *George Rogers Clark Park,* so named because Clark supposedly stopped at the site to gather forces on his way to Ohio to fight Shawnees. In the park are a few new pieces of sculpture by George Danhires. The most fun is a bronze likeness of James Bradley, an African-born slave who worked his way to freedom, crossed the Ohio River, attended seminary in Cincinnati in 1834, and went down in history as the only former slave to participate in the famous, fiery Lane Seminary debates on abolition. Bradley is depicted as reading thoughtfully on a park bench facing the river. The piece is so realistic that passersby stop talking so as not to disturb the man.

The bright blue Covington/Cincinnati Suspension Bridge, just a few blocks west of the Licking Riverside Neighborhood, has been renamed the *John A. Roebling Suspension Bridge* in honor of the engineer who designed it. When it opened in 1867, after twenty-two years of construction, the bridge was the longest of its kind in the world (1,057 feet) and served Roebling as a prototype for his later Brooklyn Bridge in New York City.

Take Garrard Street south and look on the right for the *Amos Shinkle Townhouse Bed and Breakfast,* circa 1854. What was once a posh residence for one of Covington's early big businessmen, Amos Shinkle, is now an impressive bed-and-breakfast facility. Co-owners Bernie Moor-man and Don Nash have taken pains to maintain such interesting features as the original murals on the walls of the front staircase. Rooms range from a master suite with a whirlpool to a converted carriage house that is ideal for families. Prices range from $95 to $165 and include a full breakfast. Call (859) 431–2118 or (800) 972–7012.

Another handsome place of lodging is the **Sandford House Bed and Breakfast** at 1026 Russell Street in an area known as the Old Seminary Square Historic District (from Eighth to Eleventh Streets). Built in the early 1820s for politician Thomas Sandford and sold in 1835 to the Western Baptist Theological Institute, the house was caught in the middle of one of Kentucky's hottest disputes. Northern and Southern trustees feuded so severely over the slavery issue that the seminary was forced to split into two separate schools, one in Georgetown and one in Findlay, Ohio. Hosts Dan and Linda Carter keep an award-winning garden and, in mild weather, serve breakfast in a gazebo surrounded by award-winning landscaping. The penthouse offers a beautiful view of downtown Cincinnati. Prices begin at $55 a night. Call (859) 291–9133 or (888) 291–9133 for reservations.

Although **Main Strasse** has been billed as a miniature German village in downtown Covington, historically the area is ethnically heterogeneous. German, Irish, and African-Americans have lived in this architecturally fascinating neighborhood, which has been developed into a shopping district for tourists. You can find everything from antiques and doll boutiques to restaurants and bakeries. At the edges of the developed area are local pubs with Irish names.

One of the best restaurants in town is not German, but Cajun and Creole. **Dee Felice Cafe,** at 529 Main Street, Covington 41011, next to the Goose Girl Fountain, is hot. The food is spicy, and the jazz is cool. From a bowl of gumbo for about $5.00 to spicy blackened seafood and chicken (dinner entrees range from $15.95 to $28.95), the flavor tugs at the Southern palate. It's hard to believe that the ornate building was originally a pharmacy. No Super-X can hold a candle to these pressed tin ceilings and miniature Corinthian columns, details of which are preserved in the restaurant and painted audacious colors. Every night a live band plays Dixieland, blues, and lots of jazz on a stage behind the long bar. The founder, the late Dee Felice, was a jazz drummer in his own right; he used to play with James Brown, Mel Torme, Sergio Mendez, and others. Lunch hours are 11:00 A.M. to 2:30 P.M. Monday through Friday. Dinner begins at 5:00 P.M. nightly. The phone number is (859) 261–2365. Reservations are suggested for dinner.

Iron Horse history buffs, take note of the *Railway Museum of Greater Cincinnati* at 315 West Southern Avenue, Covington 41015. This museum has a number of immaculately preserved items, such as a 1906 Southern Railroad open platform business car, a diner built for the Golden Rocket, several locomotives, sleeping cars, post office cars, cabooses, and more. The grounds are open March through October, Wednesday and Saturday from 10:00 A.M. to 4:00 P.M. You can watch as volunteers restore antique engines and equipment. Guided tours are given on Sunday from 12:30 to 4:30 P.M. Admission is charged. Call (859) 491–RAIL for more information.

Unique knickknack nautical decor and more awaits you any hour of the day or night at *Covington's Anchor Grill* (438 Pike Street, Covington 41011; 859–431–9498). Eating with neighborhood locals becomes a dining experience when you put a quarter in the jukebox. The mechanized C.C. doll band display comes to life in the corner of the grill while overhead a rotating ballroom star light sets the mood.

Perched high on a bluff above Covington, the interstate, and the Ohio River is the *Behringer-Crawford Museum* (859–491–0003) in Devou Park, a 700-acre recreational green space at 1600 Montague Road, on the west side of I–75. This unique museum houses a really impressive collection of fossils and prehistoric artifacts from the immediate region in addition to exhibits featuring Civil War relics and other artifacts from more recent history. Some of the Ice Age animal specimens were collected by archaeologist Ellis Crawford from the prehistoric site at Big Bone Lick. Hours are Tuesday through Friday from 10:00 A.M. to 5:00 P.M., 1:00 to 5:00 P.M. on weekends.

Now that you've been high above the Ohio River and looked down at its

Wilder Spirits

*S*ome of the wildest ghosts in Kentucky have been spotted at **Bobby Mackey's** *(44 Licking Pike, Wilder 41071; 859–431–5588), a country-and-western club in Wilder, not far from Newport. Over the years, more than thirty people, employees and patrons alike, have reported seeing ghosts. And these aren't your friendly ghosts—one man claimed to have been attacked by a ghost in a club rest room. Local legend has it that the hauntings are the result of the building's use for satanic worship in the nineteenth century, and its speakeasy days during the 1920s. The owner has tried exorcism and has even posted warning signs so patrons know that not all the spirits at this nightclub come in bottles.*

serpentine, sparkling surface, wouldn't you like to go below it to see inside the river? The *Newport Aquarium* (859–261–7444) has a 53-foot-long wall of clear acrylic that brings you eye level with native species of the Ohio River—big bottom-feeding catfish, nightmare-inducing gar, soft-shell turtles, shovelnosed sturgeon (probably not named Boris), and more than you never imagined. The aquarium is a state-of-the-art facility with exhibits focused on the rivers of the world, a shoreline museum (with an area designed for visitors to touch creatures like starfish and sand dollars), a collection of dangerous and deadly aquatic life (including electric eels and red-bellied piranha), and more. One exhibit allows you to walk through a clear tunnel through shark-filled waters. Titillating and educational, the aquarium is located in a super-modern building with nautical imagery of masts and sails. Go toward the Ohio River on Third Street until you see the Newport on the Levee complex. Open daily at 10:00 A.M. Admission is $14.95 for adults, $8.95 for children.

Northern Kentucky ushered in the new millennium with a very visible and permanent monument. Not far from the aquarium, at Fourth and York Streets in *Newport,* is the *World Peace Bell,* billed as "the world's largest free-swinging bell." The bell weighs 66,000 pounds and is 12 feet in diameter and 12 feet high. (By comparison, the Liberty Bell in Philadelphia is a mere 2,080 pounds.) The bell was the result of a community effort led by a local businessman, Wayne Carlisle, who envisioned marking the millennium with a symbol of freedom and peace. Designed by a family-owned company based just across the Ohio River in Cincinnati, The Verdin Bell Company, the bell was actually cast in France. (The foundry in Nantes was one of the few in the world with a furnace that could melt the 100,000 pounds of bronze.) After the casting—on December 11, 1998, the fiftieth anniversary of the Universal Declaration of Human Rights in Paris—the bell was shipped to the United States, arriving in New Orleans in July 1999. As it traveled up the Mississippi and Ohio Rivers, the bell made stops at cities along the way to great fanfare. In October 1999 it was installed in the glass and steel pavilion that was to be its permanent home. The first northern Kentucky swinging of the bell was at midnight on December 31, 1999, to welcome the year 2000. Pictures on the bell represent significant achievements of mankind, from the Gutenberg press to the first step on the moon. If you want to see it swing and hear its deep, resonant ring, come at noon. The bell also chimes on the hour. For more information, call (859) 261–2526.

Across the Licking River and northeast of Newport is the *Weller Haus Bed and Breakfast,* in Bellevue's Taylor Daughters' Historic District at

319 Poplar Street, Bellevue 41073 (2 blocks south of Highway 8). For $79 to $149 you can eat a classy breakfast and sleep peacefully amid eighteenth-century antiques in an attractive, folk-style Victorian house. According to AAA, this is a three-diamond bed-and-breakfast. Call (859) 431–6829 or (800) 431–HAUS for reservations.

Since 1939 *Schneider's Sweet Shop,* at 420 Fairfield Avenue, Bellevue 41073, (Route 8), has been *Bellevue*'s most exquisite temple of the sweet tooth. Using old-fashioned equipment and timeless craftsmanship, Jack Schneider creates truly fantastic homemade ice creams and candies. The place is famous, especially during the winter holiday season, for its "opera creams," unusual little chocolate candies with rich, creamy centers, available in the tri-state area only. Schneider's other famous originals include the summer top-seller, Ice Ball with Ice Cream, a scoop of vanilla ice cream with shaved ice packed around it and a healthy dose of specially concocted syrup poured over the top. They have won the award for best caramel apple in the Cincinnati area and have the popular vote for Jack's own favorite, cookies 'n' cream ice cream. This heaven is open Monday through Friday from 10:00 A.M. to 8:00 P.M., Saturday from 11:00 A.M. to 8:00 P.M., and Sunday from noon to 8:00 P.M. Call (859) 431–3545.

The patron saint of travelers is ready to welcome you in Bellevue. One of the most interesting and unusual bed-and-breakfasts in the area, *Christopher's Bed & Breakfast,* 604 Poplar Street, Bellevue 41073, is housed in a former church. Built in the late 1800s, the 8,100-square-foot structure originally housed Bellevue Christian Church. In 1996 Steve and Brenda Guidugli purchased the century-old building and converted it into a residence. They retained all of the original stained-glass windows. Two guest rooms and one suite are available, each with private baths with whirlpools. The suite has a two-person Jacuzzi. Rates are $70 to $130 per night. Call (888) 585–7085 or (859) 491–9354 for reservations.

Buffalo Trace Area

The river towns strung along the mighty Ohio and the areas that spread away from them are usually historically significant and, for that reason, often a touch schizophrenic, caught between the stillness of the past and the fluid present. *Augusta,* in Bracken County, is one of the few such towns that has struck a happy balance while remaining scenic. From Covington or Newport either hug the banks of the Ohio River by following Highway 8 east, or buzz along the newer

Covered Bridge

"AA" Highway 546, which connects Alexandria and Ashland. If you take the AA, watch for its intersection with Highway 1159. Turn left (north) and meander around for a moment at the **Walcott Covered Bridge,** a 75-foot-long wooden bridge spanning Locust Creek, which was active from 1824 until 1954. Walk into the bridge and read the descriptions of bridge types, definitions of terms, and explanations for methods of construction.

The **Beehive Tavern,** on the north corner of Main Street and Riverside Drive, is an elegant Colonial-style restaurant and bed-and-breakfast located in a 1790s row house facing the river. Drinks are served from noon until closing Wednesday through Saturday on the upstairs balcony, which has a perfect river view. Dinner is served Wednesday through Saturday, with lunch served Thursday through Saturday. The menu changes every two weeks and includes items such as roast pork with fried apples, corn bread stuffing, and some Spanish dishes, reflecting the heritage of owner Luciano Moral, who was born in Cuba to Spanish parents. Entrees range from $10.95 to $16.50. Be sure to save room for dessert; the blueberry trifle cake and caramel flan are primo. Call (606) 756–2202 for information.

Directly across the street is the **Augusta Ferry** (606–756–3291), one of the very few functional ferries on the Ohio River. It's operational year-round during daylight hours and, although a trip schedule exists, the captain will carry you across any time. The ride costs $5.00 per car.

Imagine yourself crossing the water when the town was new and the ferry was powered by mules.

Just a block from the river and next to Augusta Park is **The Parkview Country Inn,** a charming bed-and-breakfast decorated with art and antiques. The building dates to the early 1800s as an inn. In the early days it also included a tavern, which now is the lobby area. There are eight guest rooms and two suites, and you'll be pampered with luxurious lines and plush towels and robes. Guest rooms range from $75 to $140 per night; the River Loft suite is $125 to $225. Call (606) 756–2603 for reservations or information. The innkeepers also operate the **Augusta General Store,** a great place to stop for sundries and much more; there's an ice cream soda fountain, bakery, deli, and grill. Call (606) 756–2525.

A popular event in the area is *"The Old Reliable" Germantown Fair,* held the first week in August at the Germantown fairgrounds on Highway 10. No one seems to be able to explain the "Old Reliable" aspect beyond the fact that it happens every year. Germantown straddles the Bracken-Mason county line. Thirty-three yards from that county line, in Germantown, is a classic country cooking restaurant called the **Ole Country Inn** (606–728–2912). There's nothing particularly German about the place, but fast food can't hold a candle to the speed of the cooks, and you get a real meal to boot. Hours are 7:00 A.M. to 7:00 P.M. Monday through Saturday and 8:00 A.M. to 3:00 P.M. Sunday.

Follow Highway 8 along the river to Maysville. If you arrive from the west, there is a functional *covered bridge at Dover.* Highway 1235 crosses Lee's Creek by means of this 61-foot-long "Queensport truss" bridge, which had a tollbooth at one end when the oldest part was built in 1835.

Maysville is the next town upriver, the site of the closest bridge to the

Lights, Camera, Action!

Y ou may have already seen Augusta if you watched the television miniseries Centennial, *because the town was used to film scenes taking place in St. Louis, Missouri, in the 1880s. Because Augusta has no flood wall, Water Street (or Riverside Drive) was a ready-made set, except for a few details—the film crew put down 4* inches of dirt on the street to cover the pavement and pulled down power lines and business signs. The houses along the river were, as they always are, picture-perfect. Since then, several Public Broadcasting System (PBS) productions have been filmed in Augusta, including the classic Huckleberry Finn.

north, and the hub of activity for the whole area. To steep yourself in area history, go to the **Mason County Museum** (606–564–5865), at 215 Sutton Street, Maysville 41056, in an 1878 structure originally built to be the town's first library. Because of the historic significance of the area as an early point of access to the west, the little museum tells the bigger story of the expansion of America. Hours are 9:00 A.M. to 4:00 P.M. Monday through Friday, 10:00 A.M. to 4:00 P.M. Saturday.

In downtown Maysville, right next door to the Ohio River bridge, the visitors bureau shares space with the **National Underground Railroad Museum** (115 East Third Street, Maysville 41056; 606–564–9411), which displays documents, photographs, and other items relating to the flight to freedom slaves took through a network of brave abolitionists. Maysville was a key point along the railroad, from which escaped slaves from Kentucky and points farther south crossed the Ohio River. Right now the museum's collection is small, but plans are that it will grow and eventually move to its own location. The museum is open Monday through Saturday from 10:00 A.M. to 4:00 P.M. A small admission fee is charged.

The downtown flood wall in Maysville is becoming an art gallery on a grand scale, with the creation of huge murals depicting scenes from the area's history. The larger than life **Maysville Flood Wall Murals** are privately funded and are created by Louisiana artist Robert Dafford, who has painted more than twenty murals for the city of Paducah in western Kentucky. At press time three murals had been completed, showing the town's pioneer landing spot. Limestone Landing, as it might have looked in the 1700s, 1800s, and 1900s. Maysville has many historic buildings and sites, from a pioneer graveyard, to the 1850s New Orleans–style homes of Mechanics Row, to the childhood home of singer Rosemary Clooney. Pick up a free walking tour brochure at the visitors bureau.

Follow Second Street past Sutton and park anywhere. On the north corner of Sutton and Wall Streets is the shop of a fine furniture maker. **Joseph Byrd Brannen & Co., Antique Furniture Reproductions** is an inspirational one-person operation. Joe Brannen is asked to make all manner of hardwood furniture, but his true love is for traditional eighteenth- and nineteenth-century American furniture in cherry, walnut, mahogany, and curly maple, a wood with delicious figuring and a mean grain from which many woodworkers keep a respectful distance. Joe does use power tools, but he finishes all of his work by hand, using planes or scrapers that are fueled by pure elbow grease. The difference is noticeable and worth the extra cost. He always has a few finished pieces of furniture on hand and welcomes visitors Monday through Saturday from 9:00 A.M. to 5:00 P.M., except on Thursday. For a brochure and price list, write 145 West Second Street, Maysville 41056, or call (606) 564–3642.

Directly across the street on the corner is *Gantley's Shoe and Harness* (144 West Second; 606–564–9875), another impressive one-craftsperson operation. Joe Gantley can do just about anything with leather. Although he is set up for small work like making belts and repairing shoes and purses, he prefers working on equine equipment. Joe and his wife, Deedee, are known all over the state as fine riders and trainers of American saddlebreds, standardbreds, and Hackney ponies. Ask him about the horse-show photos in his shop. Joe's shop is open weekdays 9:00 A.M. to 5:00 P.M. and from 9:00 A.M. to 1:00 P.M. Saturday.

Drive west another 2 blocks to Rosemary Clooney Street, so named when the singer's first motion picture premiered in Maysville, her hometown. Go toward the river and you'll find the only active Amtrak station in Kentucky and a great place to eat called *Caproni's Restaurant.* Its national fame began in the 1930s, when it was just a cafe at which eastbound soldiers stopped during train layovers. Today, two long balconies look out over a wide, slow-moving part of the Ohio River. The other selling points are super food, high-quality local and foreign wines, and imported beers. You can have the usual range of country cooking, done with unusual class, or you can indulge in a savory plate of fettuccine Alfredo for a mere $5.95, a New York strip steak for $12.95, or a variety of seafood. Call (606) 564–4119.

Another of Kentucky's few remaining covered bridges is east of Maysville

The Tables Do Turn

*T*he Maysville-Washington area was settled by Simon Kenton, who first claimed the land. Kenton later sold it for 50 cents an acre to Arthur Fox and William Wood, who laid out the town of Washington. Like a good imperialist, Kenton had come to the area in search of sugar cane so that he could get rich making Jamaican-style rum. The hills were indeed covered with cane, but it was wild Kentucky cane, a tall, woody native grass, the only bam-boo species native to North America. Nothing sweet about it. Like a good capitalist, Kenton realized his error and went on to exploit some other aspect of the land. He eventually opened a small store in a cabin in Washington; that cabin now stands next to the visitors center. Legend has it that Kenton couldn't pay his bills and was thrown into debtor's prison in Washington, the very town he founded. The tables do turn . . .

in Lewis County. From Maysville take Highway 10 through Plumville and turn left (east) onto Spring Creek Road. Just as you cross the county line at the intersection with Cabin Road you'll see the **Cabin Creek Bridge** on the south side. The 114-foot-long bridge was built in 1897 and closed to traffic in 1983.

Driving the 4 miles straight uphill on Highway 68 between Maysville and Washington will take you a matter of minutes. In the eighteenth century, however, the climb consumed a whole day. Heavily loaded wagons and carts that had just come across the Ohio River at Maysville (then called Limestone) were worn out by the time they reached the ridge, so they stopped at Washington for a rest. I wouldn't call these pioneers tourists, but their patronage caused the town to grow from a few humble cabins into a bunch of humble cabins.

When Kentucky joined the Union in 1792, people west of the Alleghenies thought that **Washington,** population 462, might become the capital of the United States. (Obviously, the other Washington got the vote.) If time could have frozen at that moment, you probably would have seen a town much like the historic restoration that stands today. You can get a more complete story of the town and its characters from one of the tour guides at the visitors center, which is located in one of the original 119 cabins from 1790. Guided tours of the town are offered Monday through Saturday from 11:00 A.M. to 3:00 P.M., Sunday from 1:00 to 3:00 P.M. From December through mid-March the center is open only on weekends. The tours cost $3.00 for adults, $1.00 for children. Call (606) 759–7411 for more information.

Washington is full of small antiques and specialty shops selling everything from rare books to homemade candies to clocks, yarns, dried herbs, and copper lamps. The place to eat in town is **Brodrick's Tavern Food & Spirits** (606–759–0313) at the corner of Main and "C" Streets. This place has been licensed since 1789, when the first court of the new Mason County, for which Washington served as county seat, granted David Brodrick permission "to keep an ordinary in his home." This is where those tired hill climbers rested before heading down the buffalo trace, the place where the buffalo crossed the river. Hours will vary depending on the season; call ahead for reservations.

Just a few miles from Washington off Highway 68 is the community of **Mays Lick.** Founded in the late 1700s, this tiny community has numerous historic buildings and churches and a couple of small shops.

Highway 68 follows a north-south path made by buffalo traveling to and from the salt deposit at Blue Licks. From Maysville go south on the buffalo trace to the **Blue Licks Battlefield State Park** (859–289–5507). The place had always been one of importance to the native people as well as to the settlers who mined salt there. Its connotation darkened when in August 1792 more than sixty Kentucky pioneers were killed in a bloody Revolutionary battle against Native Americans and Canadian soldiers ten months after the British surrendered at Yorktown. All this in a fifteen-minute battle! A large granite obelisk at the park marks the area where the fighters, including Daniel Boone's son Israel, were buried in a common grave.

Take a hike along the buffalo trace beginning in the parking area. This fifteen-acre area is set aside as a state nature preserve in order to protect one of the last and largest stands of Short's goldenrod, a federally endangered species. Notice how the goldenrod grows thickest in the open areas. It is speculated that grazing and trampling by buffalo, now nonexistent in Kentucky, helped the plant survive; the buffalo also may have carried the seeds in their thick fur and thus spread the graceful yellow plant. (Goldenrod, by the way, is not responsible for your hay fever. Blame ragweed.) Goldenrod blooms in September, but as tempting as it is, please don't pick any.

The displays in the park museum are concerned with the cultural and geographic history of the area. Several original pieces of Daniel Boone's salt-making equipment are in the museum, donated by descendants of Simon Kenton. In 1778 Boone and a few others made a salt expedition and were taken prisoner by the Shawnees, who adopted many of the

Premium Hospitality

*H*ad I driven into a time warp? At Henderson Chevron in Tollesboro (east of Maysville), there were no self-service pumps. "Fill her up?" the attendant asked. I hadn't heard those words in years. Owner Paul Henderson even checked under the hood for free. A big orange tabby dozed in the front window. "That's Ol' Yellow—he just came around one day," explained Henderson. Across the road, there was a miniature golf course behind the "White's Hams" building. Nobody was around, but there was an honesty jar to leave the money in if you wanted to play. Small things like these are one of the reasons traveling the back roads is so enjoyable, and Kentucky has many small towns like Tollesboro where you'll find old-fashioned values and friendliness. Folks like Paul Henderson like it that way: "Some folks have told me I ought to go self-service. But we've always done it this way since I started in this business with my dad in '64, and I think we'll just keep it that way."

white men into their families. Boone was adopted by the chief, Black-fish. Later Simon Kenton retrieved the equipment. Today the park has fishing facilities and all the usual recreational trappings. A new lodge offers rooms from $42 to $59 per night. Cottages are also available. The lodge dining room serves breakfast, lunch, and dinner daily. Call (859) 289–5507 for information. In mid-August the park sponsors a historic reenactment of the battle during a festival that features period demonstrators and other related entertainment.

This is definitely the region of covered bridges. *Johnson Creek Covered Bridge* crosses the creek on the original buffalo trace just north of Blue Licks Battlefield State Park. Built in 1874, the dilapidated structure is 114 feet long and 16 feet wide, with Smith-type trusses. Take Highway 68 east from the park, then take Highway 165 north to Highway 1029 and watch for the bridge, which is closed to traffic.

In Fleming County, south of Maysville, there are three covered bridges. The first is the 60-foot-long **Goddard (White) Covered Bridge,** the only surviving example of Ithiel Town truss design in the state, a lattice-like design that uses rigid, triangularly placed beams as supports. Photographers love this spot because a picturesque country church can be seen through the bridge. From Maysville go to the county seat, Flemingsburg, by way of Highway 11 south. Then follow Highway 32 east almost 6 miles to Goddard. This time, you can drive over the bridge. For more information, call (606) 845–5951.

Follow Highway 32 down the road a piece and turn right (west) on Rawlings Road, or north on Highway 1895 (Maxey Flats Road). At *Ringos Mills* you'll find an 86-foot-long bridge built in 1867 that was part of a large nineteenth-century gristmill.

A more utilitarian-style covered bridge is a few miles away near Grange City. The 86-foot-long **Hillsboro Bridge** is roofed and sided with corrugated tin, and the abutments are made of "red stone." The construction is of the burr truss design with multiple king posts. It's a sight! It's also a shame that it's too run-down to use. To get there from Flemingsburg, drive south on Highway 111, pass Hillsboro, and watch the right side of the road.

Seven miles south of Blue Licks is a rural community called **Carlisle,** which boasts some 350 buildings that are on the National Register of Historic Places. One of them is said to be made of the only Daniel Boone cabin logs in Old Kentuck' that haven't turned into humus—actually, the cabin is still standing. Tours are offered by appointment. In downtown Carlisle the *Old Nicholas County Jail* and jailer's home have been refurbished down to the dungeon-like cells. Tours are offered by appointment, and on the third Thursday of every month, a delicious four-course lunch is served for $8.00 per person. Reservations are required, and fill up fast. For information about the Boone cabin tours or the jail, call Carlisle/Nicholas County Tourism at (859) 289–5174.

MORE GOOD LODGING IN NORTHERN KENTUCKY

AUGUSTA

Doniphan House, 302 East Fourth, 41002; (606) 756–2409. B&B in an 1825 Georgian-style house. Three guest rooms.

White Rose Bed and Breakfast, 210 Riverside Drive, 41002; (606) 756–2787. Three guest rooms in an 1850 house owned by innkeeper Bob Kelsch's family since 1917.

BELLEVUE

Mary's Belle View Inn, 44 VanVoast, 41073; (859) 581–8337. Two guest roms and a suite with a great view of the Cincinnati skyline.

BURLINGTON

First Farm Inn, 2510 Stevens Road, 41005; (606) 586–0199. Bed-and-breakfast in an 1870s home on a working horse farm. $89 and up.

CARROLLTON

Days Inn, I–71 at Highway 227; (502) 732–9301. Around $55.

General Butler State Resort Park, Highway 227 North; (502) 732–4384. $42 to $162.

General William O. Butler Bed and Breakfast, 713 Highland Avenue, 41008; (502) 732–6154.

Highland House, 1705 Highland Avenue, 41008; (502) 732–5559. B&B in a Mediterranean period revival-style home on the Ohio River.

COVINGTON

Carneal House Inn, 405 East Second Street, 41011; (859) 431–6130. Six guest rooms in a Palladian- and Georgian-style mansion. $100 and up.

The Claire House, 1311 Greenup, 41011; (859) 491–0168. B&B in a 1900-era row house and artist's studio.

Licking Riverside Historic Bed & Breakfast, 516 Garrard Street, 41011; (859) 291–0191. An 1870s Greek Revival house with river views and Jacuzzis for two.

CYNTHIANA

Side Saddle Inn, P.O. Box 564, Route 36, Tricum Pike, 41031; (859) 234–8600. Guest rooms in a country setting.

DRY RIDGE

Super 8, I–75, exit 159; (859) 824–3700. Around $50.

FALMOUTH

Back in Time, 804 West Shelby Street, 41040; (859) 654–6100. Six rooms with private baths.

Red Brick House B&B, 201 Chapel Street, 41040; (859) 654–4834. Four guest rooms in a Gothic-style Victorian close to Kincaid State Park.

FLORENCE

Best Western Inn, 7821 Commerce Drive, 41042; (859) 525–0090. $55 and up.

Wildwood Inn Fundome and Spas, 7809 Highway 42, 41042; (859) 371–6300. $75 and up.

FORT MITCHELL

Drawbridge Estate, I–75 at Buttermilk Pike; (859) 341–2800. Adjacent to Oldenberg Brewery. $70 and up.

GHENT

Ghent House, 411 Main Street, 41045; (502) 347–5807. Bed-and-breakfast in an antebellum home overlooking the Ohio River.

The Poet's House, Main Street and Highway 42; (502) 347-0161. A Federal-style home overlooking the Ohio River.

HILLSBORO
DH Mountain Lake Manor, Stockton Creek Road; (606) 876-5591. Four rooms in a luxurious manor house on a 1,500-acre riding and fishing resort. $75 to $95.

MAYSVILLE
French Quarter Inn, 25 East McDonald Parkway, 41056; (606) 564-8000. $69 and up.

Kleier Haus, 912 Highway 62, 41056; (606) 759-7663. Three rooms in a renovated early-twentieth-century house.

NEWPORT
Ash-Ley House B & B, 310 East Third Street, 41071; (877) 272-5767 or (859) 291-1114.

Gateway Bed and Breakfast, 326 East Sixth Street, 41071; (888) 891-7500 or (859) 581-6447. Spacious rooms in an Italianate-style townhouse. $85.

WILLIAMSTOWN
Days Inn, I-75, exit 154; (859) 824-5025. $45 and up.

Red Carpet Inn, exit 154 off I-75; (859) 824-4305. $55 and up.

MORE FUN PLACES TO EAT IN NORTHERN KENTUCKY

CARROLLTON
Churchill Manor Restaurant, 1408 Highland Avenue, 41008; (502) 732-6314. Steaks, seafood, and daily specials.

Cooper's Restaurant, 214 Park Avenue, 41008; (502) 732-4990. Catfish, barbecue, steaks, and sandwiches.

General Butler State Resort Park, Highway 227 North; (502) 732-4384. Varied menu with buffet.

Welch's Riverside Restaurant, 505 Main Street, 41008; (502) 732-9118. For breakfast, lunch, and dinner.

COVINGTON
CoCo's, 322 Greenup Street, 41011; (859) 491-1369. Southwestern food with jazz music.

Mike Fink's, Greenup Street at Ohio River; (859) 261-4212. Dine aboard an authentic stern-wheeler.

Scalea's, 320 Greenup Street, 41011; (859) 491-3334. Italian cuisine in a casual yet chic atmosphere.

Wertheim's, 514 West Sixth Street, 41011; (859) 261-1233. Traditional German fare plus pasta and chicken dishes.

CRITTENDEN
B & E Log Cabin Restaurant, I-75, exit 166; (859) 428-2907. Home cooking and homemade desserts.

CYNTHIANA
Biancke's Restaurant, 3 South Main Street, 41031; (859) 234-3443. Always a big local crowd. Good Italian and American cooking for reasonable prices.

DRY RIDGE
Little Shrimp Restaurant, 20 Broadway, 41035; (859) 824-5000. Sandwiches and ice cream.

FLORENCE
Grand Cafe, 7373 Turfway Road, 41042; (859) 371-9779. Fine traditional food and a great wine list.

FORT MITCHELL
Gatehouse Tavern, 2577 Royal Drive, 41017; (859) 341-3800. American food in an Old English castle setting (complete with moat).

Indigo Bar and Grill, 2053 Dixie Highway, 41017; (859) 331-4339. Salads, pastas, and gourmet pizza.

FORT THOMAS
El Midway Cafe, 1017 South
Fort Thomas Avenue,
41075; (859) 781–7666.
Great fajitas and other
mesquite fare in a restored
1890s saloon.

MAYSVILLE
deSha's Restaurant,
1166 Highway 68 South,
41056; (606) 564–9275.
Varied menu with wide
selection of appetizers,
homemade meat loaf, and
other specials.

Tippedore's (in French
Quarter Inn), 25 East
McDonald Parkway, 41056;
(606) 564–8000. Seafood
and Cajun dishes.

WASHINGTON
Marshall Key's Tavern,
2111 Old Main Street,
41096; (606) 759–5803.
Homemade soups, sand-
wiches, daily specials, and
pies.

WILLIAMSTOWN
Alice's Restaurant,
115 North Main Street,
41097; (859) 824–7633.
Home cooking.

South-Central Kentucky

K ids aren't the only people who need to play and learn. This region's parks and large dammed lakes are like big playgrounds for adults. There are two of the world's natural wonders, Mammoth Cave, which highlights the most spectacular manifestations of Kentucky's unique karst geography, and the breathtaking Cumberland Falls, the second largest cataract in this hemisphere and one of two in the world with a moonbow. South-central Kentucky is also associated with history. The north is Lincoln country and home to the state's only African-American history gallery, and the south boasts the beautiful Big South Fork National Park. *Bowling Green,* the largest city, is known, in part, for having the world's only Corvette plant. The whole region is spiced up with amusing town names, quirky craftspeople, and zany festivals.

From Caves to Culture

B eing in the heart of Western Kentucky University's campus on Adams Street in Bowling Green, *The Kentucky Museum* is not off the beaten path, but its contents are unique. This is one of the best collections of objects pertaining to Kentucky history and culture housed in one place. The museum also makes a special effort to exhibit fine traveling shows and to put together displays using borrowed objects that otherwise would never be in the public view. Traditional Kentucky quilts are the museum's forte. There's a Christmas crazy quilt made of silk hat liners, for example. During the holidays, a passel of relatives were snowbound for several weeks, so instead of flipping on the tube and watching game shows, they made a quilt together. Some of the quilts are political, such as the 1850 Henry Clay quilt with his portrait in the middle in crewel work, which was a presentation piece from Mrs. Henry Clay to the wife of Senator John Jordan Crittenden. And some quilts are downright fascinating; for example, the dizzying 66,000-piece *Spectrum Quilt,* which is rare in that it was made in the 1930s by a man, a jeweler who had heard that the work would keep his fingers nimble. The list goes on. Museum hours are 9:30 A.M. to 4:00 P.M. Tuesday

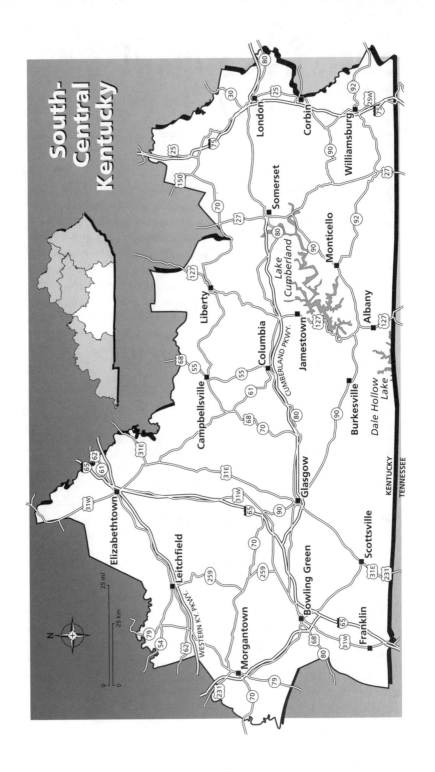

South-Central Kentucky

through Saturday, 1:00 to 4:00 P.M. Sunday. Admission is $2.00. Call (270) 745–2592 for further information.

Another downtown museum in Bowling Green is **Riverview at Hobson Grove,** which grandly overlooks the Barren River. In the late nineteenth century the river was bustling with commerce, so that homes facing the river had to be worthy of the attention they received. The Hobsons built a magnificent, three-story, brick Italianate mansion, which has been restored and filled with period antiques. Excellent guided tours are given for $3.50, from 10:00 A.M. until 4:00 P.M. Tuesday through Saturday, 1:00 to 4:00 P.M. Sunday. Riverview is closed in January. The house comes to life for visitors, thanks to an award-winning photographic and oral history exhibit called *If Only These Walls Could Talk.* To get there, follow Main Avenue north to the outside of the Victoria Street bypass (Hobson Lane), pass the Delafield School, and watch for the sign. Call (270) 843–5565 for more information.

Mariah's Restaurant, downtown at 801 State Street, Bowling Green 42101, (270–842–6878), is located in Bowling Green's oldest brick house, the circa 1818 home of Mariah Moore, daughter of one of the town's first white settlers. The Southern-style food is very good, and the restaurant is famous for its homemade appetizers, sauces, and more than thirty variations of chicken dishes. Open from 11:00 A.M. to 10:00 P.M. Monday through Friday, 11:00 A.M. to 9:00 P.M. Sunday.

Corvette devotees are already aware that General Motors's only Corvette assembly plant in the world is in Bowling Green. The fascinating, hour-long tour of the plant itself is offered at 9:00 A.M. and 1:00 P.M. Monday through Friday, except during model changes and on holidays. It's best to call and confirm at (270) 745–8419. The **National Corvette Museum** at exit 28 off I–65 gives fans a good look at the history and glory of the racy, powerful, best sports car made in America. There are nostalgic displays and lots of souvenirs. One thing sure to spark your

ZOE'S TOP PICKS IN SOUTH-CENTRAL KENTUCKY

The American Cave Museum, Horse Cave; (270) 786–1466

Appalachia—Science in the Public Interest (ASPI), Mount Vernon; (606) 256–0077

Barthell Mining Camp, Stearns; (888) 550–5748

Battle of Tebbs Bend Civil War Batttle Site, Campbellsville; (270) 465–3786

Cumberland Falls (especially the moonbow), Corbin; (606) 528–4121

Elizabethtown Historic Walking Tours, Thursday nights in the summertime, Elizabethtown; (270) 765–2175

Highland Games and Gathering of Scottish Clans, late May, Glasgow; (270) 651–3141

The Kentucky Museum, Bowling Green; (270) 745–2592

Mills Springs Civil War Battle Reenactment, a three-day event in October, Mills Springs; (606) 679–5725

Wolf Creek National Fish Hatchery, Rowena; (270) 343–3797

True Blue

curiosity is the building itself, an unusually ugly, asymmetrical, yellow, almost conical structure with a huge red spire. A query about the design to a museum employee elicited the following explanation: "Well, when the museum opened, the newspaper said that some Corvettes of the '50s and '60s had a red cone coming out of the back light. Later, someone told us that from the air, the building looked like part of the dashboard. Finally, we called the architect, who said that neither was the case; he had simply wanted to create a building that was completely different." Which it is. Admission is $8.00 for adults, $4.50 for ages six to sixteen, and $6.00 for ages fifty-five and older. Hours are 8:00 A.M. to 5:00 P.M. daily. For museum information, call (270) 781–7973 or (800) 53–VETTE.

While you're in an automotive mood, take Highway 68/31W from the Corvette plant through Bowling Green to the intersection with Highway 231. There you'll find **Holley Performance Products World Headquarters,** a one hundred-year-old company that makes the carburetors for NASCAR vehicles (as well as privately owned hot rods). A free forty-five-minute tour shows you the engineering labs, manufacturing processes, and distribution center. Tours are given Tuesday and Thursday at 9:00 A.M. and 1:00 P.M. Call (270) 745–9527 for reservations.

Now that you've properly paid homage to the almighty gas combustion engine, how about a little culture?

Feather Crowns

*Y*ou can't help liking Curiosity Hall, a narrow hall on one side of Bowling Green's Kentucky Museum filled with unusual relics with unusual ties to Kentucky. The oddities include things such as doll heads supposedly used during World War I to transport spy messages and an item known as a "death crown" or "feather crown," a ring of feathers found inside the pillow of a deceased person. Some say that the crown means that the person has gone to heaven. Others say that the feathers form a ring slowly during one's life, and when the ring is complete, the time has come to die. A friend told me that this belief was so deeply instilled in her during childhood that, despite her logical nature (she's an accountant), she still beats her pillows every morning to fight fate and destroy the feather ring. After a year of marriage, her husband got irritated enough with the habit to ask why in tarnation she did it. When she explained, he answered, "That's pathetic, honey. These are foam pillows."

There are several downtown sites worth exploring. The **Capitol Arts Center**, 416 East Main Street, Bowling Green 42101, is a classic over-the-top art deco movie theater. It's been renovated and now houses the Houchen Art Gallery and is used for all sorts of cultural events throughout the year. Call about what's playing or stop by the gallery, Monday through Friday from 9:00 A.M. to 4:00 P.M. (270) 782–2787.

Local thespians called the Public Theater of Kentucky perform everything from drama to comedy to musical shows nearby at the **Phoenix Theatre**, 545 Morris Alley, Bowling Green 42101. Call (270) 781–6233 for more information about shows, which are scheduled from September through June.

It's designed for kids, but adults can't help but have fun at **BRIMS, the Barren River Imaginative Museum of Science**, at 1229 Center Street, Bowling Green 42101. The museum features some permanent and some rotating exhibits, or rather, experiential zones. Admission is $3.50

Adventures in Good Eating

*D*uncan Hines is truly a household name, even today, fifty years after the food label was established. Today, however, the name brings to mind processed foods and, the truth be told, culinary mediocrity. Originally, however, the power of the name Duncan Hines was comparable to the power of the current star-rating system used to classify restaurants and hotels. Mr. Duncan Hines, who was born in Bowling Green in 1880, had a celebrated reputation for recommending eateries. As a young man he'd been a traveling salesman and had to eat out often. Unsanitary conditions at roadside food stands, which were ubiquitous at the turn of the century, caused deadly food poisoning. As he traveled, Hines made careful notes about places that met his standards of quality.

In the early 1930s Hines and his wife traveled extensively in the United States and made a list of "superior eating places," which they mailed to friends as a Christmas present in 1935. The list, a guide to the Hines's most highly recommended restaurants, was wildly popular and resulted in a book the next year titled Adventures in Good Eating. In 1938 they published a companion book of recommended inns called Lodging for a Night. A sign in front of any such establishment stating "recommended by Duncan Hines" almost guaranteed the business success with travelers.

Bowling Green hosts an annual Duncan Hines Festival in honor of this native gourmet every June. You can also drive the **Duncan Hines Scenic Byway**, beginning with a site on Highway 31 marking the Hines's former home and office. (Ask for a map at the visitors center, 352 Three Springs Road, Bowling Green 42104, off I–65 at exit 22, or call 270–782–0800.)

for "overgrown" and $2.50 for regular children. Hours are Thursday through Saturday from 10:00 A.M. to 3:00 P.M., Sunday from 1:00 to 4:00 P.M. Call (270) 843–9779.

Weekdays from 9:00 A.M. to 3:00 P.M. you're free to tour the beautiful, Gothic *St. Joseph Catholic Church* at 434 Church Street, Bowling Green 42101. (270) 842–2525.

If you drive the Duncan Hines Scenic Byway, you'll go through a little town called *Smith's Grove,* 14 miles north of Bowling Green, where a short walking tour of the 19th Century District includes a stop at the Smith's Grove cemetery, where Patrick Henry's sister is buried. (Get a tour map at almost any local business.) In Smith's Grove follow Sixth Street to *Cave Spring Farm Bed and Breakfast and Caverns,* a grand antebellum house, farm, schoolhouse, 1840s servants quarters, a large bird sanctuary, and private cave that is said to have the country's longest cave gate. Cave tours are offered daily except Tuesday. Admission is charged for nonfarm guests. Call (270) 563–6941.

Another cave claim to fame can be seen at the *Lost River Cave Valley,* where the cave is said to have the shortest, deepest river in the world and the largest cave opening east of the Mississippi River. It also has a short hiking trail and a butterfly house, the only one in the state. Open daily from April through October; admission is $7.00. To get there from Bowling Green, take Highway 31W out of town about 3 miles. Call (270) 793–1023. Canoeing aboveground is available on the Barren River through *Barren River Canoeing* (270–796–1979). Boat rentals, including drop-off and pick-up at the river, run between $25 and $35.

In its heyday, *Woodbury* was a busy little town on the Green River at the site of Lock and Dam Number 4. After the log structure there, which

The Heck with Straight Lines

*N*otice on your map how the Kentucky border bulges just a bit to the south in this area? Legend has it that when the border was surveyed and this land was to be relegated to Tennessee, the owner of this land, a farmer named Sanford Duncan, invited the surveying team to a party at the Duncan Tavern (about 6 miles south of Franklin), a popular spot for travelers on the Louisville-to-Nashville trek because of the fine food and Kentucky liquor served there. The surveyors were so appreciative (and drunk) that they agreed to survey all of Duncan's land into Kentucky. The heck with straight lines.

was finished in 1841, washed away in 1965, the Butler County Historical and Genealogical Society developed Woodbury into a museum complex. What was formerly the lock keeper's home has been transformed into *The Green River Museum* (270–526–2133), a visual history lesson about the riverboat era in Woodbury. The remains of the lock and dam structure are visible from the museum's big porch. From mid-April through Labor Day, the free museum is open on weekends from 1:00 to 4:00 P.M., or by appointment.

North of Woodbury on Highway 403, high on a bluff over the Green River, is *Morgantown,* a river-dependent port town in the 19th Century District. Every Fourth of July the town celebrates with the Green River Catfish Festival, downtown in the municipal park. River commerce brought wealth to the town late in the nineteenth century, evidenced by some of the remaining architecture, such as the *Hammers House,* built in 1890 and listed on the National Register of Historic Places. You can tour the house and see the original oak stairway, "riverboat carpenter trim," and Tiffany glass. By appointment only. Call (270) 526–2304 or (270) 526–4325.

Note: Keep an eye on the earth's undulations along the Green River near Morgantown, because there are supposed to be numerous ancient Native American burial mounds there.

If you travel northeast of Bowling Green, you will be in some of the most spectacular cave country in the world. Second to the Kentucky

Kilroy's Ancestors

*T*he **Old Simpson County Jailer's Residence** in Franklin was being renovated, and since it was expected that little if any original plaster could be repaired, workers weren't being terribly careful as they ripped out old paneling and wallpaper. Until they found, in a second-story room of the building, something that made everyone stop and stare in astonishment: drawings, possibly in charcoal, some almost life size, portraying Civil War soldiers, both Union and Confederate, including a portrait of the famous Confederate raider General John Hunt Morgan.

Though it may never be known exactly who created these sketches, it is known that the building was occupied by Union troops and used to house Confederate prisoners of war, and it is thought that what is left on the walls is authentic and rare Civil War graffiti. The building, now home to the **Simpson County Archives and Museum,** *is at 206 North College Street, Franklin 42135, about 21 miles south of Bowling Green. Hours are Monday through Friday from 9:00 A.M. to 4:00 P.M. Admission is free. Call (270) 586–4228 for more information.*

Derby, **Mammoth Cave National Park** is the best nationally known tourist attraction in the state, and for that reason, travelers can get information about cave history and trips anywhere within a hundred-mile radius. While definitely a well-beaten path (about 2.1 million people visit every year, and during the summer months it can be incredibly crowded), Mammoth Cave does have lesser-known aspects. Explore the cave in an old-fashioned way on a Gothic Lantern Tour. Or take a Wild Cave Tour and crawl through tight passages. Whatever tour you decide to take, if you're coming in the summer, especially on weekends, it's a good idea to reserve your cave tour well in advance. Call (270) 758–2328 or (800) 967–2283.

Aboveground there are more than 70 miles of wonderful hiking trails. Visit the **Old Guides Cemetery,** near the Heritage Trail near the Cave's Historic Entrance. Among those buried here is Stephen Bishop, the cave's preeminent explorer in the 1800s. Bishop, like many of the people who helped map underground passages and served as tour guides in antebellum days, was a slave. His owner purchased Mammoth Cave around 1838. Bishop's many discoveries led to national renown and resulted in his freedom in 1856. He hoped to purchase the freedom of his wife and son and emigrate to Liberia but was unable to do so before his death in 1857. Mammoth Cave is open every day but Christmas.

The **American Cave Museum and Hidden River Cave** on Main Street

Funky Cave Projects and Artifacts

*T*o date, the navigable cave system in the Mammoth Cave area is more than 300 miles long. The cave has provoked some odd projects, such as an underground hospital for tuberculosis victims. The cool, clean cave air would have been good for any victim of lung disease, but smoke from the cooking fires accumulated in the chamber where they lived and killed them quickly. What the doctors needed was more basic than holistic thinking—they needed common sense. Other cave project artifacts include leaching vats, which remain from the time when saltpeter (sodium nitrate or potassium nitrate) was extracted for making gunpowder during the War of 1812. Also make sure you hear the whole story of the explorer Floyd Collins. For many years his casket was on display in the Crystal Onyx Cave, to which he had been searching for a new entrance when he died. In 1929, when local cave owners were competing fiercely for tourists, someone stole Collins's body and dumped it in the Green River because it was a popular attraction. His remains have since been reinterred in a less public place.

in *Horse Cave* is an environmental education museum developed by the American Cave Conservation Association, Inc. The association's worthy mission is to educate people, especially those who live on karst lands, about how the land works and about how our actions affect the health of the system. Venial sins like dumping trash in sinkholes become mortal sins in karst areas, where the whole groundwater system can easily be contaminated. Just the entrance to Hidden River Cave is accessible through the museum (for the first time since 1943). Previously, no one wanted to go near the cave and its underground stream because it reeked of raw sewage.

Other exhibits in the museum include a whole wall display devoted to bats, a large cross-section of a karst region, and stories and artifacts from mines, bootlegging operations, early tourist endeavors, prehistoric shelters, and ceremonial sites. For more information, contact ACCA, Main and Cave Streets, P.O. Box 409, Horse Cave 42749, or call (270) 786–1466. Hours are 9:00 A.M. to 5:00 P.M. daily, with extended hours in summer.

The *Horse Cave Theatre* is one of only eight professional theaters in rural America. From late June through October, the company stages six productions per season. The range of genres is broad—Shakespeare, modern comedies, thrillers, and experimental theater by regional playwrights—and the theater thereby maintains a loyal local audience in addition to tourists. Performances are Tuesday through Saturday evening and Sunday afternoon at the large open-thrust stage in downtown Horse Cave at 107 East Main Street, Horse Cave 42749. Call (270) 786–2177 or (800) 342–2177.

After spelunking or theatergoing, you'll probably be irresistibly tempted to retire to your own personal concrete wigwam motel room, complete with rustic hickory furniture, color television, and fake smoke hole and tent flaps at *Wigwam Village*. Take exit 53 off I–65 and turn left; at the second stoplight, head north on Highway 31W and go 1 mile until you see a semicircle of fifteen white wigwams with a red zigzag design on the side. In the center is the 57-foot-high office wigwam, all built in 1937, way before the interstate existed and before concrete construction was very sophisticated. Before Americans got their kicks on the now-legendary Route 66, these maverick lodgings rose boldly from the flat plains of south-central Kentucky. In 1935 an entrepreneur named Frank A. Redford built the first Wigwam Village in nearby Horse Cave and patented his design. The Cave City village was built in 1937,

True Blue

Munfordville is locally referred to as "Concrete Alley" because it is the source of 10 percent of all commercially fabricated concrete yard-art statues made in the eastern United States.

and later five more villages went up from Alabama to California. Only two remain, but the other one, in Holbrook, Arizona, is in poor condition. At the Cave City village, however, you can still sleep in a concrete teepee with original hickory and cane furnishings. Each has a private bath. Rates are very reasonable—$25 to $45 a night—but if you want to lodge in one of these little gems (now Historic Landmarks), especially on a weekend, reserve it well in advance. The main building, which houses a gift shop, stands 52 feet high, and is made of 38 tons of concrete and 13 tons of steel. Call (270) 773–3381.

In *Brownsville,* in the Green River Amphitheatre (270–597–2403), 5 miles west of the park near where Highways 70 and 259 merge, an outdoor drama called *The Floyd Collins Story* is performed every Friday and Saturday night at dusk from July through August. The story is based on the 1925 news event of the year, when the legendary cave explorer Floyd Collins managed to dislodge a ceiling rock and get pinned underneath it as he was entering Sand Cave. This drama is

Wigwam Village

about the attempted rescue of Collins and his consequent death. More history about Collins and his death is found just by the main entrance to the Mammoth Cave National Park on Highway 70, in the *Wayfarer and Floyd Collins Museum* on the site of the 1930s Mammoth Cave Souvenir Shop. Sand Cave is a few hundred feet away. Admission is charged. Hours are 9:00 A.M. to 5:00 P.M. daily. Call (270) 773–3366.

Just a little south of the National Park, in Park City, on Highway 255 off I–65 at exit 48, are some of the most beautiful caves in the system that are open to the public. The *Diamond Caverns* are particularly known for their spectacular colors. Admission is $10 adults, $5.50 children, and it's open daily at 9:00 A.M. Closing hours vary from 4:30 P.M. to 6:00 P.M. depending upon season. Call (270) 749–2891 for information.

And on That Farm She Had a . . .

I live on a farm, and people always ask, "How many animals do you raise there?" I often answer, "Several thousand," because, in addition to raising vegetable gardens, fruit and nut orchards, milk goats, chickens, ducks, a few cattle, a horse, and a passel of dogs, we're beekeepers. The bees are the only livestock that don't need fences or daily feeding. They're not pets in that I don't have an emotional relationship with them, but they are producers of the very best sweetener in the world, and they pollinate many of the plants we raise for food. We are at least the third generation in my family to buy our bees and beekeeping supplies from the **Walter T. Kelley Co., Inc.,** in **Clarkson,** Kentucky, about 40 miles southwest of Elizabethtown, or 4 miles east of Leitchfield on Highway 62. (The bees come through the U.S. Mail as buzzing masses in screen-and-wood boxes, and the post office calls at 5:00 A.M. for us to "come and get these durn things.") This company was started some seventy-five years ago and has a huge national customer base. It continues at its original location, where wooden beehives, supers, and frames are manufactured; beeswax is processed into comb foundation; and all sorts of other supplies are made, from stainless-steel tanks and centrifical honey extractors to protective coveralls. Kelley's can also coordinate the sale and shipping of the gentle and hard-working three-banded Italian bees in swarms (sold by the pound) and their queens, all of which come from its bee yards deeper in the South. Visitors are welcome to stop by the office and see live bees in a glass-sided observation hive and to purchase honey and supplies. Beekeepers and educational groups can schedule full tours of the plant (by appointment only). A guided beekeeping museum is scheduled to open in 2002. Call or stop by Monday through Friday between 7:30 A.M. and 4:00 P.M. (except for lunch hour at noon), or on Saturday from 7:30 A.M. to noon. (270) 242–2012.

True Blue

Although Kentucky never left the Union during the Civil War, a Confederate capital was established at Bowling Green.

Kentucky was a state deeply divided during the Civil War, and exhibits at the **Hart County Museum** (109 Main Street, Munfordville 42765; 270–524–0101) in Munfordville, 3 miles north of Horse Cave, demonstrate this point well. Among the Civil War artifacts at the museum are items belonging to two Hart County residents who fought in the conflict. Confederate general Simon Bolivar Buckner and Union major general Thomas Wood were childhood friends and West Point classmates who later found themselves fighting on opposite sides of the conflict. The Munfordville battleground site is being preserved by the county historical society. A museum staff member can guide you there.

Several Amish communities are located in Hart County, and in summer months, you can buy fresh produce and other items on the courthouse lawn. Year-round, it's worth a drive out Logdson Valley Road to **Anna's Kitchen.** Anna Miller makes delicious jellies and relishes; stop by any day except Sunday. Call (270) 524–0820 for information.

East of Bowling Green, the next sizable town is **Glasgow,** host of the **Highland Games and Gathering of Scottish Clans,** held near the end of May or in early June at Barren River Lake State Resort Park, east of Glasgow on Highway 31. The games begin with a musical extravaganza called the Tattoo, then clan and society members get together for a Tartan Ball and Scottish Country Dancing. Last but not least exciting are the athletic and battle-ax competitions, which originated as martial exercises under

Running to the Loo

*U*nassuming as it looks, Tompkinsville has a bizarre reputation to uphold. On the Saturday before Labor Day this town hosts the most popular event in the **Monroe County Watermelon Festival, the Privy Grand Prix.** Yes, it's an outhouse race, and it's professional. The outhouses (3 feet wide by 3 feet deep by 6 feet high) must be made of wood, except for the wheels and roofs, and teams must consist of two people pulling, two pushing, and one sitting on the john, who must wear a seat belt and crash helmet and weigh at least 100 pounds. Contestants dream of breaking the toilet-paper ribbon in a shower of glory. The festival's main theme is watermelons, however, so there has to be a seed-spitting contest. In 1982, the first year of the Privy Grand Prix, the announcer for the spitting contest got tongue-tied and made a first call for "speed-sitting." Thus, serendipity gave birth to a new, perfect name for the outhouse race. Call (270) 487–9548 for more information.

King Malcolm Canmore in Scotland around 1060. It's amazing to watch these manliest of manly men wearing skirts (ahem, kilts) while "tossing" logs the size of telephone poles. The best-known aspect of the gathering, however, is the Ceilidh, another set of musical performances by American and international musicians—praised by Fiona Ritchie of National Public Radio's *Thistle and Shamrock* show. For more information, contact Glasgow Highland Games, Inc., 119 East Main Street, Glasgow 42141, or call (270) 651–3141.

The **Hall Place Bed and Breakfast** is a handsome place to spend the night and have a big country-ham breakfast. From downtown Glasgow take Highway 31E south (South Green Street) for 1¹/₂ blocks and look for the sign on the right. Although the house was built in 1852, the three B&B rooms have modern, private baths and phones. Rates are $45 per night for a single, $50 for a double. Call (270) 651–3176 for more information.

From Glasgow take Highway 63 south to **Tompkinsville,** the Monroe County seat. Take Highway 90 to Highway 163 south of town for about 3 miles to the **Old Mulkey Meeting House.** Built in 1804 during a religious revival that swept through the region, it is not only the oldest log meeting house in the state, but it is probably the only example of highly symbolic log architecture. The building's twelve corners represent the twelve apostles, and the three doors are meant to be reminders of the Trinity. Daniel Boone's oldest sister, Hannah, is buried in the cemetery alongside other early settlers.

Living History Country

"The pause that refreshes will make husband more helpful." What pause? Every experienced American consumer knows that it's Coca-Cola; the famous phrase was printed on a drink tray in 1934, when a Coke cost 5 cents. Over the years—from the early days when it was advertised as a mouthwash (and contained a small quantity of cocaine, an ingredient eliminated in 1905) to the modern era of "Classic Coke"—the famous beverage has been advertised on everything from posters to pencils to toys.

Elizabethtown is home to one of the world's largest private collections of Coca-Cola memorabilia, owned by the Schmidt family, who for decades owned the local bottling plant and set up a museum on the second floor. After their retirement, *Schmidt's Coca-Cola Museum* closed for a while, but it has reopened, albeit somewhat scaled down, in a room at the Elizabethtown Tourism Bureau, 1030 North Mulberry Street, Elizabethtown 42701. It's on the right from exit 94 off I–65. Items from the collection will be shown on a rotating basis. The tourism bureau is open from 8:00 A.M. to 5:00 P.M. October through May, staying open until 6:00 P.M. and on Saturday from 10:00 A.M. to 2:00 P.M. from May through September. Call (800) 437–0092 for information.

You'll also likely find an antique or collectible car on display at the tourism bureau, as advertising for another local attraction, **Swope's Cars of Yesteryear Museum.** Bill Swope, a retired longtime auto dealer in town, has a collection of about thirty vehicles from the 1920s to the 1960s. You'll find the rest of them on display at 1100 North Dixie Highway, Elizabethtown 42701. It's next door to the Swope dealership now run by Bill's son. The free museum is open from 9:00 A.M. to 5:00 P.M. Monday through Saturday. Call (270) 652–2181 for more information.

Polarities can be wonderful teachers. Leave the Coke memorabilia and old cars and please, please, please take time to get an education at the **Emma Reno Connor Black History Gallery.** Go southeast of the courthouse on East Dixie Avenue, veer left onto Hawkins Drive, and look immediately for a white stucco house on the right with a sign that says BLACK HISTORY GALLERY. This was the childhood home of the late Emma Reno Connor, a teacher who recognized a disgraceful dearth of information about the lives and accomplishments of African-Americans. She supplemented her lesson plans with pictures, articles, and stories of African-Americans and later organized these teaching materials into museum displays.

An amateur museum that is comprised of well-organized cutouts from magazines, original pen-and-ink portraits of great people, poems by Ms. Connor, and newspaper articles, this is also a powerful place full of love, knowledge, and opportunities to learn about the African-American experience. You'll enjoy learning about the lives and accomplishments of Satchmo (Louis Armstrong), Josephine Baker, Langston Hughes, Sojourner Truth, Gwendolyn Brooks, Frederick Douglass, and Martin Luther King Jr., to name a few outstanding people. Hours are noon to 5:00 P.M. Saturday and Sunday or as posted. On weekdays make an appointment with Charles Connor, Emma's widower, at (270) 769–5204 or with her sister Ruby Williams at (270) 765–7653. A tour of the gallery with Mr. Connor brings nationally known figures to life, and Ms. Williams knows the personal histories of local heroes. Together they could change your life.

Many towns of historic significance offer walking tours of their downtowns, but few resurrect the characters in living color. In the summer try the *Elizabethtown Historic Walking Tours,* during which you meet and see a brief "performance" by Sarah Bush Johnston Lincoln (Abe's stepmother), P. T. Barnum, Jenny Lind, Carrie Nation, and eight other historical figures portrayed by local people dressed in period costumes who are well versed in their figure's history. Carrie Nation, for example, runs down the street with a Bible in one hand and her famous hatchet in the other to shut down Jim Neighbor's bar. (In real life she was prevented from destroying the joint when someone knocked her out with a bar stool.) The tour covers twenty-five buildings and takes about an hour. Tours are scheduled for Thursday at 7:00 P.M. and start at the Brown-Pusey House on North Main Street. Call (270) 765–2175 or (800) 437–0092.

> ## True Blue
>
> *The Squire Pates House on Highway 334 near Lewisport was the site of Abraham Lincoln's first trial. He defended himself against charges of operating a ferry across the Ohio River without a license.*

The *Brown-Pusey House* (270–765–2515), was Elizabethtown's first public lodging house for travelers. You can't stay overnight now, but you can take a free guided tour of the very stately Georgian Colonial building. General George Custer and his wife stayed here sometime in the 1870s. A genealogy library is also housed here. Hours are 10:00 A.M. to 4:00 P.M., Monday through Saturday.

Elizabethtown has another unusual seasonal event worth the trip to town. From the Wednesday before Thanksgiving until January 2 every year, Freeman Lake Park (directly behind the Coca-Cola plant on Highway 31W North) is transformed into a glittering wonderland during *Christmas in the Park.* Cut your headlights and take the luminaria-lined drive around the lake past more than seventy lighted Christmas displays built and donated by local businesses, including a huge swan floating in the water and Santa in a boat. The show is on from dusk until 11:00 P.M. nightly.

From June through September in the Freeman Lake Park you can you can visit the *Lincoln Heritage House,* which Thomas Lincoln, Abe's father, a carpenter by trade, helped to construct, and the *Sarah Bush Johnston Lincoln Memorial,* an early-nineteenth-century cabin that re-creates the home of the woman who married Thomas Lincoln and became Abe's stepmother when the President-to-be was only ten years old. Nearby there is also a renovated 1892 one-room schoolhouse. Hours are 10:00 A.M. to 5:00 P.M. daily during the season. Call (800) 437–0092 for information.

If you didn't get enough of old cars at Swopes, head northwest of Elizabethtown on Highway 1600 (Ring Road) to Rineyville. There you'll find the *Model "A" Ford Museum,* a collection of everything from coupes to antique oil cans. There are about forty unrestored Fords from 1928 to 1931. The museum is open by appointment (call 270–862–4671), and admission is $2.00 for adults, $1.50 for children.

Take Highway 220 northeast of Rineyville and get on Highway 31W to reach Fort Knox Military Reservation, with a couple of attractions worth seeing. To America's World War II generation there was perhaps no greater hero than General George S. Patton. The *Patton Museum of Cavalry and Armor* (270–624– 3812) at Fort Knox was dedicated in the general's honor on Memorial Day 1949, four years after Patton's death. In addition to a section dedicated to Patton's life, the museum includes a display of tanks and a variety of other military items—even a section of the Berlin Wall. The museum is on Fayette Avenue near the Chaffee Avenue entrance to the base. It's open weekdays year-round from 9:00 A.M. to 4:30 P.M. It opens at 10:00 A.M. on weekends, closing at 6:00 P.M. May through September and at 4:00 P.M. October through April. Admission is free.

Not far from the Patton Museum is the *United States Treasury Department Gold Depository,* America's "Gold Vault." Although no visitors are allowed inside, you can view the building from the outside and imagine the inside, where the nation's cache of pure gold bars is stored in a two-level vault protected by a 20-ton door and armed guards.

Right at the northern edge of the Fort Knox Military Reservation in a deep bend of the Ohio River is the little town of *West Point.* Ask any local shop owner for a map showing the path of a walking tour that directs you to more than twenty buildings on the National Register of Historic Places. On the south side of town is *Fort Duffield,* a park site where Union soldiers were stationed and built earthworks in 1861. On Wilson Road, south of Highway 31, are two hiking trails. The Bridges of the Past trail is a 1-mile walk along the old Louisville and Nashville turnpike that takes you by three pre–Civil War stone bridges. On request you can be guided through the area by an interpreter. The walk takes about an hour. Call (800) 334–7540. Originating nearby, the Tioga Falls Hiking Trail is a 2-mile circuit that crosses into areas sometimes used for military training. (The trail is closed in that event.)

Excessive exposure to military equipment is bound to make a soul world-weary. To restore some sense of faith in the world's good things, try a hike in the 730-acre *Vernon-Douglas State Nature Preserve,* located 15 miles east of Elizabethtown just off Highway 62. In the early spring the woods here are full of delicate, breathtaking wildflowers.

A great place for lunch or dinner is south of Elizabethtown in a historic little railroad community called **Glendale**. Go south of town on Highway 31W for about 5 miles, then take Highway 222 west to Glendale. In the early 1970s James and Idell Sego transformed the old Glendale hardware store, which is smack-dab next to the railroad tracks on Main Street, into the **Whistle Stop Restaurant** (270–369–8586), where they now serve really, really good Southern food for reasonable prices in a cozy, depot atmosphere. Famous for its open-faced hot brown sandwich—a mountain of roast beef on bread, smothered with a rich cheese sauce—the restaurant's menu ranges from homemade soups to ham and asparagus rolls to fried chicken and taco salad. Desserts clarify the meaning of sin. Hours are 11:00 A.M. to 9:00 P.M. Tuesday through Saturday.

All of Glendale seems to be in a time warp. Though the village is small, it has a functional general store and several antiques and gift shops. During the first weekend in December, every building is decked out for a **Christmas in the Country** event, open to the public. Or come to Glendale on the third Saturday in October for the **Glendale Crossing Festival,** when the spirit of the old-time trading days pervades the town.

In the midst of this pretend atmosphere is an 1870s farmhouse with a big, inviting front porch. This is the **Petticoat Junction Bed & Breakfast** (223 High Street, Glendale 42740; 270–369–8604). Six overnight rooms are available, two of which have private baths (one bath has an old-time claw-foot tub and the other a state-of-the-art Jacuzzi). Two rooms are in a small, private cottage out back. Rates range from $60 to $90.

You've always tried to avoid places that are lame, but once you hear this, you'll want to set foot in a place that's limp—well, that's called Limp. From the Elizabethtown or Glendale area, take Highway 62 south. Just past Big Clifty, take Highway 720 to the right (north), then Highway 920 (Salt River Road) to the right and look for the **Three Springs Farm Orchard** on your left. Dale and Yvonne DePoyster and their family have a fruitful farm with blackberries to pick in the summer, and in autumn they sell apples, pears, pumpkins, honey, cider, and apple butter. In early September they offer guided orchard tours and tastings. Call (270) 862–3528 for fruit-ripening dates and an events calendar. Come hungry.

The **Official Kentucky State Championship Oldtime Fiddling Contest** is an event for beginner and virtuoso musicians or for anyone who just likes to listen to bluegrass music. Fifteen to twenty different contests, including harmonica, flat-top guitar, mandolin, banjo, bluegrass band, and even jig dancing, are held annually at **Rough River State**

Dam Park in northern Grayson County during the third week in July. This is a recommended place to have a breakdown—take your choice of "Tennessee Breakdown," "North Carolina Breakdown," "Straw Breakdown," or "Cheatum County Breakdown." When the region's hottest fiddlers compete in the Governor's Cup Fiddle Off, you'll want to cry at the music's sweetness—but the wind from the musicians' lightning-quick bow action will dry your tears before they can hit your cheeks. Camping is available, and folks are invited to come early for the informal jam sessions that go on all week prior to the main contest. For more information about the park or the contest, call (270) 257–2311. Also ask about the park's other special events such as the "Dulcibrrr" in February, a weekend for fans of lap and hammered dulcimers.

In the town of **Leitchfield,** 18 miles southeast of the State Resort Park, you can make an appointment to tour the **Jack Thomas House** (270–230–8989), the oldest house in the county and a grand Federal-style mansion. The original two-room house, built in 1815, became the south wing of the expanded building. Tours are given Tuesday through Friday from 10:00 A.M. to 4:00 P.M.

Not everything in the area is caught in the past. John and Lisa Brittain of the **Nolin River Nut Tree Nursery** have become famous for per-

The Bigger Apple!

*F*ast-food restaurants really weren't the first to "supersize" it. As evidence, there's the annual Casey County Apple Festival, held in Liberty the last full week in September. This festival has been an annual event since 1974, often attracting up to 50,000 visitors. Undoubtedly they follow their noses to this small south-central Kentucky town, because cookin' big is a centerpiece of the event.

The folks in Casey County, you see, have a special supersized oven, and they set it up in the city parking lot at festival time. The feasting begins Wednesday night, when they bake a giant chocolate chip cookie. Then on Thursday night, guests can share in a giant pizza. All of this is just a warm-up, however, for the main course, which gets under way Saturday morning, when volunteers start assembling "the world's largest apple pie." Mix thirty bushels of apples, 200 pounds of sugar you get the idea. The result: a 1,200-pound pie with a buttery crust 8-feet in diameter. (It takes a forklift to get it into the oven.) The pie bakes and bakes until noon Saturday, when it is scooped into bowls for the drooling crowd. Got a major sweet tooth? Call the Casey County Chamber of Commerce at (606) 787–6463 for more information about this all-American feast.

forming nutty modern-day miracles. Of the more than one hundred varieties of nut trees grown in their nursery, most are grafted. You're not supposed to be able to graft most nut trees because the sap tends to run so much that the grafts don't take—that is, heal and fuse to the rooted tree—yet these growers make expert use of an obscure method called a coin purse graft. They also are able to dig and ship nut trees up to 5 feet tall—that's 4 feet taller than the "rules" claim to be possible without fatally damaging the taproot.

The Brittains can probably answer any question you have about nut trees and sell you just about any variety your heart desires. They now have more than 175 varieties available, plus 15 kinds of persimmons and 4 varieties of pawpaw. For between $16 and $30 per tree, you can choose from a number of walnuts, heartnuts, butternuts, chestnuts, hickories, pecans, and hicans (a cross between hickory and pecan). Order as far in advance of spring as possible, and call if you plan to visit. For a catalog, write Nolin River Nut Tree Nursery, 797 Port Wooden Road, Upton 42784, or call (270) 369–8551. Be sure to call ahead if you want to visit.

Abraham Lincoln has put **Hodgenville** on the map and kept it there. From Elizabethtown take Highway 61 south to Hodgenville and follow signs to the **Abraham Lincoln Birthplace National Historic Site** (270–358–3137), just south of town. A humble log cabin like the one in which Abe was born on February 12, 1809, is enshrined in a huge, stone-columned building prefaced by fifty-six steps, which represent the years of Abe's life. The park is open from 8:00 A.M. to 4:45 P.M. daily, with hours extended until 6:45 P.M. in summer. Go through town on Highway 31E to tour Lincoln's boyhood home on **Knob Creek Farm,** open daily from April through October. There is a replica of the cabin where young Abe's first memories were formed; this was the last place he lived in Kentucky. This site is maintained by the National Park Service. Admission is $1.00. Call (502) 549–3741 for more information.

Downtown on Lincoln Square near the bronze statue is a small **Lincoln Museum** (270–358–3163), open Monday through Saturday from 8:30 A.M. to 5:30 P.M., Sunday from 12:30 to 5:00 P.M. Admission is $3.00. The museum features twelve scenes from Lincoln's life (with wax figures) and a display of memorabilia. Ask about the **Lincoln Days Celebration** held in town during the second weekend of October. The festival features a few odd events, including Lincoln look-alike contests and a very manly rail-splitting tournament. Call the LaRue County Chamber of Commerce at (270) 358–3411 for more information.

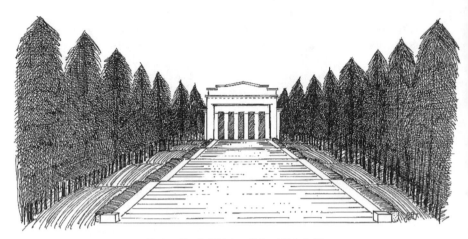

Abraham Lincoln Birthplace National Historic Site

Heading south past the Lincoln Birthplace, turn left on Highway 61 to Highway 470 and you'll come to the tiny community of Buffalo and the *Buffalo Antique Mall* (270–325–3900). Owner Allene Hager said her building with tin ceilings is pretty typical for an early-twentieth-century general store, which is what it was built to be. The balcony that runs the perimeter of the front room gave the store owner a clear view of what was going on in every nook and corner, she explained. For her, the railing is the perfect display rack for a type of collectible she especially loves: quilts and coverlets. Dozens hang in the shop, their bright colors a pleasing contrast against the white walls. Hager is herself a quilter. Stop by to see her latest quilt top, browse the three levels of just-about-everything, and chat about quilts or antiques. Hours are Monday through Saturday from 9:00 A.M. to 5:00 P.M., Sunday from 1:00 to 5:00 P.M.

Lakes and Knobs Region

oing east from Glasgow, the high road leads to Columbia, the low road to *Burkesville.* Take Highway 80 or the Cumberland Parkway to *Columbia.* Few people know that on April 29, 1872, Jesse James and his gang held up the Bank of Columbia and killed a cashier, R. C. Martin. Nor do most know that Mark Twain's parents, Jane Lampton and John Marshall Clemens, were married in Columbia in 1823. Fewer still realize that Maxwell House coffee was developed by a Burkesville boy named Joel Owsley Cheek. After a brief career as a traveling (by horseback) salesman, Cheek started experimenting in the late 1870s with roasting and mixing blends of coffee that were usually sold to the stores green and unground. The first place to sell the expensive blend was the Maxwell House hotel in Nashville, Tennessee. The rest is history.

On the campus of Lindsey Wilson College in downtown Columbia is an architectural treat worth taking a side trip to see, wherever you're going. The *John B. Begley Chapel,* at 210 Lindsey Wilson Street, Columbia 42728, was designed by E. Fay Jones, a Frank Lloyd Wright disciple who is said to be the world's foremost chapel architect. For more information, call (270) 384–8400.

North of Columbia, just off Highway 55, is the *Green River Lake State Park* and the starting place for a self-guided tour of sites associated with the *Battle of Tebbs Bend,* fought in early July 1863. This battle marked the beginning of Confederate general John Hunt Morgan's daring campaign, known as the Great Raid into Indiana and Ohio, which ended later in July when he and his men were captured in Ohio. The battle at this site ended when the Confederates were demoralized by what they mistakenly thought to be Union reinforcements arriving. The Union commander, Colonel O. H. Moore, had fooled the Rebels into thinking back-up troops were arriving all night by having his men go back and forth over a bridge crossing the Green River. One other fascinating deception in this battle was revealed afterward when one of the Union wounded turned out to be a sixteen-year-old girl named Lizzie Compton, from London, Ontario, who was posing as a man. There have been reenactments of the battle in years past, but they were suspended a few years ago after, as one observer put it, "the North and the South REALLY got into it with each other." Disagreements over whether to stage the battle authentically or to have the Rebels win led to the event's demise. You can get information about the battle at the park or at the Taylor County Tourism Commission, 107 West Broadway, Campbellsville 42719. The commission's phone number is (800) 738–4719.

In the park, stop by the interpretive center and request the key to the *Atkinson-Griffin House,* a 1½-story double-pen log building used by the Confederates as a hospital after the battle, which now houses some Civil War exhibits and even has bloodstains on the upstairs bedroom floor. Also, get the little map and list of other battle sites.

The next major town to the north is *Campbellsville,* in which there are two relatively obscure historic sites that are worth a stop. In Campbellsville at 1075 Campbellsville Bypass, visit the *Jacob Hiestand House,* an exquisite Federal-style stone house built in 1823 by a German

True Blue

During the 1918–1919 school year there were 7,067 one-room schools operating in Kentucky. What may have been the last one, in Perry County,

tanner who had moved to Kentucky from Pennsylvania. The house that is there now was moved (try to imagine that task!) from its original site because it was endangered by sprawling development. Though there are many stone houses in this state, this one was is particularly well crafted. From mid-June to mid-August, the house is open Tuesday through Saturday from 10:00 A.M. to 3:00 P.M. or by appointment. Call (270) 789–4343 or (270) 465–8601 for more information.

Another building that was moved from its original location for the sake of preservation is the *Friendship School,* a humble little one-room schoolhouse built in 1918 and now located behind the Taylor County High School at 300 Ingram Avenue, Campbellsville 42718. People are welcome to visit the schoolhouse on Sunday afternoon between 1:00 and 4:00 P.M. from July through December, or by appointment if you make arrangements with Pat Webster (270–465–5410) or Shirley Newton (270–465–5106). This little school is a classic example of Kentucky's one-room schoolhouses, which were built inexpensively and run by teachers who were legendary for their level of devotion and self-sacrifice. The Friendship School, like many of its kind, had a class size of between eight and forty students, ranging in grade from first to eighth. Like the current hours Friendship School is open, the school year ran from July through December from 8:00 A.M. to 4:00 P.M. regardless of weather conditions. Such tiny schools were located within walking distance of a few families who could pay the teacher. (This may come back into vogue and would certainly be considered radical.)

Campbellsville is a great place to visit if you're in the market for fine handmade cherry furniture. There are four companies in town that manufacture the furniture: *Campbellsville Cherry Reproductions, Inc.,* on Saloma Road (270–465–6003); *Campbellsville Hand Made Furniture,* on the Water Tower Bypass (270–789–1741); *Gary Humpress & Sons,* on East Main Street (270–465–2786); and *McMahan's Furniture Company,* on West Main Street (270–465–4831). All welcome visitors and have showrooms of beautiful beds, chests, tables, and other pieces. If what you want is not in stock, you can order it and have it shipped. "Campbellsville cherry" graces houses all over the world.

In a little town called *Mannsville,* east of Campbellsville about 10 miles on Highway 70, is *Penn Country Hams,* at 8812 Liberty Road, Mannsville 42758, a place that might be familiar to a ham fan since it sells more than 50,000 a year. You can tour the facilities and do some taste testing before you purchase. Call (270) 465–5065 for information. Hours are 8:00 A.M. to 6:00 P.M. Monday through Saturday.

West of Campbellsville about 13 miles in the town of **Greensburg** there stands the oldest existing courthouse west of the Alleghenies. It was built in 1803 and now houses a regional museum. Around town you can see a number of other historic buildings, many of which are on the National Register of Historic Places, including a log cabin, circa 1796; an old railroad depot; and a 445-foot-long pedestrian bridge. You can see the area like the early pioneers did, from the water. Take a guided or an unguided canoe trip (from May through September only) down the Green River near Greensburg for $30 to $45 per canoe. There are even some Class I rapids occasionally. Call **Canoe Kentucky** (Green River) to schedule a trip at (800) K–CANOE–1.

South of the Campbellsville/Columbia/Greensburg area is **Dale Hollow,** a large manmade lake that straddles the Kentucky-Tennessee line. Take Highway 61 to Burkesville and watch for signs. The area is full of small marinas, motels, and fishing camps. It is said to be one of the cleanest lakes in the state, and since there are myriad inlets and islands, Dale Hollow is good place to swim. **Dale Hollow Lake Resort Park** has a lodge and offers horseback riding and hiking.

Northeast of Dale Hollow is **Lake Cumberland,** one of the largest fabricated lakes in the United States; its peak surface area is more than 55,000 acres. It is also said to have more walleye, bass, and crappie than any other American lake. Although there are water-oriented businesses all around the lake, you may want to stop by the headquarters of the Lake Cumberland State Resort Park (off Highway 127 just south of Jamestown; 270–343–3111) to get specific information. If you boat around the big, clear lake, you'll find endless little coves to explore, places to swim, fossils over which to ponder, and almost no commercial development to distract you. The park also has a lodge with a restaurant, cottages, an indoor pool, campgrounds, and a marina.

Don't you want to know where all those fish in the lake come from? (Well, not all the fish— birds transport some.) Follow Highway 127 south from the park and watch for signs for the

Unwanted Static

Besides Dale Hollow lake, another thing shared by Kentucky and Tennessee is a little town with a rowdy reputation called **Static,** *which sits directly on the border where Highway 127 goes through. Kentucky says Static belongs in Tennessee, and Tennessee says the town is all Kentucky's. With a town name that means "showing little change," it's no wonder no one claims the place. To make things worse, legend has it that Static was named after a local farmer's one-eyed bulldog.*

Wolf Creek National Fish Hatchery (270–343–3797), where thousands of rainbow and brown trout are raised. Auxiliary pleasure begins if you take time to watch wild birds, like the ever-so-svelte great blue heron or the sassy belted kingfisher, feast on the easy pickings. Deer feed near the dam daily at dusk. The hatchery has some interpretive displays that explain the process of mass raising fish. Open from 7:00 A.M. to 3:30 P.M. daily.

Starting from the state park, take Highway 1058 west, then Highway 379 south through Creelsboro; when the road almost touches the Cumberland River, watch for signs for the *Creelsboro Natural Bridge.* Though there are many rock bridges in Kentucky, this 75-foot arch has been designated a National Natural Landmark because it is limestone rather than the more common sandstone.

True Blue

The state bird of Kentucky is the cardinal.

A town named *Touristville* makes a person suspicious, and rightly so. Some chamber of commerce type was on the ball that hot summer day in 1929 when the post office was named. For a time Touristville did profit from the flow of vacationers through nearby *Mill Springs,* which sits very near what is now Lake Cumberland. *Dunagan's Grocery & Supply* in Mill Springs now serves as post office for both towns. The anachronistic store really is an attraction for nostalgia buffs and curiosity seekers. In 1935 Everette Dunagan's father moved the store to its present site from about a hundred yards across the road employing one pair of mules, a bunch of logs used as rollers, some cable, and two days' worth of ingenuity. Since then precious little has changed. He carries a little bit of everything, as a good country store owner must; there's even a great little photo postcard of Dunagan's. Take your own picture or make a sketch. The place has been painted by several artists. Mr. Dunagan keeps his place open from 8:00 A.M. to 5:00 P.M. every day but Sunday. To visit, take Highway 90 to Highway 1275 and go 1 mile west. Trust me—you'll love it.

To get to Mill Springs, go to Monticello in Wayne County and follow Highway 90 to Touristville. Turn west on Highway 1275 and you'll see signs for the *Mill Springs Mill,* "largest over-shot waterwheel in the world." That's a slightly overrated waterwheel, but as it turns out, the wheel is 40 feet, 10 inches in diameter, making it the third largest in the nation and among the top ten in the world. It may be the only one of the biggies to still be functioning as a gristmill. The first cereal grinding mill was built around 1817 at this site, where thirteen springs gushed out of the hillside. The waterwheel also powered a cotton gin, carting factory, and wagon production line. After a fire and several remodelings, in 1908 the Diamond

Dunagan's Grocery & Supply

Roller Mills's 40-foot wheel was installed. Today the mill is open at no charge to the public from Memorial Day to Labor Day, 11:00 A.M. to 5:00 P.M. daily. On weekends cornmeal is ground with the old equipment. For specifics call (606) 348–8189.

The mill is the site of a tide-turning Civil War battle in January 1862. Confederate general Felix Kirk Zollicoffer set up camp at a house near the mill, the Metcalfe House. Zollicoffer lost the Battle of Logan's Crossroads and thereby left the first gap in what was a long, strong Rebel defense line in Kentucky. Just west of Somerset on Highway 80 in a town called Nancy are the **Mill Springs Battlefield** and the Zolli-coffer Park and burial site, where more than a hundred rebel troops are buried under one stone, all from the Mill Springs battle. Driving tour maps of the battlefield are available at the park. From the ceme-teries you can see (and smell and taste and climb) the fruit trees at the adjacent **Haney's Appledale Orchard** (270–636–6148), one of the state's best and largest apple orchards. The orchard is open mid-June through Christmas.

If you venture into **Somerset,** you'll not be excited by the seemingly end-less strip-type development, but there is one place that may be worth

True Blue

stopping: Call (606) 677–6000 for a schedule of
performing arts events at the **Center for Rural
Economic Development.**

If you leave Jamestown and **Russell Springs** to the
north, you leave the lake area and enter the Knobs
again. Take Highway 127 north into Casey County,
known as the **"Gate Capitol of the World."** Most gates, truck racks, and
round-bale feeders are made of tubular steel, a concept first developed in
1965 by Tarter Gate in Dunnville, the first and largest of the gate companies in the county, producing more than 1,000 gates a day.

Due to the isolation and beauty of this hilly country, a large number of
Mennonites have moved into the area. It's always inspirational to see
their neat, well-tended farms, but these people are not interested in
intrusion from the outside world. This community has two businesses
that are open to the public. Going north on Highway 127 from Russell
Springs, turn southeast on Highway 910. Go about 3½ miles and turn
east onto South Fork. This is a beautiful drive past both secular and
Mennonite farms (watch for "shocked" corn and draft horses in the

Mysteries of Dark Skies

*I*f you happen to be driving along
Kentucky Highway 78 near Liberty
after dark, take a few moments to
glance skyward. You are at the site of a
true unsolved mystery. It happened on
January 6, 1976. Three Casey County
women, two of them grandmothers
and all avid churchgoers, were returning from dinner at a Stanford restaurant. Between Hustonville and Liberty,
they saw what they thought was a
plane about to crash. Next thing they
knew, it was an hour and twenty-five
minutes later and they were 8 miles
down the road, with severe headaches
and burnlike red marks on the backs
of their necks. The car's electrical system was malfunctioning, and the paint
on the hood was blistered. Shaken and
confused, the women returned to Lib-

erty, where a neighbor asked them to
draw what they had seen, and their
aircraft looked suspiciously like a UFO.
Soon, a veritable army of UFO investigators, and the national tabloids,
descended upon this small Kentucky
town. Under hypnosis the women told
a story that seems almost commonplace today, but was then quite rare:
They had been taken aboard a spacecraft and examined by creatures with
huge, pale blue eyes. Later they even
passed a polygraph test. These unlikely
UFO abductees have long since moved
away from Liberty, Kentucky; they
grew tired of hearing the ridicule and
laughter. The case, however, remains
unsolved, a mystery to be pondered by
those who gaze upon the night skies of
Casey County.

field). It's hilarious to see the contrast in styles: Watch to the right side of South Fork for the gaudiest house in the world; the obviously secular yard is thick with whirligigs, holiday yard art, and endless junk.

At the other extreme and just a few miles away, **Bluegrass Wood and Leather Craft** (Furniture, Chairs, Tables, Harnesses and Leather Goods) is a remarkable place run by remarkable people. The store is a large building on the right filled with furniture (mainly in oak) upstairs and leather goods downstairs, all of excellent quality. Because the Mennonites in the area do much of their farming with horses and mules, the leather items are primarily horse-related, but there aren't many limits to these craftsmen's abilities. The fellows in the shop are more than willing to answer questions, and if you're serious about a purchase, they are glad to take a special order as long it falls within their way of working. There's no phone, but they are usually open on weekdays during business hours.

Back on Highway 910, go "just a little piece" farther south to **Dutchman's Market,** a small Mennonite general store in the basement of their community elementary school. To remain apart as much as possible from the corrupt aspects of today's culture, these Mennonites often employ low-technology methods for farming, building, and living in general. So, if you are in search of something unusual, a modern instance of an old model of any kind of equipment, like a hand pump for your cistern, inquire about it at Dutchman's. Let me also recommend the local sorghum molasses. Alan Oberholtzer, the local molasses meister, keeps this store well stocked. You'll want to speed home to make a mess of biscuits just to have an excuse for draining what promises to be the first of many jars.

Head south again and make your way toward Somerset. Along the way, if you want to stop for lunch or dinner, try the **Yosemite** (pronounced YO-seh-mite) **Country Store.** The homemade chili is hot—a liquid

The Underwater World of "Atlantis"—in Kentucky

*B*urnside, just south of Somerset on Highway 27, is not only the only town on Lake Cumberland—it is the only town under the lake. In the late 1940s the U.S. Army Corps of Engineers moved the entire town to higher ground because the lake area was being impounded. The durable remains of old Burnside become visible during the winter when the lake's level lowers. It's eerie seeing foundations, porch steps, and sidewalks emerge from the mud and debris.

atomic fireball. This is one of those groceries that makes its own pickled eggs. What's funny is that the homemade eggs are kept next to a jar of commercial eggs, which are dyed a sickening hot pink. The manager told me it increases sales of the homemade ones. Smart. Yosemite is on Highway 70 going southeast from Liberty. You can stay on Highway 70, which becomes Highway 635 and runs into Highway 27, which leads into Somerset.

Nearby in **Burnside,** on Highway 27 south of Somerset, is **General Burnside State Park,** a 430-acre island that's right in the middle of a deep bend in the Cumberland River as it's widening into lake status. You can camp here, launch a boat, even play golf. What the heck?! You're on an island in Kentucky! Call (606) 561–4104 for any information. At Christmas the park sponsors a lavish 3¹/₂-mile drive-through light show with several hundred displays and more than a million lights. Lucky for them electricity is cheap in Kentucky.

If you're not a camper, you can enjoy luxurious lodging at **Raintree Inn Bed & Breakfast,** located on Lake Cumberland south of Somerset. This beautiful antebellum home with huge columns looks like something out of a movie—and it is. The place takes its name from the movie starring Elizabeth Taylor and Montgomery Clift, and was one of the Kentucky locations where the film was shot. Owner Gwen Ison has lovingly restored the home and filled it with antiques. Three guest rooms in the main house, as well as the carriage house and guest rooms in the barn, are available for $90 per night ($145 for the carriage house). A full country breakfast is served. On the property you can also explore a real tobacco barn and remnants of an 1800s stagecoach stop. Call (606) 561–5225 for reservations or information.

The Shortest Creek in the World

Stab, *a short name for a small town with a short creek, is 10 miles east of Somerset along Highway 80 near the Pleasant Run Baptist Church. Short Creek emerges from a hillside cavern at an impressive width of about 25 feet. It flows in a semicircle for maybe 150 feet and ducks back underground in a small cave. There's no doubt, this is the shortest creek in* *the world. Elwood Taylor, who owns the creek, says that there was a gristmill at one end and that the creek formerly was used for wintertime baptisms because the water is always 54 degrees Fahrenheit. The Taylors own the small grocery at Stab, too. Stop by their store and ask permission to have a picnic by the creek. You may hear some good stories.*

The **Natural Arch Scenic Area** was once Cherokee country and is now a beautiful place to take a few short but spectacular day hikes. (If you're feeling energetic, you could actually cover all the trails in one day.) From Somerset take Highway 27 south for 21 miles, then turn right (west) on Highway 927 and follow the signs for 4 miles. The natural arch for which the area is named is a majestic 50-by-90-foot span of sandstone that curves above the forest below. Short trails go to some spectacular overlooks and fertile deep valleys. Early spring is a great time to go; every week brings a different set of wildflowers, including the rare lady's slipper. For trail maps or trail condition reports, contact the Somerset District Office, 135 Realty Lane, Somerset 42501, or call (606) 679–2010.

You absolutely must pay a visit to some or all of the Appropriate Technology Demonstration centers owned and operated by **Appalachia— Science in the Public Interest,** or ASPI. Make your way toward Mount Vernon via I–75, exit 49; Highway 150; or any of the small but beautiful and navigable roads that wind that way. This place marks the western edge of one of North America's most diverse ecoregions, the Mixed Mesophytic Forest, a highly varied hardwood forest. This also marks a theoretical borderline into the foothills of Appalachia, a region much beset by economic and ecological abuse. ASPI's vision is to demonstrate and promote the economic and political power found in self-sufficient living, simple living that is healthy for people and for the environment. Although Appalachia desperately needs this vision, the sustainable practices promoted by ASPI apply to everyone in every situation: Use locally available materials and apply good science in order to live compatibly with your natural surroundings. In the 1970s there were many demonstration sites like this across the nation. This is one of the few remaining centers, and it's more active than ever.

There are two beautiful and educational ASPI sites for people to visit. The appropriate technology demonstration center near **Livingston** on Highway 1329 features a thirty-two-acre site with all sorts of architectural experiments like a cordwood building; a total solar house with solar water heaters, space heaters, and greenhouses; five kinds of dry composting toilets; a yurt; a geodesic dome; artificial wetlands (which purify the center's greywater); organic gardens; miles of hiking trails; and camping sites. A 7,000-volume library is an excellent research facility, and the self-guided tours of sustainable forest practices are fascinating. Downtown Mount Vernon is ASPI's main headquarters and houses a small-town demonstration site with a wonderful intensive garden nestled surprisingly right in the midst of asphalt parking lots. The office is open from 8:00 A.M. to 4:00 P.M. on weekdays. Call ahead to make an appointment to visit the demonstration center; (606) 256–0077.

Cumberland Falls is not really off the beaten path, but it's such a flamboyant, unusual cataract that it must be recognized. Follow I–75 to Corbin, get off on Highway 25W, veer west on Highway 90, and follow the signs to Cumberland Falls State Resort Park (606–528–4121). The wide, humble Cumberland River explodes dramatically as it crashes over the curving precipice and becomes the largest American waterfall east of the Rocky Mountains, except for Niagara. When the entire disk of the moon is illuminated and the skies are clear, a long moonbow arches from the top of the falls to the turbulent waters below. The only other moonbow in the world is at Victoria Falls along the Zambezi River in southern Africa. The Cumberland Falls is so powerful that the mist fans way out and above the water; when the wind is right, you get a gentle shower on the rocks at the top. More than 65 feet high and 125 feet across, the waterfall is believed to have retreated as far as 45 miles upstream from its original position near Burnside. In a process that takes many millennia, the water wears away the soft sandstone under the erosion-resistant lip at the top.

The park, which is open all year, has another smaller but beautiful falls called *Little Eagle Falls.* If it's hot, the pool below Little Eagle Falls is a divine swimming hole. Ask for information at the park lodge about hiking trails, rooms, cabins, and special events. Within the park is a state nature preserve left to its wild state. It boasts more than fifteen species of rare plants and animals including endangered mussels and plants like the box huckleberry, brook saxifrage, goat's rue, and riverweed. A guided hike can be a real education.

Another way to "get into" the river, and to have a rip-roaring good time, is to hook up with a guided canoeing or white-water rafting trip down the river. Write to *Sheltowee Trace Outfitters,* P.O. Box 1060, Whitley City 42653, or call (800) 541–RAFT.

The other big playground in this region is at the *Big South Fork National River and Recreation Area* in McCreary County and below the border. Take Highway 27 or I–75 south to Highway 92 and go west to Stearns. If you're arriving via Highway 27, check out the natural rock bridge just off Highway 927, which goes to Nevelsville. You can also get to Big South Fork on Highway 700, which intersects Highway 27 near Whitley City. The latter route brings you directly to *Yahoo Falls,* Kentucky's highest at 113 feet.

The whole Big South Fork area is beautiful. Deep, jagged gorges are frequent surprises, and the variations in the landscape, from cool woods to hot, high, open-faced rocks, are endlessly pleasing. That the area was once extensively logged and mined is apparent. From early April through the end of October, the U.S. Forest Service operates the *Big South Fork Scenic Railway,* which takes visitors on a three-hour trip through the Stearn Coal and Lumber Company's former logging and mining empire, now mostly second-growth woods. Call (800) 462-5664 for information and excursion times. You can also drive or take the railway to an abandoned coal mining camp called *Blue Heron,* or Mine 18. This isolated company town was built in 1937 and nearly abandoned by the late 1950s, and the original buildings were ingeniously rebuilt as "ghost structures" in 1989. Life-size photographs of miners and their families occupy the skeletal structural and corrugated-steel spaces, and recorded voices depict life in the camp through a kind of time-delay oral history. The walk across the coal tipple bridge is breathtaking—you can't help but appreciate the engineering. Another camp, circa 1910, called the *Barthell Mining Camp,* is accessible only by train. You can even lodge overnight in one of the mining cabins. The appointments have improved over the days when miners slept here, however: Each cabin includes two bedrooms with queen-sized beds, and kitchens with microwaves. Rates are $95 to $125 per night, depending on the season. Call (888) 550-5748 for information.

The *Stearns Museum* (606-376-5730) fills out the picture with historic artifacts. The sandstone tree stump in front of the museum was unearthed in a strip mine just below the Tennessee line. Apparently the two-ton stump is not petrified wood but a sandstone cast of a tree (possibly an oak) that died about 315 million years ago. When the tree rotted or dissolved, the space was filled with sandstone silt, which then hardened.

True Blue
In 1818, while drilling for salt along the Big South Fork, workers inadvertently discovered oil. So began the first commercial oil well in America.

At the peak of a hill in Stearns is the *McCreary County Museum* (606-376-5730), located in the nearly century-old former Stearns Coal and Lumber Company office building. The history, depicted by displays, begins with pre-European Native American culture and ends in the present with a gallery devoted to local contemporary artwork. The museum is open Tuesday through Saturday from mid-April through October.

Take exit 11 off I-75 and keep an eye peeled for a new brick Colonial-style building on the campus of Cumberland College in *Williamsburg.* This is the *Cumberland Museum, Lodge, and Center for Leadership*

Studies. Students work in the facility to help pay for their tuition and to learn real-world skills in hotel management. The restaurant and lodgings have a great view of the surrounding mountains. Rates are around $70; call (606) 539–4100 for information. Among other things, the eclectic Cumberland Museum has an Appalachian lifestyle exhibit, a Native American artifacts collection, a very unusual collection of more than 6,000 Christian crosses, and a "life science" collection that consists of actual, preserved animal specimens, such as polar bears and shrews, shown in displays that mimic their natural habitats. There is an admission charge. For more information, call (606) 539–4050. Hours are 8:30 A.M. to 6:00 P.M. Monday through Saturday.

Jellico, Tennessee, just across the border on I–75, is (or was) the number-one place for underage Kentuckians to get hitched. In Jellico they do it fast, legal, and without parental or priestly consent: "I do, and he does, too."

Just east of Williamsburg is *Friendship Mountain Crafts,* one of many fruitful mountain craft cooperatives in the Appalachian region. Because this one is near a beaten path, the folks are prepared to show visitors around. For example, women who quilt together regularly often have some beauties for sale at the center. Activities change, so call ahead at (606) 549–1617. From Williamsburg go 9 miles east on Highway 92, turn right (southeast) on Highway 904, and watch for the sign.

Corbin sits on the adjoining corners of Whitley, Laurel, and Knox Counties and serves as the commercial hub for the whole area. Although Corbin is not famous the world over, its native son, Colonel Harland Sanders, is. From Tokyo to Moscow to London, England, and London, Kentucky, the Colonel's red-and-white portrait, complete with the almost sinister goatee, smiles out on chicken consumers everywhere going through the doors of Kentucky Fried Chicken. Corbin is the home of the original restaurant—it's even listed on the National Register of Historic Places. At *The Harland Sanders Cafe & Museum,* see Harland's kitchen as it was in the 1940s and eat in a dining area restored to resemble the original restaurant. To get there, go north of Corbin and take Highway 25E south; turn right at the second traffic light.

London, the next town to the north, is trying to get in on the chicken action, too, and holds an annual *World Chicken Festival* downtown at the end of September. In addition to the usual festival activities, all the great cooks in town compete for coveted cook-off prizes. The real winners are the tasters. Call (800) 348–0095 for specifics.

If you think the interstate near London looks busy now in a postindustrial, highway-laced world, ponder the years between 1775 and 1800, when more than 300,000 people came into Kentucky from the east through this area when it was wild. The **Levi Jackson State Park** is situated at the intersection of the Wilderness Road and Boone's Trace, the two main frontier "highways." The park is just 2 miles south of London on Highway 25. The Mountain Life Museum gives newcomers to the area a glimpse of pioneer history with a reproduction pioneer settlement stocked with period furniture and Native American artifacts. Also at the park is McHargue's Mill, a completely operational restored gristmill, circa 1812, that serves as a kind of mill museum and has what may be the world's largest collection of millstones. On park grounds is the only marked burial ground along the Wilderness Road (though historians believe that there are many other cemeteries lacking headstones). To ask about hiking, camping, or any park information, call (606) 878–8000.

Ask at the area visitors center, off I–75 at exit 41 (800–348–0095), about **Camp Wildcat Civil War Battle Site.** The "Battle of Wildcat Mountain," as it's also called, was four days of skirmishing that took

Lost and Found

Unless I'm in a big hurry, I rarely worry about getting lost, because I know that almost any Kentucky road is going to end up somewhere interesting. And if it doesn't, well, you just turn around. So I wasn't too concerned that my directions to the Amish store near Munfordville that April Saturday were somewhat vague. "It's outside of town a little piece," the quilter who told me about the store said.

"I'm not sure which store you mean, but if you turn left at the yellow flashing light and head out of town, then turn left again after a ways, you'll come to an area where a lot of Amish people live," offered a gas station attendant. Now, that was something to go on. When I saw the sign at Logsdon

Valley Road for Yoder's Harness Shop, I figured that had to be the turn.

"Look! Something's going on over there," my travel companion exclaimed. Indeed, there was. Dozens of vans, trucks—and even more horse-drawn carriages—were parked in a field, and hundreds of people, Amish and "English" of all ages, were gathered under a tent. It turned out to be a consignment auction to benefit the Amish community school, with everything from handmade bookshelves to goats going on the block. In between bidding you could fill up on just-grilled hamburgers and homemade baked goods. Best bad directions I ever had.

place October 1861. Collectively, the encounters are considered the first major battle and Union victory in Kentucky. The battle site off Hazel Patch Road includes various monuments and rough terrain.

The Rockcastle River, the lower part of which has been designated a Kentucky Wild River, runs through some gorgeous country in the Daniel Boone National Forest. Riding its currents is probably the perfect way to see the land in this area. No matter what your skill in a canoe or kayak, you will be challenged. Between March and October three area outfitting companies offer trips along the Rockcastle, which, by the way, has rapids rated between Class I and IV. *Sheltowee Trace Outfitters* (800–541–RAFT) offers guided trips for between $20 and $35 per person. *Rockcastle Adventures* (606–864–9407) rents canoes and kayaks for self-guided trips along the river, Buck Creek, or Wood Creek Lake with shuttle service and primitive camping for between $20 and $40 per person. And *Rockcastle River Runners* (606–864–8208 or 606–843–9999) lets you cruise either way, with or without guides, for between $15 and $25 per canoe. It also has camping sites available.

The next town to the north is *Mount Vernon.* Mount Vernon is considered a kind of gateway to the Knobs, the serious hills that skirt the Appalachian Mountains. For a double delight—beautiful mountains and wonderful people—take a drive straight uphill from the caution light in downtown Mount Vernon at the junction of Highways 150 and 1249. Exactly 10 miles later you'll find yourself on a hillside in front of a redbrick ranch house on the left, home of *Betty Thomas Teddy Bears.* Betty works at home and welcomes visitors but requests that you call first at (606) 256–5378 to see her fine dolls and stuffed animals— everything from realistic Canada geese and goslings, decoy-size mallard ducks, debonair foxes dressed in traditional hunt clothing and hard hats, Old World–style teddy bears, mice, cats, dogs, unicorns, soft-sculpture baby dolls, and on and on. Most of her pieces have hinged joints, and all are stuffed so tightly that they stand independently; all are made of high-quality wool, satin, or cotton in delicious colors.

Ms. Thomas's patience, persistence, and skill with her hands come by her honestly. Her parents raised thirteen children in a log cabin in a holler (hollow) just across the road from her present home. Her father, William McClure, is rightfully considered a kind of legend among folk-culture enthusiasts. For years his handmade wooden roof shingles were in constant demand in all the surrounding states, as were his handsome carved dough bowls. You can see some of his work on the roof of the Aunt Polly Hiatt house at Renfro Valley (coming up next). They say that although that roof has gaps in it so big you can see sky through them, it doesn't leak a drop. Long live the McClure family!

Here's the lineup: "Banjo Pickin' Gal," "Winking at Me," "Chicken Reel," "Cackling Hen," "Barbara Allen," "Poor Ellen Smith," "Tramp on the Street," "Matthew 24," and "Old Shep." These could be the names of thoroughbreds in the starting gate at the Derby but are, in fact, some of the best country songs ever written and some of the first ever performed at **Renfro Valley**, "Kentucky's Country Music Capital." Many folks in the region remember when they first heard John Lair's silk-smooth voice in 1939 broadcasting an all-country-music radio show live from his big tobacco barn in Rockcastle County. Those humble beginnings have led to the establishment of a large complex of buildings and traditional music and entertainment programs at Renfro Valley; the radio shows are now transmitted to more than 200 stations in North America. In addition to performance events in the auditorium (a luxury barn), there are on the grounds a craft village with mountain craft demonstrators, a gift shop, the Renfro Valley Museum, a bakery, a hotel, and a restaurant. Go north from Mount Vernon a few miles on Highway 25; for the more scenic route, to the Renfro Valley exit. For more information, show tickets, or reservations, call (800) 765–7464. Renfro Valley is open March through mid-December.

MORE GOOD LODGING IN SOUTH-CENTRAL KENTUCKY

BOWLING GREEN
Alpine Lodge,
5310 Morgantown Road,
42101; (270) 843–4846.
Swiss chalet–style B&B with five rooms and two suites. Full country breakfast.

Best Western Motor Inn,
I–65, exit 22;
(270) 782–3800 or
(800) 343–2937. About $60 per night.

1869 Homestead Bed & Breakfast,
212 Mitzpah Road, 42101;
(270) 842–0510. Historic home on fifty-five acres, with three guest rooms and numerous hiking trails.
$69 to $99.

BRANDENBURG
Doe Run Inn, Highway 448, northwest of Fort Knox; (502) 422–2982. Rustic country inn decorated with antiques. About $50 per night.

BURKESVILLE
Cabin Fever, 630 Davidson Road, 42717;
(270) 358–4415. B&B in wooded setting.

Cumberland House,
P.O. Box 7069, 42717;
(270) 433–5434 or
(800) 727–5850. B&B with sauna.

CORBIN
Best Western, I–75, exit 25;
(606) 528–2100. About $45 per night.

Cumberland Falls State Resort Park, Highway 90 southwest of Corbin;
(606) 528–4121. Rustic stone lodge and sixteen cabins; open year-round.
$42 to $155.

EUBANK

I. E. Payne House, 185 Ellison-Pulaski Road, 42567; (606) 379-2014. B&B in 1904 Victorian house, on the National Register of Historic Places. Excellent breakfast and evening dessert.

FORT KNOX

Best Western Gold Vault Inn, 1225 North Dixie Highway, 40160; (270) 351-1141. $60 to $70 per night.

GLASGOW

B&B Country Cottage, 1609 Winn School Road, 42141; (270) 646-2940. B&B in a rural setting near Barren River Lake.

Four Seasons Country Inn, 4107 Scottsville Road, 42141; (270) 678-1000. Twenty-one guest rooms with private baths. $60 to $90 per night.

Mammoth Cave Hotel, Mammoth Cave National Park; (270) 758-2225. Rooms and cottages; pet kennel available. About $75 per night.

307 B&B, 307 West Brown, 42141; (270) 651-5672. Circa 1900 Williamsburg-style house.

GLENDALE

Glendale Crossing Gate Bed & Breakfast, 883 West Glendale Hodgenville Road, 42740; (877) 357-4283. Six guest rooms with tennis, fishing, and hot tub on seven-acre setting.

JAMESTOWN

Lake Cumberland State Resort Park, Off Highway 127; (270) 343-3111. Two lodges and thirty cabins; open year-round. About $45 to $126 per night.

LEITCHFIELD

Rough River Dam State Resort Park, Highway 79; (270) 257-2311. Lodge and cottages. $42 to $115 per night.

MAMMOTH CAVE

The Mello Inn, 2856 Nolin Dam Road, Mamoth Cave 42259; (502) 286-4126. Newly constructed Victorian-style house on twelve acres. $65 to $75 per night.

MONTICELLO

Mill Springs, Highway 1275; (606) 348-0780. B&B next to the mill with a view of Lake Cumberland. Fishing boats available.

MORGANTOWN

Helm House, 309 South Tyler, 42261; (270) 526-2743 or (800) 441-4786. An 1898 Victorian home overlooking a city park. There's a playground for the kids.

RUSSELL SPRINGS

White Pillars, 100 Thrasher Court, 42642; (270) 866-7231. B&B in an 1876 antebellum home.

SMITHS GROVE

Victorian House Bed and Breakfast, 130 Main Street, 42171; (270) 563-9403. Four rooms with private baths and fireplaces; located in antiques district 10 miles north of Bowling Green. About $105 per night.

SOMERSET

Osborne's of Cabin Hollow, 111 Fietz Orchard Road, 42501; (606) 382-5495. B&B in a log home in the woods. Open only March through November.

STEARNS

Marcum-Porter House, Highway 1561; (606) 376-2242. Bed-and-breakfast in a historic house built by Stearns Coal and Lumber Company. $55 to $65 per night.

WILLIAMSBURG

Cumberland Lodge Marriott, 649 South Tenth Street, 40769; (606) 539-4100. About $70 per night.

More Fun Places to Eat in South-Central Kentucky

Bowling Green
The Fletcher House and Parakeet Cafe, 1129 College Street, 42101; (270) 781-1538. Casual dining downstairs and fine dining up, with outdoor courtyard area and gazebo.

440 Main Restaurant and Bar, 440 East Main Avenue, 42101, (270) 793-0450. Elegant dining in a restored historic home.

Brandenburg
Doe Run Inn, Highway 448, northwest of Fort Knox; (502) 422-2982. Country ham, skillet-fried chicken, and other regional favorites.

Cave City
Hickory Villa, Highway 90; (270) 773-3033; Home-smoked barbecue.

Sahara Steak House, 413 Happy Valley Road, 42127; (270) 773-3450. Steaks, seafood, and country-ham dishes.

Watermill Restaurant, Highway 70; (270) 773-3186. Large buffet or order from the menu.

Corbin
Cumberland Falls State Resort Park, Highway 90, southwest of Corbin; (606) 528-4121. Wide variety of sandwiches and seafood entrees, plus regional specialties such as country ham, served in a family atmosphere.

Dale Hollow Lake State Resort Park, Highway 1206, south of Lake Cumberland; (270) 433-7431. Variety of American dishes and regional specialties. Dinner buffet Friday through Sunday.

Elizabethtown
Stone Hearth Restaurant, Highway 62; (270) 765-4898. Home cooking.

Leitchfield
Rough River Dam State Resort Park, Highway 79; (270) 257-2311.

Renfro Valley
The Lodge Restaurant, I-75, exit 62; (800) 765-7464. Country cooking, with great soup, beans, chicken and dumplings, and chocolate pie.

Somerset
Shiloh Roadhouse, exit 41 at I-75; (606) 877-9363. Steaks, chicken, and ribs, with free peanuts and rolls.

Western Kentucky

The sky seems bigger in the vast, open land of this western region. Sunsets are beautiful, and you can see a storm coming for hours. There's plenty of room for everyone, and everyone's here, from coal miners and bluegrass musicians to Amish farmers and master quilters. There must be something in the soil here because legendary figures have sprung up like weeds: Robert Penn Warren, Edgar Cayce, Casey Jones, Jefferson Davis, and John James Audubon, to name a few. Western Kentucky also boasts some of the best museums in the state, such as Shakertown at South Union, the most southern of all Shaker communities; the Museum of the American Quilter's Society; and the Owensboro Museum of Fine Art.

Most dear to Kentuckians is the Land Between the Lakes, a clean, gorgeous, wild land surrounded by Lake Barkley and Kentucky Lake, a double paradise for fisherfolks. There must be more resorts and marinas per square mile around the Land Between the Lakes area than anywhere else in the state. Stop and ask about camping, cottages, fishing, restaurants, or anything else your heart may desire. American bald eagles also find this region attractive and make their homes here and along the shore of the Mississippi River in the far southwestern region. You'll find western Kentucky quiet, not overdeveloped, yet full of fascinating surprises. The fact that people here have uniquely open spirits gives the traveler a chance to absorb and deeply enjoy the culture of this place.

Jackson Purchase

On the fourth Sunday in May, if you are anywhere near **Benton,** west of the lakes on Highway 641, plan to attend **Big Singing Day,** the only American singing festival that uses the 1835 *Southern Harmony Book* of shape note tunes. (Shape note singing is a traditional form of a cappella that represents the four notes—mi, fa, sol, la—on the staff by a different shape; i.e., diamond, triangle, circle, square, respectively.) This wonderfully nonhierarchical group-singing event has been happening here since 1843. There is no leader and no instrumental

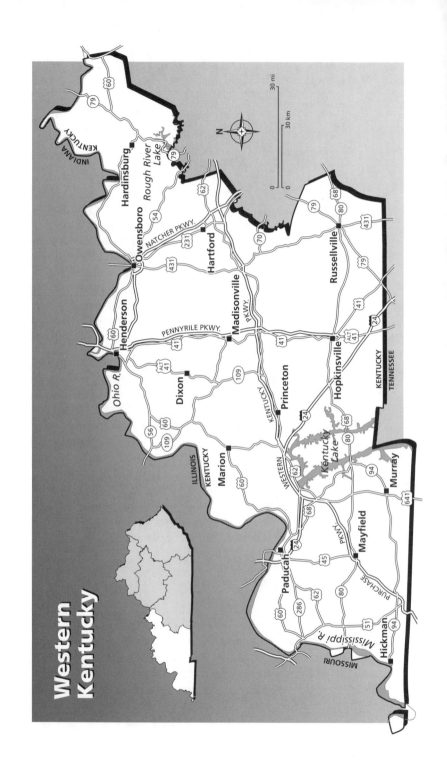

accompaniment, and the songs, usually traditional Welsh hymns, are arranged in parts such that no one sings beyond his or her range. Weather permitting, the singing happens outdoors on the courthouse lawn.

The other big event is Benton's *Tater Day,* held on the first Monday in April since 1843 and one of the world's few events dedicated to the delectable sweet potato. Pay your homage to a great food and enjoy a friendly small-town festival. Activities run the whole weekend, leading up to the day itself.

Just outside Benton in *Draffenville,* the music continues. On any Saturday night of the year and on Fridays in June, July, August, and December, a live country music show is performed by Clay Campbell's *Kentucky Opry.* Locals love this show, so if you're serious about getting to know this region, you've got to stop by and "give a listen." It's a family-oriented place, so children are welcome but alcohol is not. The specialties are country, gospel, and some really hot bluegrass. Regular admission is $9.00 for adults and $4.50 for kids, although tickets for celebrity concerts might be higher. Call (270) 527–3869 or go high-tech and log onto www.kentuckylake.com/kentuckyopry.

While you're aboard the Internet, also check out www.hsrr.com, so you can plan a train excursion aboard the *Hardin Southern Railroad,* based in Hardin, south of Benton via Highway 641. On Saturday and Sunday from Memorial Day through the end of October, two-hour train trips into the beautiful Clarks River Valley depart from the station off Highway 80. When the excursions began in 1994, it had been more than forty years since a passenger train had traveled the route, but at one time the Nashville Chattanooga & St. Louis Railway corridor through western Kentucky was a busy and stylish operation. The railroad works with the Mid-South Rail Heritage Foundation to preserve the 110-year history of rail service in the area, along with antique steam and electric engines. It's a largely volunteer effort, a labor of love for those who escort you on this nostalgic journey. Excursion tickets are $9.95 for adults, $6.00 for children. If you prefer to get

---

ZOÉ'S TOP PICKS IN WESTERN KENTUCKY

American Quilter's Society National Quilt Show and Contest, late April, Paducah; (270) 898–7903 or www.AQSquilt.com

Ben E. Clement Mineral Museum, Marion; (270) 965–4263

The Homeplace 1850, Land Between the Lakes; (270) 924–2000 or (800) 525–7077

John James Audubon State Park, Henderson; (270) 826–2247

Mantle Rock, Joy (care of The Nature Conservancy); (606) 259–9655

Paradise Steam Generation Power Plant Tour, Paradise (near Drakesboro); (270) 476–3301

Seaman's Church Institute, Paducah; (270) 575–1005

Shakertown at South Union, South Union (near Auburn); (270) 542–4167

Trail of Tears Intertribal Pow Wow, the weekend after Labor Day, Hopkinsville; (270) 886–8033

Wickliffe Mounds Research Center, Wickliffe; (270) 335–3681

True Blue

Kentucky is one of only four states to use the designation commonwealth, *meaning government based on common consent of the people.*

your travel information the old-fashioned way, write Hardin Southern Railroad, Inc., Railroad Avenue and Second Street, P.O. Box 20, Hardin 42048, or call (270) 437–4555.

Going south on Highway 641 brings you to the peaceful town of *Murray,* which Rand McNally ranked the "number one retirement location in the country" because of the proximity of outdoor recreational areas, the low crime rate, and the low cost of living. On the Murray State University campus, you can get a free crash course in the history of the region by visiting the *Wrather West Kentucky Museum* (270–762–4771). Hours are Monday through Friday from 8:30 A.M. to 4:00 P.M., Saturday from 10:00 A.M. to 2:00 P.M. The *Clara M. Eagle Gallery* (270–762–3052), on the sixth floor of the Doyle Fine Arts Building on the corner of Olive and Fourteenth Streets, features a wide variety of exhibits from faculty shows, plus nationally touring exhibitions of fine art and fine craft.

For classy lodging in Murray, consider the *Diuguid House Bed and Breakfast* (603 Main Street, Murrary 42071; 888–261–3028). Hosts Karen and George Chapman serve a full breakfast, avoiding what they refer to as the four basic elements of Southern cooking: "salt, sugar, grease, and grit." The very Victorian house, which is now on the National

Authentic to the End

*C*ivil War reenactors (and Kentucky has a slew of them) often take their reenactment quite seriously, insisting on meticulous detail and authenticity in their uniforms and accessories, and often adopting the total identity of soldiers from the past. Carrying this thought to its ultimate conclusion was one of the inspirations for **Bert & Bud's Vintage Coffins,** of Murray. Roy "Bud" Davis and Albert "Bert" Sperath, respectively the former and current director of the Clara M. Eagle Art Gallery at Murray State University, create nineteenth-century "toe pincher–style" and other unique coffins at a studio in Sperath's

garage. So far, business hasn't been exactly lively, but one Murray antiques buff ordered a coffin for use as a coffee table, and a Nova Scotia customer plans to use one in a theatrical production. Meanwhile, they're looking at lighter sidelines. They also built a whimsical coffin that looks like a dollhouse for Davis's wife. "She has no intention of using it for a long time," he noted. "Our market is really not for people who need a coffin now, but for people who want something different and tend to plan ahead." Give Davis a call at (877) 371–9279 or (270) 753–9279 if you're interested in stopping by while you're in Murray.

Register of Historic Places, affords guests all kinds of spaces for living, from private nooks for reading to a large veranda for socializing. Rooms start at $40 per night.

Speaking of socializing, **Rudy's Restaurant** (270–753–1632), on the west side of the courthouse square, is so crowded at lunchtime that you may have to sit with a stranger if you're determined to have a fresh hamburger and homemade onion rings. This little place has been open since the early 1930s, when the original Rudy made it famous for its consistently good country cooking and cutting-edge gossip. Rudy, a short, roly-poly fellow whose lip never knew the absence of a cigar, collected money and spread the news of the day from a stool behind the big brass cash register. Monday through Saturday breakfast starts at 5:00 A.M., and lunch ends at 2:00 P.M.

True Blue

In addition to an official state song ("My Old Kentucky Home" by Stephen C. Foster), Kentucky also has an official bluegrass song, "Blue Moon of Kentucky" by Rosine, Kentucky, native Bill Monroe.

Take Highway 94 East and go about 8 miles out of downtown Murray. Watch for a shop on the right side of the road with curving bent willow chairs in the yard and a sign by the driveway indicating the **House of Willow.** This is the workshop of Alfred Duncan, an extraordinary, thrifty chair maker. Regardless of the fact that this style of outdoor furniture, sometimes called "stick furniture," is in vogue at the moment, this craft has lasting integrity. Just like the gypsies who sold willow chairs in this area in the early 1930s, Alfred and his master-teacher from down the road a piece, George Beard, go to riverbanks in Kentucky and all over swampy areas of the South to gather red and white willow trees, which are bent and nailed into place while green. Nothing is wasted; the large stock is used for heavy supports, thin branches are twisted into decorative backs or armrests, and the very thinnest trees, some as young as six months, are used as "benders," pliable pieces that make accommodating seats. Sit in any chair, love seat, or rocker and your body will understand that the Shakers couldn't have designed them better. The choices of branch size and spacing create a simple and visually stunning effect. Beard has become something of a regional treasure. In 1978 the Smithsonian bought one of his hooded chairs in red willow for its permanent collection; a dark red Indian willow love seat is in a museum in Utah; and the Kentucky Museum in Frankfort exhibits a settee and child's chair. George claims not to be able to tell his own work apart from Alfred's. These are craftsmen not to miss. Alfred works every day during business hours, including weekends. For more information. call (270) 759–9595.

Hazel, just south of Murray on Highway 641, was one of the towns that sprang up in the 1890s as the railroad connected western Kentucky with the rest of the world. The town may have been named for the daughter of the conductor of the first through train, although other Hazels are also in contention. Samuel H. Dees, who founded the Hazel Post Office, also had a daughter named Hazel. Some think the name refers to the thick hazel groves that grow in the area. In more recent times, Hazel has made a name for itself as an antique lovers' haven. The town's charming turn-of-the-century storefronts are now home to dozens of antiques malls and shops; one count placed more than 250 dealers active in the community. So bring your measuring tape, your magnet, your price guides, and your checkbook, and plan to spend all day wandering from shop to shop. *Charlie's Antique Mall* on Main Street also has an old-fashioned soda fountain.

As you leave Bell City, going north on Highway 97, watch for **Murdocks' Mausoleum,** a semiunderground building with a sign on the top that reads, STOP SEE A ROAD MAP TO HEAVEN. Who wouldn't stop? On the wall of the porch is a large painted sign describing how one can get to heaven—the gospel of John is heavily quoted. Behind a decorative iron door and window one can view the burial area. The graves of two women take up perhaps a sixth of the burial space, leaving the rest free for future occupants.

Get back on Highway 94 and head west to Cayce. On the west side of town, look for the *Henson Broom Shop Museum.* What appears to be a perfectly maintained old country store is actually Richard N. Henson's broom-making shop. With a few simple pieces of equipment, three generations of skill, piles of sticks, heaps of broom straw, and lots

Selected Sources of Travel Information for the Jackson Purchase Area

Kentucky's Western Waterland Tourist Information Center,
721 Complex Drive, Grand Rivers 42045; (270) 928–4411. Stop by in person by taking exit 31 off I–24 at Grand Rivers and follow the signs. (Note the small herd of buffalo on the opposite side of the highway.)

Mayfield Tourism Commission, *201 East College Street, Mayfield 42066; (502) 247–6101*

Paducah/McCracken County Convention and Visitors Bureau,
128 Broadway, Paducah 42001; (270) 443–8783, (800) PADUCAH, or www.paducah-tourism.org

of energy, Henson makes hundreds of graceful, functional brooms. His grandfather, also Richard N. Henson, started making brooms in 1930 when the American economy was faltering and the family needed more income. The elder Henson liked to say, "A Hoover put me into business, and a Hoover put me out of business," referring to the President and the vacuum cleaner, respectively.

Today the third-generation broom maker is rarely out of work. During the summer and fall, Henson converts his horse trailer into a portable workshop, dons a costume, and travels to festivals where he does historic craft reenactment, educating the public while he works. (He has been winning blue ribbons for his craftsmanship all over the country.) Brooms have changed very little during the past hundred years. If you watched the television show *Dr. Quinn, Medicine Woman* before it was canceled, you probably saw Henson's brooms for sale in the show's general store and in use by the characters. To his array of old-fashioned kitchen, shop, whisk, cabin, Colonial hearth, Shaker, and parlor brooms, Henson has added a fancy, twisted-handle design he calls the "Jane Seymour Broom" in honor of the show's star. Prices range from

A Festival Whose Ap-peel Is Remembered

*F*ulton, Kentucky, a fence-sitting town on the Kentucky-Tennessee border (South Fulton is in the Volunteer State), reminds me of that old song, "Yes, We Have No Bananas." Once, Fulton, had plenty of 'em. For decades, wholesalers from all over the country came to Fulton to buy bananas, which were shipped from South America via New Orleans to the largest icehouse in the United States in, you guessed it, Fulton. In 1962 the town started the annual International Banana Festival, which featured the "world's largest banana pudding." One year the publicly made pudding topped 2 tons in order to make it into The Guinness Book of World Records. Changing times, however, were catching up with Fulton, and in the festival's last years,

the town had to practically beg for bananas. So in 1992, the festival was disbanded. In a way, though, you can still experience it, in a children's illustrated story published online by Indiana author and illustrator Jerry Jindrich. Through tales and drawings, Jerry and his wife, Susan, have created an educational fantasy world online called the "Island of Meddybemps, home of Chateau Meddybemps." One of the stories, titled "But That Wasn't the Best Part," was inspired by the International Banana Festival, which Jerry attended one year. Wonder what the best part was? Visit www.meddybemps.com and find out a little about a Kentucky town's festival that will always ap-peel to the imagination.

$5.00 to more than $50.00 He's glad to have visitors, so stop by any-time. You can call him at (270) 838–6652 or write him at 101 Clinton Street, Hickman 42050.

R. N. Henson likes his town, and although the mailing address is in Hickman, he puts Cayce on his business cards. Another young man who put this town on the map was the daredevil railroad engineer John Luther Jones (better known as Casey Jones), who was "yanked-up" here. When he got his first job with the Illinois Central, there were so many Joneses that his boss nicknamed him "Cayce." The legend that developed around him after his death somehow also corrupted the spelling to "Casey," but folks here haven't forgotten.

True Blue

Mark Twain called Hickman "the most beautiful town on the Mississippi."

In downtown **Hickman,** next to the chamber of commerce, is the shop of **J. M. Cooper,** Old World–style tinkerer extraordinaire. Although he makes and repairs guns and jewelry, Cooper is best known for his work on clocks. The shop is filled with all kinds of modern and antique clocks, some of his own, some belonging to townspeople (the mayor told me that J. M. has had at least ten of her clocks for at least a decade), but his pride and joy—the courthouse clock—rises high above everything else on the bluff. In 1974 J. M. completely rebuilt the innards of the old Seth Thomas, originally installed in 1904. The clock parts weigh almost 2 tons, the bell about 2,800 pounds, and the striking hammer a hefty 40 pounds. Few such clocks are in operation, and fewer yet are still wound by hand; every eight days "Coop" climbs the long stairs of the clock tower and winds. On slow days, when he's feeling up to it, he'll take people up. His shop hours are by chance, so call the chamber ahead at (270) 236–2902 to find out if J. M. is in.

The **Warren Thomas Black Museum,** 603 Moulton Street, Hickman 42050, preserves history of the town's African-American community. The building itself is one of the most significant artifacts; it's an 1890 church, Thomas Chapel, founded by former slaves. The chapel was named for "Uncle Warren" and "Aunt Sally" Thomas, who gave the land for the building. Warren Thomas was the congregation's first minister. In 1895 the original building burned and the present building was built to replace it. For decades it served as a school and center of community life for African-American citizens in Hickman. The old Thomas Chapel building became a Kentucky Landmark in 1978. Tours are given by appointment; call (270) 236–2535.

From Hickman you can take the **Hickman-Dorena Ferry** across the Mississippi River to Missouri. A one-way trip is $8.00; round trip is $12.00. The ferry runs daily except Christmas Day.

From Hickman you can also follow Highway 94 southwest to **Reelfoot Lake.** The part of the lake that is in Kentucky (most is in Tennessee) is wild, beautiful swampland. During the winter of 1811–12, a series of earthquakes along the New Madrid fault shook the whole region so violently that the tremors made bells ring as far away as Pittsburgh, Pennsylvania. Reelfoot Lake was created when the quakes caused the Mississippi River to run backwards; when it returned to its usual flow, it straightened out and left behind one of its old curves. Look at your map and the abandoned bend will become obvious. Admire the large stands of bald cypress trees. Their lower trunks are broad, flaring like upside-down flying buttresses; the needles are feathery and fine; and they're surrounded by their own "knees," or cone-shaped roots, which seem to emerge from the water independently. These roots make it possible for the large trees to remain upright in the muddy soils. Follow Highway 94 southwest to the Reelfoot Lake National Wildlife Refuge and talk to the rangers about the local wildlife.

The only way to go farther west in Kentucky is to drive down Highway 94 into Tennessee, where it becomes Highway 78. From Tiptonville, Tennessee, follow the signs to the Madrid Bend, also known as Kentucky Bend or Bessie Bend. A few families have the peninsula to themselves to farm however they please.

North of Hickman and "inland" a bit, on Highway 51, is the town of **Clinton,** home to the new **Hickman County Museum,** which is a testament to the spirit of local devotion to local history. Volunteers and a museum board renovated an 1870s house (once belonging to Captain Henry Cruse Watson, who fought with the Confederate army) at 221 East Clay Street, Clinton 42031. Each of nine rooms presents thematically grouped artifacts (all of which were donated), from the College Room to the Medical Room. Items on display range from historic military uniforms, an early 1900s fire-hose cart designed to be pulled by two men on foot, political mementos associated with "local boy" Alben W. Barkley, pottery made by prehistoric peoples called Mound Builders, and all sorts of agricultural tools. Hours are 1:00 to 4:00 P.M. on Wednesday

True Blue

Alben W. Barkley was born in 1877 in Graves County and raised there in relative poverty before his steady political climb from law clerk to county attorney to U.S. congressman, senator, and finally, in 1949, to vice president in the second administration of President Harry S. Truman.

and Saturday, or by appointment. Admission is $1.00. For more information, call (270) 653–6566.

In the center of the Jackson Purchase region is the town of *Mayfield,* known to outsiders for *The Wooldridge Monuments,* "the strange procession that never moves," in the cemetery. The entrance to the Maplewood Cemetery is in town at the intersection of the Highway 45 overpass and North Seventh Street. The eighteen-figure group in sandstone and Italian marble was erected in the late 1890s by an otherwise inconsequential bloke named Henry G. Wooldridge. Though he is the only person buried on the site, the figures represent him on his favorite horse, Fop; him standing by a podium; two hounds, a fox, and a deer; and his three sisters, four brothers, mother, and two great-nieces, one of whom, rumor has it, actually resembles Henry's first love, Minnie, who died in her youth. Legend has it that when the statues were en route from Paducah, a drunk climbed on the flat railcar and mounted the stone horse behind the stone Wooldridge to ride into Mayfield, the drunk king of a mute parade.

If you aren't sure whether or nor you are really in the South, you will be when you encounter another memorial in town in right in the center of town square, because it's dedicated to Mayfield's Confederate dead. More local history is explained just blocks away in the *Western Kentucky Museum* at 120 North Eighth Street, Mayfield 42066, at the corner of West North Street. The museum of artifacts dating back to the late nineteenth century includes lots of regional business and agricultural paraphernalia, particularly pertaining to tobacco. Also housed in the restored

Bobbie Ann Mason

*M*ayfield is the hometown of Bobbie Ann Mason, one of America's most perceptive and powerful writers. If you've read her work, you'll feel you've been in this region before. Her fiction is intensely crafted and rich in realistic detail, and her characters seem familiar, not at all larger-than-life. Mason says, "Like me, these characters are emerging from a rural way of life that is fast disappearing, and they are wondering where they're going to end up." Her novels include Feather Crowns, Spence + Lila, *and the powerful work about the effect of the war in Vietnam on rural Americans,* In Country, *which was made into a well-loved movie by the same title. She has written many short stories and recently published a selection of her favorites called* Midnight Magic, *which will make you seek out all her short fiction. Mason lives in Kentucky and still has family in Mayfield.*

icehouse building is the *Graves County Art Guild,* which showcases local painting and sculpture. Both are open Tuesday through Saturday from 10:00 A.M. to 4:00 P.M.

Stanley Boekout has built houses and furniture all of his life. Upon retirement, however, he switched scales and now builds dollhouses. He even creates customs-built miniature replicas of real-world homes, complete with miniature furniture, carpets, kitchen accoutrements, lamps that plug into outlets (yes, he can wire them for electric service), and birdhouses for the yard. His shop, *Wood 'n Crafts,* is attached to his house, just south of Mayfield at 1312 Highway 303, Mayfield 42066, and he welcomes visitors. Most every day the shop is open from 8:00 A.M. to 5:00 P.M. Custom orders are welcome, so bring blueprints.

A great place to eat in town is the *Hills Barbecue* (270–247–9121). Coming from Murray by Highway 121 north, it's on the left at the Y intersection of Cuba and Paris Roads, next to McDonald's. In business since 1949, the place is known for homemade pies and any-way-you-want-it sandwiches. It has a big porch for summer eating, a drive-in window, indoor tables, and a long sociable counter. The decor has definite allure. I tried, in vain, to buy an old tin John Ruskin cigar sign—best and biggest. Hours are 7:00 A.M. to 10:00 P.M. Monday through Saturday.

Fiery debates and pit barbecue are at the heart of the *Fancy Farm Picnic,* perhaps the sole survivor of grassroots political-campaign picnics in America. *The Guinness Book of World Records* lists it as the world's largest one-day picnic, not surprising when more than 15,000 pounds of fresh pork and mutton are cooked annually. The first Saturday in August at 10:00 A.M., games and entertainment begin, country-goods booths go up, and local, state and national political figures rile the crowds, one way or another. Speeches are given from a red, white, and blue bunting-covered flatbed wagon, just like in 1880, when the picnic was established as the last opportunity for candidates to meet before the August primaries. Because the primaries are now held in May, the picnic functions as a debate forum for the final candidates. Fancy Farm is 10 miles west of Mayfield on Highway 80, at its junction with Highway 339.

Does talking politics make your head reel? Try reeling in a live fish instead. (Though both can emanate less-than-delicate aromas . . .) West of Fancy Farm, near Arlington at the corner of Highway 80 and County Route 1130, is *Grogan's Pay Lake* (270–655–2470). If your luck leaves your line empty, bring a catch home anyhow from the Fresh Fish Market.

Due west on Highway 80 in Hickman County is the low-lying river town of *Columbus.* Slightly upriver, between Columbus and Clinton, the

Where, Oh Where Did Wolf Island Go?

*H*ickman County is missing a tooth. Sometime between 1820 and 1870 a channel of the Mississippi River shifted to the east, leaving a 9,000-acre chunk of Kentucky land stranded in Missouri, nearly a mile west of the rest of the county. Despite its new location, in 1871 the Supreme Court awarded the land, now called Wolf Island, to Kentucky, thereby denying the big daddy of all waters the power to move official boundaries.

Columbus-Belmont Battlefield State Park (270–677–2327) perches on 200-foot-high palisades. The park marks the Civil War site of the westernmost Confederate fortification in Kentucky. Rebel soldiers installed a whopping mile-long chain, held afloat by wooden rafts, across the Mississippi River to prevent Union gunboats from moving south. Each link of the chain weighed 15 pounds, and the anchor attached to it was six tons. Cannons were lined up on the face of the bluffs. Shortly after the fortification was complete, Union forces led by Ulysses S. Grant took the town in 1861 when Confederate forces were crumbling everywhere. It's a pleasantly dizzying picnic and camping site, and the park has a little museum of early Native American artifacts and Civil War relics, including chain links, the anchor, and cannons from the river blockade. The museum is open only on weekends in April and October, daily May through September.

True Blue

Kentucky Lake and Lake Barkley together form one of the largest engineered lakes in the United States.

Follow Highway 123 north to Bardwell, then take I–51 north to Wickliffe. Every Memorial Day weekend from Wickliffe to Fulton, on the Tennessee border, Highway 51 is lined with flea markets and yard sales. If you can't find junk to your heart's desire on that weekend, you ain't never gonna find it.

Go through Wickliffe as if you were crossing the river to Cairo, Illinois, and look for signs to the ***Wickliffe Mounds Research Center*** (270–335–3681). You'll understand why the Mississippian Indians chose this site as a town or ceremonial grounds when you stand on the highest mound and look out toward the wide sparkling junction of two massive rivers, the Ohio and the Mississippi. The scene is exhilarating. In addition to the intact, four-sided, flat-topped "ceremonial mound," three excavation areas have been preserved and interpreted for the public.

True Blue

Paducah was founded in 1827 by William Lewis (of Lewis and Clark).

One of the most significant displays is in the cemetery. Without being eerie or morbid, the space is moving. The bodies were buried close together, each surrounded by a few significant belongings, each facing east as if to remain in contact with the cycle of days and nights. The display explains how archaeologists determine diet, illnesses, typical injuries, and physical appearances by analyzing the remains of people who weren't radically different from us. All the actual human remains and burial goods have been replaced with plastic replicas in their original positions. This seriously self-examining display deals with various points of view, including a Native American view, about the appropriate study and treatment of human remains. The curators and Native American advisers are working toward making Wickliffe Mounds into a ceremonial site, as it was thousands of years ago. Hours are 9:00 A.M. to 4:30 P.M. daily from March to November. Admission is $4.00 for adults, $3.00 for children. If you want to try your hand at excavation, check into summer field school at the Mounds. Write to the Wickliffe Mounds Research Center, P.O. Box 155, Wickliffe 42087.

About 6 miles northeast of Wickliffe on Highway 60 is the town of Barlow, and in it a museum called the *Barlow House Museum,* on the corner of Broadway and Fifth Street, which pays tribute to the early history of Ballard County by preserving the home and belongings of a family that helped settle the region. In 1849 Thomas Jefferson Barlow bought land but didn't want to farm, so he opened a general store and started selling lots for houses. Like many an American town, that's how Barlow was

The Most Debated Place Name in Kentucky

*I*f you've become hooked on digressions, here's an opportunity to indulge. Continue from Barlow on Highway 60 east to La Center and take Highway 358 north, then go west on Highway 473 through Ogden (once called Needmore) to **Monkey's Eyebrow,** the most debated place name in the state of Kentucky. There is no post office, hence no official name, but we argue nonetheless. Journalist Byron Crawford submits the idea that, if one looks at the shape of the northern boundary of Ballard County, the Ohio River forms a rough profile of a monkey in such a way that this community is just where the eyebrow would be. Others say that there was a store owned by John and Dodge Ray, the brothers who settled the sandy loam ridge in the late nineteenth century, and behind it was a berm that resembled a monkey's eyebrow because it was covered with tall grasses. New theories are welcome fuel for the fire.

born. The fully restored 1903 Victorian home belonged to Thomas's oldest son, Clifton J. Barlow, and remained in the Barlow family until 1989. The house is open to the public for tours Monday, Friday, and every other Sunday from 1:00 to 4:00 P.M., or by appointment, and also for meetings, receptions, and so forth. Contact Della Johnson for more information at (270) 334–3010 or (270) 334–3691.

To get in touch with nature, go east on Highway 60 until you reach Future City. Turn left (northeast) on Highway 996 and go almost 6 miles to where the road ends in a strange swampy landscape. The Kentucky State Nature Preserves Commission has purchased **Metropolis Lake** in order to protect this intriguing little naturally formed body of water and the surrounding river floodplain from destructive development. Fishing is permitted here because anglers drool over the lake's population of fish and because people take good care of the area. Although the lake area used to be a developed commercial recreation area, today it is more pure, an enchanted dreamscape with bald cypress and swamp tupelo trees casting strange shapes against the sky and even stranger reflections on the water. Beavers, kingfishers, wildflowers, and seven rare aquatic species are among the many living creatures that share this special space. If you have questions, call the commission at (502) 564–2886.

Stay on Highway 60 and go east into **Paducah,** the urban center of the Jackson Purchase region. As you near the downtown area, look for Noble Park on the west side of the road. Stop when you come across an enormous, haunting sculpture of a Chickasaw Indian. The piece, called **Wacinton,** or "to have understanding," was carved from a 56,000-pound red oak tree by Hungarian-born sculptor Peter "Wolf" Toth in 1985. Toth donated the piece to the city of Paducah and the state of Kentucky in honor of the Native American people who lived in the area before the Jackson Purchase, in 1818. In 1972, at the age of twenty-five, Toth decided to carve a giant Native American sculpture for every state in the Union. He refuses pay. His "trail of whispering giants" is his gift to our national conscience. He identifies with the suffering of Native Americans because he and his family lost everything when they fled Hungary in 1956 just before the communist revolution. Paducah's *Wacinton* is his fiftieth sculpture. After the United States, he says he'll be carving in Canada, then Mexico.

The people of Paducah have renovated and preserved a once-dilapidated Classical Revival mansion by making it into the **Whitehaven Welcome Center,** south of town on I–24, and filling it with antique furniture from the area. Get travel information here, or call the center at (270) 554–2077. Tours are available from 1:00 to 4:00 P.M. daily.

Wacinton

In downtown Paducah between Broadway and Kentucky Avenues is the Market House, the hub of business and trade since 1836. Today the building houses three arts organizations. The **Market House Museum** (270–443–7759) is a regional history museum that includes the reconstructed interior of an 1877 drugstore. Hours are noon to 4:00 P.M. Tuesday through Saturday from March through December. Admission is $1.50. The **Yeiser Art Center** and gift shop (270–442–2453) hangs traveling exhibits of contemporary and traditional art. Hours are 10:00 A.M. to 4:00 P.M. Tuesday through Saturday. Admission is $1.00. Also in the building is the **Market House Theatre** (270–444–6828), a not-for-profit community theater—check its busy production schedule.

Across the street, the **Paducah Harbor Plaza** is a five-story yellow brick building with stained-glass windows and ornate sandstone cornices. Beverly McKinley has opened a bed-and-breakfast on the second floor, making accommodations available in high style as they were when the place was called the Hotel Belvedere. For between $65 and $125 a night, one or two people get a renovated bedroom appointed with antiques and handmade quilts, and a continental breakfast. In the morning, guests get first crack at the women's apparel and rich fabrics, buttons, and quilt and clothing patterns in Dogwood Lane, a store on the first floor of the plaza that caters to quilters. For lodging information, call (270) 442–2698 or (800) 719–7799.

When people think of Kentucky crafts, quilts are often the first things that come to mind. Since April 1991, Paducah immediately comes to mind as the quilt capital of America, thanks to the *Museum of the American Quilter's Society,* downtown at the corner of Second and Jefferson Streets. Those of us who have grown up around (or under) handmade quilts and have taken them for granted can't help but be awestruck with the beauty and variety of the quilts in the museum. Unlike many collections in the region, this museum is primarily devoted to the modern quilt. Those who appreciate abstract painting may find a new passion in the bold shapes and colors of these "canvases."

In addition to the main display area of more than 150 quilts from the permanent collection and the two additional galleries with quilts from traveling exhibitions, the 30,000-square-foot building has a climate-controlled vault, classrooms, a gift shop, and an excellent bookstore that features more than 400 books pertaining to quilting and textiles. The museum is open Tuesday through Saturday from 10:00 A.M. to 5:00 P.M. year-round. From April through October it is also open Sunday from 1:00 to 5:00 P.M., Monday from 10:00 A.M. to 5:00 P.M. Admission is $5.00 for adults, $3.00 for students. For more information, call (270) 442–8856. Three-day quilt-making workshops taught by renowned quilters from across the country are offered every year. For schedules, write MAQS/Workshop Program, P.O. Box 1540, Paducah 42002-1540.

Also contributing to Paducah's position as Quilt City USA is the annual *AQS National Quilt Show and Contest,* sponsored by the Paducah-based American Quilter's Society. This national quilt extravaganza is held in late April at the Executive Inn Convention Center in downtown Paducah. More than 400 quilts from all over the world are displayed and judged to win a part of the $75,000-plus in cash awards. During that week the whole city is overflowing with quilts. Special workshops and lectures are offered, quilt supply vendors set up shop, and there's even a fashion show and contest. Hotel space is at a premium during the show, so plan ahead. For show information, write to AQS, P.O. Box 3290, Paducah 42002-3290, or call (270) 898–7903. Or visit the Web site at www.AQSquilt.com.

Within sight of the Museum of the American Quilter's Society are two other sites not to be missed by quilt aficionados. Look for a huge painted mural of a quilt on the side of a building at 119 North Fourth Street. Inside is *King's Quilting Studio* (270–444–7477), the showroom, studio, and classroom of Sara Newberg King. In addition to fine quilts, you'll find hand-dyed silk scarves and other wearable art by King. Ask about special classes and lectures. And if you're saturated with looking and ready to get to work, continue up the street to 420 North Fourth Street, where *Quilter's Alley* offers a plethora of quilting supplies and gorgeous fabrics. Classes are offered regularly, and these knowledgeable folks can make appraisals. For more information call (270) 443–5673.

Right in the hub of old downtown Paducah at 114–118 Market House Square is the business you wish was next door every day. Five generations of German bakers have titillated taste buds at *Kirchhoff's Bakery and Deli* since it was established in 1873. Traditional as the skills are, the owners have stayed current and now offer a range of gourmet market items, deli cheeses, and fresh vegetables, as well as to-die-for breads and pastries. Lunch is served daily from 11:00 A.M. to 2:00 P.M., and the calzones go fast. Hours are Monday through Friday from 7:00 A.M. to 5:00 P.M. and Saturday from 8:00 A.M. to 3:00 P.M.

One of Paducah's most unique and geographically relevant institutions is the *Seaman's Church Institute,* which is perched just to the dry side of the confluence of the Tennessee and Ohio Rivers at 111 Kentucky Avenue. This is the only official Center for Maritime Education that trains riverboat captains to navigate freshwater inland rivers. Take a tour to watch students learn the ropes in a sophisticated river navigation simulation system. Because it is a busy, professional school, you must make reservations in advance by calling (270) 575–1005. Adjoining the maritime school is the brand new *River Heritage Museum,* housed in a beautifully restored 1843 Federal Bank Building (said to be the oldest remaining structure in the downtown area) at 117 South Water Street, Paducah 42001. Some exhibits are already open; when completed, the museum will feature an interesting blend of traditional displays of artifacts, photographs, and so forth, with high-tech fiber optics maps and interactive touch-screen computer stations. The focus is on the cultures of the region shaped by the Ohio, Tennessee, Mississippi, and Cumberland Rivers, beginning with the survival techniques of early indigenous peoples and ending with an exploration of life on the rivers in the present. Call (270) 575–9958 for additional information and hours. If you're reading this

True Blue

before the museum opens, you can make an appointment to view the work in progress.

When you step outside the front doors of the museum, you're facing the confluence of two of the four rivers, the Ohio and the Tennessee. You're also facing a marvelous artistic vista that was created along the city's flood walls—some twenty-two murals showing scenes from Paducah history. The **Paducah Flood Wall Murals** were all created by Robert Dafford, a Louisiana artist noted for his large-scale public works in the United States and Europe.

Downtown Paducah itself seems somewhat larger than life itself during the summer **After Dinner Downtown Paducah** events. Each Saturday night, from the first Saturday in May through the second weekend in October, is like a mini-festival, with music on the street corners, antique car displays, carriage rides, and late shop hours. The events attract lively crowds. Contact the tourism office at (800) PADU-CAH for more information.

Civil War buffs, take heed! The taking of Paducah by the Union in 1861 marks a significant moment in the war—when Kentucky finally lost its neutrality. The Union was responding to the recent Confederate victory at the nearby Mississippi River town of Columbus. This and other war stories are explained through artifacts, documents, and photographs at the **Tilghman Civil War Heritage Center,** at the corner of Seventh and Kentucky Avenues. The restored house was once home to a Confederate general, Lloyd Tilghman, who defended the Tennessee and Cumberland Rivers and was finally killed in action near Vicksburg. Tours of the center are available by calling (270) 575–1870. Eight other relevant Civil War sites in downtown Paducah can be seen on a free walking tour. Stop by the visitors bureau at 128 Broadway, Paducah 42001, for a map.

Pennyroyal Region

Tennessee Valley Authority's (TVA) **Land Between the Lakes** national recreation area is considered the "crappie fishing capital of the world," not to mention the huge populations of largemouth and smallmouth bass—an angler's dream come true. The Tennessee River was dammed to make Kentucky Lake, and Lake Barkley was formed from the mighty Cumberland River. Together they comprise 220,000 acres of clean, safe water and form a 40-mile-long peninsula, which the TVA has developed for recreation and education.

For bird lovers, Land Between the Lakes, or LBL, is one of a scant hand-ful of places where one can get a glimpse of wild bald eagles. In the 1960s poaching and the use of chemicals such as DDT reduced the number of breeding eagles to fewer than 600 pairs, making our national mascot nearly extinct on this continent. The wildlife management peo-ple at LBL successfully got the numbers back up by returning raptors to a natural habitat with very little human contact. Ask about eagle and wildlife programs at the Woodlands Nature Center. During the winter, eagle field trips are scheduled for the weekends.

Photographers can get close-up pictures of these marvelous creatures in captivity at the nature center, or if you're lucky and very patient, in the wild. Throughout the year there's plenty for nature enthusiasts to see and do. In addition to plenty of lake access ramps, there are great hiking trails, ranging from 0.2 to 65 miles in length. (The easy **Center Furnace Trail** goes past a historic iron furnace.) You can also rent a bicycle or a canoe. One of the natural programs has been an effort to reintroduce endangered wildlife species. LBL is home to the nation's largest public herd of bison, and in 1996, elk were released into the area. You may be able to see these animals along a self-guided driving tour of the **Elk & Bison Prairie.** At the Golden Pond Visitors Center, there's a small planetarium. And if you drive to the southern end of LBL (actu-ally in Tennessee), you can walk around **The Homeplace 1850,** set up as a working nineteenth-century homestead. Enter the park from any direction—Highways 68, 94, 641, 24, or in Tennessee, Highways 79 or 76—and go to the North, South, or Golden Pond Visitors Centers for directions and information about the park. For information about any of the attractions in Land Between the Lakes, call (800) LBL–7077.

If you're not in the mood for camping but are in the mood for unusual lodging, try **Our Kentucky Home Inn,** 8534 Canton Road (Highway 68), Cadiz 42211. Not far from Lake Barkley Resort Park, this is a con-verted leather shop building with large beams and cathedral ceilings. Rates are $49 to $59. Call (270) 924–5850 for reservations. The inn's large dining room is open to the public.

If you're hungry and caught smack-dab between a lake and a wet place, pull into **Patti's 1880's Settlement,** home of the Mile-High Meringue Pie, the 2-inch-thick pork chop, and bread baked in a flowerpot. With five gift shops, two restaurants, a miniature-golf course, and an animal park, Patti's seems like a continuation of the dream that a young multi-millionaire, Thomas Lawson, had for the town in the 1880s when he found it nestled between the Cumberland and Tennessee Rivers. Law-son changed the town's name from Nichols Landing to Grand Rivers and built himself a resort town with the theme of Southern hospitality. Now that the rivers have been dammed, it should be renamed Grand Lakes, but . . . Patti's Restaurant, owned by the Tullar family, and a perennial favorite with both seasonal and twelve-month diners, is open year-round from 10:30 A.M. to 8:00 P.M. every day. Other activities vary some. Call (270) 362–8844 for specifics.

At the Grand Rivers exit, number 31 off I–24, Kentucky's Western Waterland regional tourism information center (270–928–4411) is an important spot to stop and gather information. While you're there, look carefully at the pasture across the highway—there's a small herd of buffalo just like those that roamed these plains in the hundreds of thousands before European settlement.

An interesting loop drive in this area is along a bit of Lake Barkley's shore. Go to **Kuttawa,** a town with a name that means "beautiful" in Shawnee: From I–24 take exit 40, turn south on Highway 62, then turn south on Highway 295. You'll curve along the rim of the lake (gorgeous at sunset) toward Kuttawa. Just as you get to town, look for a public parking area on the lake side and, if it's summer, stop for a little walk along the "Kuttawa cliffs," where you may be lucky enough to watch daring locals do some cliff diving into the deep water. In downtown metropolis Kuttawa there's a beach, marina, and harbor with a restaurant famous for its generous "Rudyburger." To complete the loop, stay on Highway 295 until

Living Near the Pokey

*I*f you stand on the lakeside near Kuttawa and look across the water, you will see a massive monolithic stone fortress perched on a peninsula that is reminiscent of Alcatraz. This is the Kentucky State Penitentiary at Eddyville, Kentucky's only maximum-security prison. Growing up, whenever kids were reprimanded, someone would say, "Keep that up, and we'll be coming to visit you in Eddyville." A woman who actually grew up in Eddyville in a house just up the hill from the pen told of being in the kitchen and hearing prisoners bang chains against their bars as a form of protest and seeing the men hang white sheets out prison windows with written pleas to the outside world stating their dire need for a new warden. It spooked her to think that the prisoners could see their free neighbors and were bold enough to attempt communication. She also remembered the more trusted old lifers being allowed to sell trinkets by the front gate on Sunday afternoon. One old man gave her a shellacked peach-pit necklace because she reminded him of his own little ones far away.

it intersects with Highway 62, at which point you can go whichever direction your trip is taking you. Both the Western Kentucky Parkway and I–24 are nearby. If you're ready to get off the highway and get out of your car, you could try climbing in the saddle and hitting the trail. *The Pebble Creek Riding Stable* offers guided tours through the woods, full-moon trail rides, and cowboy-style catered parties and cookouts. Group rates are available, but generally it costs $12 per hour per person. It's open every day, but in the winter you'll need to make an appointment. Call (270) 388–4747 for directions and more information.

The Davis House, a bed-and-breakfast in Kuttawa, offers lodging over-looking the lake. The house is named for the family that bought it in 1953 and moved it to its present location when the lake was created. Current owner Betty Dixon bought the 120-year-old house in 1989. There are five guest rooms, along with a lakeside patio and nearby boat dock. Rooms are $65 per night. Call (800) 259–4546 or (270) 388–5585 for reservations.

One bed (no breakfast) that is worth a visit ranks among Kentucky's most unusual grave markers. Stay on Main Street (also Highway 295), going north until the road splits into separate high and low lanes, and look to the left for the entrance to the city cemetery. When the cemetery driveway forces you to go either right or left, go right. In about 100 feet you will reach a grave that is on the left under a large oak tree and next to a tall obelisk. The marker is a life-size double-bed frame made of stone, beneath which are buried Eliza Jane and Charles Anderson. Married for sixty years, they moved to this marriage bed in 1901 and 1895, respectively. It's a beautiful marker and eerie, too. You'll see.

Due north of Eddyville, if you were to drive aboveground on Highway 641, you'd pass through Fredonia and Crayne before entering the busy little town of *Marion.* If you were to drive several hundred feet underground, you might just pass through sparkling veins of the amazingly beautiful mineral, fluorspar. Unlike diamond, fluorspar is beautiful in its natural state, just as you'd find in the walls of the underground highway on which you're traveling. Fluorspar, the industrial name for fluorite, the nonmetallic mineral calcium fluoride, is the primary source for the tooth-decay retardant, as well as an important material used in the production of aluminum, zinc, some ceramics, and a whole range of chemicals. During and after World War II, Kentucky was the largest producer of the mineral in the United States.

For an actual tour (not virtual or imaginary) of some of the most interesting and varied samples of these crystals to be found anywhere, head down Main Street in Marion, then right on First Street, and watch for the signs to the **Ben E. Clement Mineral Museum,** 205 North Walker Street, Marion 42064, in a former elementary school building. Year-round hours are 9:00 A.M. to 3:00 P.M., Tuesday through Saturday, and admission is $3.00. Curator Ronnie Stubblefield or an assistant will be on hand to guide you through this stunning array of fluorite crystals as well as other minerals and geological and archaeological specimens (petrified dinosaur dung, eggs, Mastadon teeth, and so forth) collected by Ben Clement over his sixty-year career in the mining business. Most unforgettable is the room full of optical fluorite mounted in vitrines that light the crystals from beneath. For more information, call (270) 965–4263.

Another little museum in town deals strictly with objects made and used by the human hand. The **Bob Wheeler Historical Museum,** just downhill from the Crittenden County Public Library, is open from April through October, Tuesday through Saturday from 10:00 A.M. to 4:00 P.M. or by appointment. Admission is free. Next to the white concrete-block building that houses an enormous range of regional artifacts is a reconstructed log cabin with period implements. It's delightfully out of sync with the rest of the neighborhood. Call (270) 965–9257 for more information.

The region north of Marion and south of the Ohio River has been settled in recent years by Amish families whose farms and houses might not strike you as much different than the surrounding non-Amish farms, but for a few subtle signals—and not just black buggies, either. See what you notice. For an interesting driving loop, take Highway 60 north, then turn left (northwest) onto Highway 654 at the community of Mattoon. On the left is a very large, active Amish farm where there is a harness shop that's open to the public. Look across the road for a sign that says MAST FAMILY BAKED GOODS and definitely stop if it is open. Continuing north (watch for a flock of emus at a farm on the right with a sign in the yard for Ray's Small Engines), make another stop 1 mile beyond the Mount Zion Church Road at **The Dutch Way Store,** a tiny, family-run general store that's primarily stocked with goods for Amish use; inexpensive footwear; spices; all sorts of dry, bulk foods; and plenty of sewing supplies. It's open from 8:00 A.M. to 5:00 P.M. every day but Sunday. One overall-clad, non-Amish man shopping there bought two pounds of powdered sage leaves. He was slaughtering hogs and thinking about sausage spices. Seasonally, you can dig your own mums at the farm next to the store. Other signs along the way might alert you to the availability of lye soap or sorghum, fresh eggs or apple butter.

To continue the loop, go back and take the Mount Zion Church Road west and turn left (south) onto a tiny gravel road called Turkey Knob. When you meet Fords Ferry Road, either turn left (south) to get back to Marion or turn right, then right again onto Highway 91 and head toward Illinois. To cross the wide and mighty Ohio River, you'll have to ride the **Cave-in-Rock Ferry,** unless the water's high, in which case you're up a creek. There's no place to cross closer than Paducah. The ferry runs daily from 6:00 A.M. to 10:00 P.M. The ride is free.

There was no way to cross the mighty waters in the bitter winter of 1838 when thousands of Cherokee traveled on foot during the forced march from their home lands in southern Appalachia to what would eventually become reservation lands in Oklahoma. This devastating march, known as the Trail of Tears, included a winter spent at a site called **Mantle Rock.** Now owned by The Nature Conservancy and preserved for its rare biological community as well as for its historic importance, this gorgeous site is open to visitors year-round. From Marion take Highway 60 southwest to Salem, then turn north on Highway 133. Continue through the community called Joy; when you have passed the junction with Highway 1436, go exactly 1.1 miles and look on the left for a bronze historical marker with the number 1675 painted on the post. It's very easy to overlook. If you pass the Cave Spring Church, you passed Mantle Rock. Park your car and take the short ($^3/_4$-mile) hike in to the most dramatic natural feature of the preserve, a 30-foot-high sandstone arch with a 188-foot span and some fabulous honeycombed weathering patterns. It was here that the Cherokee waited for the ice in the river to melt. Over 4,000 died of cold and starvation, since they were not prepared to winter over. In the spring they finally crossed into what is now Galcouda, Illinois.

True Blue
The Albany, New York, setting of the movie How the West Was Won *was filmed in Smithland, Kentucky, in 1961 by Metro-Goldwyn-Mayer.*

Preceding this bleak event by almost 10,000 years, Archaic Peoples camped on this site. Between A.D. 600–800, Lewis Peoples, who were hunter-gatherers, had a village here. Archaeologists have discovered more than one hundred stone burial mounds. Today the site is home to some rare and fragile plants, like June grass. The site is lush and quiet and so isolated that you might be able to let your mind travel to other times and other human occupations. If you want more information about the site or would like to arrange guided tours of the fragile glades (normally off-limits to hikers), contact The Nature Conservancy, 642 West Main Street, Lexington 40508, or call (606) 259–9655.

The first major town east of the lakes on Highway 68 is **Cadiz** (pronounced KAY-dizz), named, perhaps, after the hometown of an early Spanish surveyor. Since the creation of Land Between the Lakes, people say that the name means "gateway" in Spanish, since Cadiz is at the southeastern entrance to the area. Saxophone lovers pay homage here to the inimitable Boots Randolph, who was born in Trigg County. (The question is, should a golf course be named after a musician? Poor guy.) Ham lovers must have a meal in town; prize-winning hams are served everywhere—try **Broadbent's Food and Gifts** (502–522–3156), a big place to buy take-home hams, bacon, sausage, and cheeses, located 5 miles east of town near I–24. During the second weekend in October, follow your nose to the Trigg County Country Ham Festival, which features the Guinness record holder for the world's biggest ham and biscuit. Non-Southerners may learn that not all country ham can be safely compared to the salt-drenched tongue of your big brother's hiking boot. Call (270) 522–3892 for festival information.

Since you're now headed toward the land of rest and recreation, you'll need some good reading material. Check out **The Olde Book Shoppe** (270–522–6484), just 1/2 block off Main Street at 13 Marion Street, Cadiz 42211. For a small store, there's a nice range of books from antique tomes on farming to the latest by Kurt Vonnegut. The small downtown area is also full of antiques shops.

For more information about local attractions, including a walking tour of historic homes, stop by the log cabin tourist center on Main Street downtown, call (270) 522–3892, or log onto the Internet and look up www.gocadiz.com.

On Saturday, for a real treat with local flavor, stop by **Jim's Music Shop,** 8 Marion Street, Cadiz 42211, and see if there's a jam session happening. Local musicians and friends get together and play bluegrass, old-time, and a whole range of country music right there in the store. Jim also buys, sells, and trades new and used instruments. The shop is usually open from 9:00 A.M. to 4:00 P.M. Saturday. To get the scoop call (270) 522–8994.

Leaving Cadiz on Highway 68 west, there is an exciting short course in the beauty of native fauna available at the **Woods and Wetlands Wildlife Center.** If you spend time on or in the water in this region and have always wondered what was swimming around below the surface, this is your chance to find out. A 12,000-gallon aquarium houses a breathtaking range of native fish, including three kinds of gar (don't pull one of these into your fishing boat!) and cartoonlike catfish as big as the family dog. Most heart-stopping is the serpentarium, featuring over forty species of snakes; some are regional natives like the regal cottonmouth found in swampy wetlands in western Kentucky, or the much-respected timber rattlesnake; some snakes are exotic, like the giant python. Kids love to have their photo taken, for $5.00, with the huge (35-pound!) albino python named Julius. The experienced guides are helpful, and the signs identifying each species will educate you.

Outside in small but well-kept cages are the mammals and raptors, including a number of owls; three kinds of fox; bobcat; coyote; and even a mountain lion that purrs an octave below an opera tenor. The treat is being able to examine the stunning beauty of these wild animals at close range. The wildlife center is cosponsored by the industry next door, Knight and Hale Game Calls. Hours for the center are 9:00 A.M. to 6:00 P.M. daily in the summer and, the rest of the year, 9:00 A.M. to 3:00 P.M. Monday through Friday and 9:00 A.M. to 5:00 P.M. on weekends. Admission is $5.00 for adults and $3.00 for kids. Call (270) 924–9107 for more information. These naturalists also do educational programs and demonstrations with live animals from the wildlife center. Call (800) 788–0458 to learn more about programs for tourist groups, professional clubs, or schoolchildren.

There is something eerie and irresistible about stepping into a person's space and looking at the way that individual's daily life is shaped and revealed by his or her personal belongings. The **Adsmore Museum** in **Princeton** draws visitors into the lives of its early-twentieth-century residents in that almost-taboo way by presenting the house intact, changing detailed decorations and personal accessories seasonally, and building the tour around stories of the family. The interpretive staff reenacts weddings, birthday parties, and wakes (complete with wailing mourners dressed in period clothes). Details make this place a treat. That the Victorians in Europe were not morally able to utter the phrase "chicken thigh," for example, comes as no surprise when you find that the piano's legs, like a lady's, were always chastely covered with a shawl.

Built in grand late-Victorian style in 1857, Adsmore was fully restored in 1986 by the local library board to which Katharine Garrett, the last family resident, donated the building and its contents. Adsmore could have also been called "Collectsmore," for it is furnished lavishly with items from all over the world. Also on the grounds is the Ratliff Gun Shop, a restored 1844 cabin filled with antique tools. The museum and grounds are open Tuesday through Saturday from 11:00 A.M. to 4:00 P.M.

and Sunday from 1:30 to 4:00 P.M. Admission ranges from $2.00 to $5.00, according to age category. Group rates are available. Call (270) 365–3114. Adsmore, at 304 North Jefferson Street, Princeton 42445, in downtown Princeton, has been called the Natchez of West Kentucky because of its grand homes. From Cadiz the quickest route is Highway 139 north. From the Land Between the Lakes, take Highway 62, or take exit 12 from the Western Kentucky Parkway.

Princeton's oldest building, the circa-1817 Federal-style Champion-Shepherdson House at 115 East Main, has been renovated and is now home to the *Princeton Art Guild.* Like so many early settlements, Princeton began with a general store located near a big, dependable spring. A lean-to money-counting room, also used by fur traders, is now an artist-in-residence studio. The main building houses a gallery, a gift shop, and space for special events and workshops. Hours are 11:00 A.M. to 4:00 P.M. Tuesday through Saturday. For more information, write the guild at P.O. Box 451, Princeton 42445, or call (270) 365–3959.

In the not so distant past, the change of seasons was reflected in retail stores, and not just by "fall fashions" or seasonal decorations. Nowadays we often are offered the same things year-round. Not so with *Newsom's*

Fire?

*E*arly one morning, during recent travels through western Kentucky, I was driving down an old highway in that trancelike state of the traveler. Moisture was rising like liquid smoke from low places, and silver frost traced grassy meadows where shadows lingered. Everything was beautiful and slightly surreal. My eyes snapped wide open at the sight of a tall, skinny barn from which real smoke was pouring out of every crack as if it was about to lift off its rubble stone launchpad foundation and head to Mars. It was sided with a hodgepodge of corrugated roof tin, galvanized here, rusted or painted there, and long boards were leaning at steep angles against any panel that opened or was loose enough to flap in the wind. Nearly driving off the road, I looked hard. The structure was not burning, but it sure as heck was smoking. Throughout the day I saw dozens more tall skinny barns made of just about anything, uniformly and calmly smoking away. These, I realized, were curing barns for dark-fired tobacco, unfamiliar to a bluegrass resident for whom Burley tobacco, which is air-cured in sievelike open slatted black barns, is standard. Dark-fired tobacco is hung in these tall barns and carefully dried by use of slow-burning, smoldering fires usually built in pits in the floor. This year, late October was curing time. And for the traveling outsider, time *not* to call 911 at every puff of smoke.

Old Mill Store at 208 East Main Street, Princeton 42445. Garden plants are available in the spring and fresh produce is available as it comes in during the growing season. Gifts and specialty foods are offered year-round, with a special emphasis on country ham. The Newsoms sell their own aged hams, bacon, sausage, and, the favorite, hickory-smoked barbecue ham. Store hours are 8:30 A.M. to 5:00 P.M., Monday through Saturday. Call (270) 365–2482 for mail-order information.

For a historic picnic spot, stop just 1 block south of the Princeton courthouse at *Big Spring Park,* the original settlement's water source and a site where the Cherokees camped on the Trail of Tears. Also noteworthy is the Black Patch Tobacco Festival, which Princeton hosts in early September to commemorate the times when dark-leaf tobacco was harvested in the area in massive quantities. Accompanying this event is a dark and touchy history involving tobacco price wars and the night riders, a movement of farmers (made nationally famous by writers such as Robert Penn Warren) who turned to a sophisticated form of organized violence to ensure the viability of their way of life. Local historians explain the events during the Black Patch tour.

Take Highway 91 south from Princeton to downtown *Hopkinsville.* In the grand old Federal-style post office building at the corner of East Ninth (Highway 68) and Liberty Streets is the *Pennyroyal Area Museum* (270–887–4270), an impressive regional-history museum. The main display area is in the huge mail-sorting room. Notice the enclosed catwalks overhead, secret vantage points from which postmasters watched postal workers handle the mail, not to enforce efficiency (it is after all, a federal institution), but to prevent workers from stealing cash from the envelopes in a pre–checking account era.

The museum's displays address many facets of the Pennyroyal region's history, from agriculture and the Black Patch wars to reconstructed pioneer bedrooms and an 1898 law office. In the middle of the room sits a beautifully preserved original Mogul wagon, made just 2 blocks away in a large factory that manufactured every imaginable type of wagon. Mogul Wagon Company's ads in the 1920s read EASY TO PULL, HARD TO BREAK and BUY A MOGUL AND WILL IT TO YOUR GRANDSON. Railroad and early automobile artifacts compete for your attention with a miniature circus made by John Venable, which is said to have inspired Robert Penn Warren's *The Circus in the Attic,* the title piece of an early collection of short stories. Museum hours are 8:30 A.M. to 4:30 P.M. Monday through Friday and 10:00 A.M. to 3:00 P.M. Saturday. Admission is $1.00 for children under twelve and $2.00 for adults.

The Edgar Cayce exhibit is one of the most popular in the museum. The display case contains a few photographs and significant personal objects, like Cayce's dog-eared desk Bible. Cayce, who was born in 1877 in southern Christian County near Beverly, was a "strange" child who preferred meditating on the Bible to playing baseball. In 1900, after a severe illness, Cayce mysteriously lost his voice. When put under hypnosis by "Hart-The Laugh Man" in 1901, Cayce diagnosed the problem and restored his own voice by using a treatment he discovered during hypnosis. That was the beginning of his career as an internationally known clairvoyant, "the sleeping prophet." He gave 14,256 psychic readings in which he diagnosed medical problems and predicted world affairs, including natural disasters and economic changes. Today the Association for Research and Enlightenment, based at Virginia Beach where Cayce spent the last twenty years of his life, continues "The Work," as Cayce called it, by providing a library and educational programs related to his readings.

Many of Hopkinsville's visitors from the west, passing through town en route to Virginia Beach, stop to see the place where Edgar Cayce and his wife, Gertrude Evans, are buried in the Riverside Cemetery on the north side of town, just east of North Virginia Street. Seven miles south of town on the Lafayette Road (Highway 107) in Beverly are Cayce's church, the Liberty Christian Church, which is open to the public at no charge, and his school, the Beverly Academy, which is now on private property. If you're a Cayce fan, ask at the museum about other significant sites.

Hopkinsville has done more than any other town in the state to pay tribute to the Native American people who were forced to move from their southeastern homelands across the Mississippi River to Oklahoma on the infamous Trail of Tears during the winter of 1838–1839. More than 13,000 Cherokees camped in Hopkinsville and received provisions for their forced migration, during which thousands of people died.

The Trail of Tears Commission, Inc. has developed the **Trail of Tears Commemorative Park** at Ninth Street and Skyline Drive on the west edge of town. The park includes impressive, larger-than-life statues of Cherokee chiefs White Path and Fly Smith, who are buried on the property. Near the banks of the Little River is a log cabin that serves as an education center.

Although the Cherokee people fought alongside the colonists during the American Revolution and later with Andrew Jackson in the War of 1812, Jackson, as president in the late 1820s, insisted that Native Americans of numerous tribes yield and leave their homelands east of the Mississippi.

The forced removal spanned a decade, causing tremendous loss of lives in the process and leaving the survivors a legacy of hardship on barren reservations in the West. It should also be noted that gold was discovered on Cherokee land in Georgia in 1828, ten years prior to the Native Americans' forced migration. The park includes a heritage center. Hours are Monday through Saturday from 10:00 a.m. to 4:00 p.m. from April through October, and Tuesday through Saturday from 10:00 A.M. to 2:00 P.M. November through March.

The *Trail of Tears Intertribal Indian Pow Wow* has become an annual event, held during the weekend after Labor Day. Although the recent history of the Native American people is tragic, this public festival is meant to commemorate the beauty and integrity of their culture. The powwow features Native American crafts, food, storytelling, blow-gun demonstrations, and a very competitive Indian dance contest. Contact the Trail of Tears Commission, Inc., P.O. Box 4027, Hopkinsville 42240, or call (270) 886–8033.

For lodging near Hopkinsville, Melissa and Gary Jones's bed-and-breakfast, the *Oakland Manor* (9210 Newstead Road, Hopkinsville 42240; 270–885– 6400) is a truly elegant restored 1857 antebellum mansion filled with period antiques. With its ninety-five trees, gazebo, flagstone walkway, and gracious Old South country setting, it looks like a scene from *Gone With the Wind*. From April through December three rooms are available for lodging at a rate of $45 per night. From downtown Hopkinsville take Canton Pike (Highway 272) to the west, turn left on Newstead Road (Highway 164), and watch for the sign on the left side after about 3$^1/_2$ miles.

Any time of year that you travelers need to trade in your wheels for some real, old-fashioned horsepower, out of the bucket seat and back in the saddle, away from diesel exhaust and into the good clean air, try a trail ride. You don't really need to create a relationship with a rented horse. They're well trained and accustomed to anything, even people who don't know which end of a horse is friendlier. North of Hopkinsville is a fancy place called the *Copper Canyon Ranch,* which features an 1800s mining town replica and long, quiet riding trails through woods and fields. You have to make an appointment in advance, so call Tim or Carol Emery at (270) 269–2416. To get there, go north of Hopkinsville on the Pennyrile Parkway, take the Crofton exit onto Highway 800, and go to Fearsville. Take Highway 189 for 3 more miles and watch for the signs.

South of Hopkinsville, on the Tennessee border, is a small portion of the large Fort Campbell Military Reservation. Generally it's a private, no-trespassing kind of place, but the public is welcome to visit the **Don F. Pratt Memorial Museum,** a showcase of sorts, for the history of the 101st Airborne "Screaming Eagles" Division (Air Assault), which is based here. Indoors one can see exhibits from the Civil War through Desert Storm, a restored World War II Cargo Glider, and other war-related artifacts. Outdoors are a number of army aircraft, including helicopters. Admission is free, and the hours are 9:30 A.M. to 4:30 P.M. daily, except Christmas and New Year's Days. To get there from U.S. Highway 41A, go through the fort's main gate and stop at the visitors center, where you have to get a pass. Then continue on the same road, turn right on Tennessee Avenue, and left into the museum. For more information or to schedule special guided tours, call the post protocol office at (270) 798–9913.

As soon as you drive east from Hopkinsville, you are in an area heavily populated by Amish and Mennonite people. Nationally there are about 85,000 Amish, many of whom live in Pennsylvania, Ohio, and Indiana in communities that are being encroached upon by rapidly widening urban edges. Rural Kentucky has become a popular place for Amish families to relocate because the land is beautiful, isolated, and relatively inexpensive. When you visit Amish and Mennonite businesses, keep in mind that they are committed to their way of life in part because they want isolation from the rest of the world. Respect their privacy. Observe their work practices, for they are good stewards of their land and of all their resources. We could stand a little education.

About 6 miles east of town on Highway 68, at a big farmhouse with rock pillars by the driveway, Henry Hoover runs an unadvertised bulk food and farm supply business primarily meant to serve an orthodox community known as Horse and Buggy Mennonites, folks who have no cars or telephones. He will sell to the public, so stop in if you need flour, cereals, bread, cheese, and so forth. It's a great way to avoid excessive packaging and higher prices due to expensive advertising. Hours are by chance.

Pete's Custom Saddle Shop is an orderly, productive (secular) one-man leather operation on Highway 68 about 8 miles east of Hopkinsville. In addition to making and refurbishing more than a hundred saddles a year, Russell (Pete) Harry makes holsters, halters, and bridles, not to mention guns, tomahawks, and an occasional painting. Although he's geared primarily to custom work, there are always a few items for sale in the shop that will knock your socks off. Pete's original saddle designs range from a sleek bird-hunting saddle to variations on Civil War styles to a western pleasure show saddle with special braces for a local woman

True Blue

The Jefferson Davis monument in Fairview is the fourth largest concrete obelisk in the world (351 feet).

who is paralyzed below the shoulders. Even if you are not in need of tack, his stunning work and positive spirit are unique and inspirational. Because his hours are not regular, call him at (270) 886–5448 before visiting.

Half a mile east of Pete Harry's place is an Amish harness shop called **Leather Works** (look for hand-painted signs by a road called Vaughns Grove on the north side of the highway), where a young farmer named Wayne Zimmerman makes and repairs leather tack of all kinds, except saddles. That his specialty is harnesses is no accident. Except for very heavy work like plowing, he and many Amish and Mennonite farmers in the area work with mule teams. The shop is small, and he does not keep much in stock, but if you are interested in placing an order or just in seeing the operation, stop by. Hours are by chance.

One mile past the Leather Works place is **Fairview,** a tiny rural town you can't miss, thanks to the **Jefferson Davis Monument State Historic Site** looming overhead at a height of 351 feet. From miles away in any direction, the incongruous tower, said to be the tallest concrete-cast obelisk in the world, is visible poking into the sky. During the summer you can ride an elevator to the top of the monument. Jefferson Davis, the first and only president of the Confederate States, was born in March 1808 in a house called Wayfarers Rest on the site of what is now the Bethel Baptist Church in Fairview.

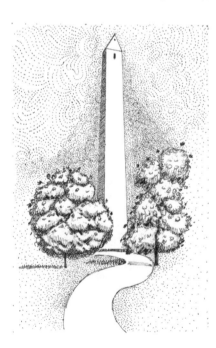

Jefferson Davis Monument State Historic Site

Adjacent to the monument is the **Zimmerman Farms produce stand,** run by harness maker Wayne Zimmerman's brothers. From late May to mid-October, you can buy delicious, organically grown fruits and vegetables. You can trust the Amish when it comes to wholesome, flavorful produce.

At *Elkton*, 8 miles east of Fairview, take Highway 181 south for about 10 miles and look to the right for *Schlabach's Bakery* (270–265–3459), an Amish bakery specializing in satisfaction. Its sourdough bread, sweet rolls, pies, cakes, cookies, and yes, even granola are delicious and always fresh. Hours are 8:00 A.M. to 5:00 P.M. every day but Thursday and Sunday. Although the owner is Abe Schlabach, you'll be more likely to meet one of his bakers, who live nearby.

Another mile or so south, at the intersection of Highways 181 and 848, is the *Penchem Tack Store* (270–483–2314), a large Amish tack and farm supply store also patronized by the general public. John H. Yoders and his sons work in the leather shop in the basement while another family member tends to retail sales upstairs. It's a great place to browse, especially if you're in the market for good functional suspenders, straw work hats, Redwing shoes, veterinary supplies, tack (commercially and locally made), or just a soft drink and candy bar. Hours are 7:00 A.M. to 5:30 P.M. Monday through Saturday.

If Amish men are among the best leather workers, the women have always been known for the fine art of quilting. *Grandma's Cupboard* (270–483–2461) is an informal sales outlet for women who make quilts, hooked rugs, and woven runners. It's open Monday through Saturday from 9:00 A.M. to 5:00 P.M. From Penchem's go left (east) on Highway 848 to Highway 79; turn left (north) and stop at the second house on the right. If you'd like to see even more quilts, visit Elmer and Mary Hochstetler, who closed their large dairy business because none of the

Amish Ingenuity

*J*ust to illustrate how the Amish in the Elkhorn area (there are many kinds of Amish communities) adjust their lives to both the community rules and the modern world, let me tell you how Betty Miller gets to work at Schlabach's Bakery every morning. Her community uses tractors and horse-and-buggy rigs, but not cars or bicycles. If she were male, she might hop on her Massey Ferguson and drive; if she were a child, she might sprint. Instead, she gets on her small tractor (a ride-on lawn mower) and commutes through yards and along the shoulder of the highway. Some churches won't allow use of any vehicle with rubber tires, so the members own steel-wheeled tractors. Other churches allow cars and trucks but insist they be painted black, even the chrome parts. Others allow congregation members to have cars and attend graduate school. And, at the other extreme, very orthodox communities use only horses and oxen.

male children stayed on the family farm. What used to be the dairy barn is now the store where the family sells everything from homemade noodles, Amish cheese, soup mixes, and Mary's famous angel-food cakes to Amish, Mennonite, and other Christian printed materials. The handmade quilts easily steal the show, however. With the help of other local quilters, Mary Hochstetler can make almost any type of quilt to order, and there are usually exquisite finished pieces for sale. Hours are 9:00 A.M. to 5:00 P.M. Monday through Saturday. Profits from quilt sales go, in part, to the Galilean Home Ministry, a Christian school in Liberty. Tell Mary and her daughters that I said hello.

If you are in the area in early summer and get that unbearable craving for strawberries (it's best to gorge), call the local *strawberry kings* Emmett Walton in Allensville (270–265–5597) or Tommy Borders near Elkton (270–265–5770) to see if they are open for picking. They'll direct you to the field on which you may sweetly graze.

Due south on either Highway 79 or 41, nestled right next to the Tennessee border, is the town of *Guthrie,* birthplace of Robert Penn Warren, poet laureate of the United States and Pulitzer prize winner for both poetry and fiction. For those who have read his work, it is enriching to walk the streets and drive by the endless fields, an environment that obviously influenced his writing. Once in town, if you want details or if you'd like to tour the *Robert Penn Warren Museum,* the house in which Penn Warren was born, contact Mrs. Dean Moore at (270) 483–2683. Tours are given 11:30 A.M. to 3:30 P.M. Tuesday through Saturday and 2:00 to 4:00 P.M. Sunday. The house is at the corner of Third and Cherry Streets.

Libby's Steakhouse & Entertainment Center is not only the biggest restaurant building you have probably ever seen, it's also bound to have the widest variety of entertainment you can imagine inside a restaurant—horse shows, professional Nashville country-music performances, open dances, rodeos, thumb pickin' contests, parties, and even beauty pageants. Upcoming country musicians perform on stage Saturday night from 7:30 to 10:00 P.M. for *Live at Libby's,* a syndicated FM radio show that has helped people such as Tracey Lawrence and Aaron Tippen get their starts. It's a "family" restaurant, so no alcohol is served, but a full Southern menu is offered. The 3-pound "West Texas Slab" rib loin steak is yours free if you can clean your plate. Libby's opens at 5:00 P.M. on Friday and Saturday only (270–265–2630). Find the place on Highway 68 at its junction with Highway 1309 in Daysville, between Elkton and Russellville.

On Highway 79, about halfway between Guthrie and Russellville in Allensville, is **The Pepper Place.** Take Highway 102 east toward town and watch for the sign in front of a large, blue, clapboard-sided house, circa 1864, with an inviting wraparound porch. The house is available for weddings, receptions, and catered meals. Many of the period antiques in The Pepper Place are for sale. Write Dr. Mack Craig, P.O. Box 95, Allensville 42204, or call (502) 265–9859 for reservations or a tour.

If you need a place to spend the night in **Russellville,** try the restored 1824 home of George Washington's third cousin, John Whiting Washington. The **Washington House** is a bed-and-breakfast with three lodging rooms, each fully furnished with antiques that are for sale. The first week in October is a great time to visit town and this B&B because of the Logan County Tobacco Festival; or try the weekend before Thanksgiving, when gorgeous old houses in town participate in the Christmas Open House. Contact Roy Gill, 283 West Ninth Street, Russellville 42276, or call (270) 726–7608 or (270) 726–3093.

Another nice area lodging is **The Log House,** a four-room bed-and-breakfast built from hand-hewn logs recovered from old cabins and barns in the Logan County area, including old buildings in Russellville. Almost 8,000 square feet in all, the house has a rambling feel and eclectic decorating featuring folk art and antiques. All for $95 per night. Call innkeepers Mike and "Sam" Hossom at (270) 726–8483. The house is at 2139 Franklin Road, Russellville 42276.

Three miles east of Auburn on Highway 68 is **South Union Shaker Village,** now a wonderfully curated museum marking the site of a once-thriving village comprising more than 6,000 acres and 200 buildings. Members of the United Society of Believers in Christ's Second Appearing, more commonly known as Shakers, lived at the South

Stick 'Em Up

The **Southern Deposit Bank** in downtown Russellville, on the corner of Main and Sixth Streets, was the scene of a great crime, the Jesse James gang's first out-of-state robbery. Prior to that day the gang was just a handful of local hoodlums. On May 20, 1868, the gang held up the bank for $9,000, shot and wounded bank president N. Long, and galloped away to join the ranks of America's famous federal fugitives. (What old Jesse didn't know was that there was an additional $50,000 in the vault.) Today the building has been restored into a classy apartment building.

South Union Shaker Village

Union community from 1807 until 1922. They supported themselves with sophisticated enterprises in garden seed, fruit preserves, fine colorful silk handkerchiefs, and farming. They also ran a large, steam-powered mill, hired out some of Kentucky's first purebred bulls for stud all over the state, and built and leased out (to "the World") a train depot, post office/general store, and tavern.

The forty-room building that now serves as the main museum was the Center House, a dwelling complete with kitchen, communal dining room, and bedrooms—men on one side, women on the other. The structure fulfills your basic expectations of a Shaker building, but in a slightly showier way—some of the trim boards are beaded, there is a nook for a clock, the first-floor window casings flare, and arches abound. From the woodstoves to the cooking utensils to the hat molds, South Union is filled with original Shaker objects, not reproductions. Even the brick dust and mustard-ochre stains on the woodwork are original (let's hear it for organic paint!). This Shaker museum also boasts the largest collection of western Shaker furniture in the United States.

The museum and gift shop are open from March 1 through November 30, Monday through Friday from 9:00 A.M. to 4:00 P.M. and Sunday from 1:00 to 4:00 P.M. Admission is $5.00 for adults and $1.50 for children ages six to twelve. Children age five and under are admitted free. Call (800)

811–8379 or (270) 542–4167, or write South Union Shaker Village, P.O. Box 30, South Union KY 42283 for information and a schedule of events. One mile east of the museum is Highway 73. Turn left (south) and go ¹/₂ mile to the **South Union Post Office** (501–542–6757), established April 1, 1826. This was the last building constructed in the Shaker community.

Directly across the road from the post office is the **Shaker Tavern,** an ornate Victorian tavern the Shakers had built to house the overflow of railroad travelers stopping at the village for lodging. The tavern was always run by non-Shakers and still is. Jo Ann Moody has turned the tavern into a combined restaurant and bed-and-breakfast and given this place the sparkle it deserves. Five classy bed-and-breakfast rooms are available for between $65 and $75 per night, and the chefs guarantee a full Southern breakfast in the morning. Call (270) 542–6801 for reservations or more information.

Yellow Banks, Green River

> *addy, won't you take me back to Muhlenberg County,*
> *Down by the Green River where Paradise lay.*
> *I'm sorry my son but you're too late in askin',*
> *Mr. Peabody's coal train has hauled it away.*

John Prine's famous lyrics give us a glimpse of Muhlenberg County's history, while traveling through the area gives us an update. *Paradise* is an enormous steam-generating power plant, the largest of its kind when it was built in the late 1950s. The county has not been hauled away completely, but you may think they're trying to do so when you see some of the monstrous earth-moving machines in the surface mines visible from several major roads. (The term *strip mine* is taboo.) Just driving through will convince you that this was the largest coal-producing county in the United States for twenty-three consecutive years until Environmental Protection Agency (EPA) regulations reduced the market for the area's high-sulfur coal. Seeing Paradise for yourself is worth the effort. From Central City take Highway 70 south to Highway 176 and go east until you get there. Don't worry, you'll know it because the landscape changes dramatically as you approach the Green River. First, there are the long train tracks with car after car of coal. There are the strange swampy lowlands, some of which are reclaimed mining areas. If you follow some of the side

---

True Blue

The first commercial mine for bituminous coal in the entire state was opened near Paradise, in Muhlenberg County, in 1820. From 1973 to 1987 Kentucky led the nation in coal production.

roads, you'll see eerie little pockets of undisturbed areas, mostly ceme-
teries, where no mining was allowed. Eventually you arrive at the power
plant, announced by massive, curving cooling towers and a horizontal
sulfurous yellow cloud, on still days. Plant tours are available between
8:00 A.M. and 3:00 P.M., Wednesday through Friday, but you must make
advance reservations by calling (270) 476–3301. The engineering is
spectacular, as is the altered landscape.

Aside from coal, great country music is this area's claim to fame. In front
of the City Building in *Central City* is a monument to the town's native
sons, Phil and Don Everly. Every Labor Day weekend the Everly Brothers
and more than 10,000 fans come to town for a benefit concert called the
Everly Brothers Central City Music Festival, the proceeds of which go
to music scholarships and other community projects. One of the favorite
events is the International Thumbpicking Contest in honor of Merle
Travis. Call (270) 754–9603 for festival information.

Greenville, just south of the Western Kentucky Parkway on Highway 62
or Highway 189, is home to several unique attractions. One is the *House
of Onyx,* a megamart of gemstones that promotes investment in precious rocks and discourages trust in the banking system. Beyond inventory and prices, its literature consists of an odd combination of claims
that the House of Onyx is a real, honest business and fortune
cookie–type moralistic quotes. One's curiosity is piqued. The business
is primarily geared toward the wholesale and mail-order markets, but if
you are in town on a weekday between 8:30 A.M. and 4:30 P.M., call
ahead for a tour of the retail showroom. The mind boggles at the sight
of rows of cases of rubies, sapphires, pearls, and myriad other stones.
Though there is no sign, the office is in the Aaron Building at 120 North
Main Street, Greenville 42345. Ring the doorbell and explain your interest, or call ahead for an appointment at (270) 338–2363.

One Interesting Town Mascot

*W*hat do bluegrass music, Scotch taxidermy, and barbecued mutton have in common? The Owensboro area. If you are approaching the area by the Bluegrass Parkway and still need con-vincing that Kentucky is far from mun-dane, head north on the Green River Parkway and take exit 69 to the tiny town of **Dundee**. When you get into town, keep your eyes to the sky. Stand-ing stiffly above the Masonic lodge is a stuffed goat, imported almost one hun-dred years ago from Dundee, Scotland. The town, which was once called Hines Mill, changed its name to commemo-rate this oddity.

A little-known fact: Greenville is the home of the **State Championship Washer Pitching Playoffs.** Washer pitching is the rural American version of the ancient game of quoits and is related to horseshoes. In the heat of late summer, the playoffs are held at the Greenville Municipal Ball Park. You'll get a schedule for the event if and when you win a district blue ribbon.

If you plan to dine or spend a night in the area, take Highway 431 south from Central City to Highway 973 in Dunmor; take a right and go 4 miles through the countryside to **Everly's Lake Malone Inn** (270– 657– 2121). Don Everly owns this hotel and big restaurant and has redecorated it with Everly Brothers memorabilia.

Fishing is fantastic in the **Lake Malone State Park.** The 788-acre lake is surrounded by a 388-acre park laced with middle-aged pine forests and sandstone bluffs and caves where the Jesse James gang supposedly hid out. (Jesse James is to western Kentucky what Daniel Boone is to the central and eastern parts—both hid everywhere, carved their initials on every historic tree and building, and are still receiving royalties for their freely interpreted deeds.)

Barbecue Doesn't Get Much Better

*I*n mid-May Owensboro comes alive for the **International Bar-B-Q Festival,** *during which time the local folks compete fiercely for culinary titles. A friend's father, "Pop Beers," concocted a darn good recipe for barbecued chicken that has won three festival championships. Because this generous soul has given me permission to pass on to you his secret recipe, I hereby command you to sensitize your palate before participating in the festival. I quote:*

Bring the following ingredients to a rapid boil on medium high heat:

1 stick butter

1 big lemon

1 tablespoon Worcestershire sauce

1 tablespoon soy sauce

5 shakes Tabasco sauce

1 teaspoon black pepper

1 teaspoon paprika

1 teaspoon garlic powder

1 teaspoon Accent meat tenderizer

1 teaspoon poultry seasoning

Cook until a brown scum forms and then goes away. Let cool and use. Won't spoil if kept. Makes enough for three 3-pound chickens. To use, cut fat (not skin) off chicken. Grill chicken on one side for 30 minutes, turn and repeat, then turn again, baste, and grill for 15 minutes; turn again and repeat. Eat!

On to the self-proclaimed *Bar-B-Q Capital of the World* and the third-largest city in the state, *Owensboro.* In this town, where there's smoke, there's barbecue. Initiate yourself by eating at one of the many "smoking" restaurants, ranging from a humble joint called *George's Bar-B-Q* (1362 East Fourth Street, Owensboro 42303; 270–926–9276), where you can sample one version of honest-to-goodness Kentucky burgoo (a super-hearty meat-and-veggie stew that originated in Wales and came here via Virginia with the pioneers), to the famous *Moonlite Bar-B-Q Inn* (270–684–8143), a huge restaurant west of town on Parrish Street where the barbecue is all hickory-pit cooked. George's is open 8:00 A.M. to 8:00 P.M. Monday through Friday and 8:00 A.M. to 9:00 P.M. Saturday. Hours at Moonlite are 9:00 A.M. to 9:00 P.M. Monday through Saturday and 10:00 A.M. to 3:00 P.M. Sunday.

My favorite landmark in Owensboro is a *sassafras tree* in the front yard of E. M. Ford & Company on the corner of Frederica and Maple Streets. At a height of 100 feet and a circumference of 16 feet, this 250- to 300-year-old droopy-armed beauty is registered by the American Forestry Association as the largest of its kind in the country and probably in the world. A Mrs. Rash saved the tree from the merciless highway department by planting herself at the base of the trunk with a shotgun in hand. She then pulled political strings, and the governor immediately installed a retaining wall and lightning rod. (I'll bet Earth First! would recruit Mrs. Rash.)

Planting Ideas

*M*ike and Marci Bland own a shop in Owensboro that carries dresses, shoes, suits, hats, backpacks, paper, shampoo, lip balm, hammocks, pizza-crust mixes, cooking oil, and a wide array of other products. Which wouldn't be unusual at all, except that the products are all made from industrial hemp (Cannabis sativa, *but grown to include little of the psychoactive ingredient in the plant's marijuana form). Stop by* **Common Sense Hemp** *(1722A Sweeney, Owensboro 42303; 270–926–4455) and you'll get a thought-provoking crash course in a* hot Kentucky agriculture issue. The Blands are among a serious contingent of Kentuckians and others advocating industrial hemp, legal in some other countries as a versatile, environmentally friendly, profitable crop for Kentucky farmers. Actor Woody Harrelson came to Kentucky in 1996 and planted industrial hemp seeds to test the issue in court. Out and about in the state is the **Kentucky Hemp Museum,** *an exhibit-on-wheels about hemp history and uses. Call its director, Craig Lee, at (606) 692–9775 to find out its schedule.*

The **Owensboro Area Museum of Science and History** (220 Daviess Street, Owensboro 42303; 270–687–2732) is a natural science and history extravaganza containing everything from live reptiles to a one-hundred-plus-seat planetarium, a tobacco-store figure of Punch, dinosaur replicas, and artifacts illustrating events in Kentucky history. Kids and uninhibited adults love the hands-on science exhibits called *Encounter* and *The Discovery Center.* Though it is said that the museum started in a church building in 1966, the truth is that it began somewhat earlier in local storyteller and natural historian Joe Ford's backyard playhouse, where he stockpiled insects, rocks, and snakeskins, some of which are still in the museum collection. Open Tuesday through Saturday from 10:00 A.M. to 5:00 P.M. and Sunday from 1:00 to 4:00 P.M. Admission is free.

Western Kentucky is almost as famous for bluegrass music as it is for barbecue. In fact, the "Father of Bluegrass Music," Bill Monroe, was born and is buried in the little town of Rosine, one county over from Owensboro. The **International Bluegrass Music Museum** (111 Daviess Street, Owensboro 42303, in Owensboro's RiverPark Center; 270–926–7891) honors Monroe and other bluegrass stars. The museum features interactive exhibits, vintage photographs, and film clips and memorabilia from a variety of performers. A major renovation began in 2000, and the museum is scheduled to reopen in spring 2002.

The **Inter-Tribal Indian Festival,** open to the public and held annually in early October, is a cultural extravaganza that includes traditional food booths, Native American drummers and singers accompanying breathtaking dance performances, storytellers, medicine men lecturing on traditional uses of plants, and demonstrations of spear throwing and flint knapping. This event is held outdoors on the campus of Owensboro Community College, which is located just off Highway 231 on the southeast edge of town. Admission is a mere $2.00, or $1.00 for students, but no carload of people will be charged more than $4.00. For more information call Libby Warren at (270) 686–4495.

One of Kentucky's largest fine art museums, the **Owensboro Museum of Fine Art** at 901 Frederica Street, Owensboro 42301, has an impressive permanent collection of works from eighteenth-, nineteenth-, and twentieth-century American, English, and French masters and a decorative arts collection of American, European, and Asian objects from the fifteenth to the nineteenth centuries. The museum has completed a $1.6 million expansion, which includes a new Exhibitions Wing; an Atrium Sculpture Court; a restored Civil War era mansion; the Kentucky Spirit Galleries, featuring rotating exhibitions of Kentucky folk art and crafts;

and the Yellowbanks Gallery, for works by regional artists. One highlight is an early-twentieth-century German stained glass collection displayed dramatically in 25-foot towers in an atrium gallery. The Mezzanine Gallery contains religious art. Hours are Tuesday through Friday from 10:00 A.M. to 4:00 P.M. and weekends from 1:00 to 4:00 P.M. Admission is free, but donations of $2.00 per adult and $1.00 per child are suggested. Call (270) 685–3181.

There are times when rest can be found in activity. Do tennis (indoor and out), racquetball, swimming, horseback riding, fishing, canoeing, and weight lifting strike you as heavy labor? Joan Ramey, owner of Ramey Sports and Fitness Center and Ramey Riding Stables, has opened *Trail's End Bed & Breakfast* to all appreciative visitors. Several cottages are now available for bed-and-breakfast lodging at $75 per night; this includes Ms. Ramey's athlete's breakfast. In addition to all these goodies, a masseuse is available. The cottages are 3 miles east of Owensboro on Highway 56. Call (270) 771–5590 or fax (270) 771–4723.

True Blue
Both Civil War presidents —Abraham Lincoln and Jefferson Davis—were born in Kentucky, one year and 100 miles apart.

WeatherBerry Bed and Breakfast at 2731 West Second Street, Owensboro 42301, offers country-style lodging very close to town. For $50 to $70 a night, depending on the size of the room, you get a private bath and a grand Kentucky-style breakfast, or a more moderate "healthful" repast. The previous residents of the impressive 1840 farmhouse had a vineyard and collected weather information for the National Weather Bureau, hence the name WeatherBerry. Call (270) 684–8760 for reservations.

In all cultures, people set time aside to take retreats, quiet time for contemplation away from the bustle of everyday life. Whether or not you are Catholic or connected to any church or creed in any way, *Mount Saint Joseph Center and Community of Ursuline Sisters* offers a quiet, respectful atmosphere to those of us yearning for space and time to absorb (or forget) life. Aside from retreats, the center offers all kinds of religious, cultural, and social programs. Call (270) 229–4103 for information. To get there, take Parrish Avenue (Highway 81) west out of town until it turns due south; take Highway 56 to West Louisville, turn right (west) on Highway 815, and look for the sign within 2 miles.

Go in the Maple Mount Farm entrance, find the Mother House, and ask to see the museum. Sister Emma Cecilia Busam or Sister Mary Victor Rogers will guide you through the museum artifacts, which range from desks of the founders to gifts from foreign missions, musical instruments, religious articles, books, and displays, such as "The Madonna Room," which houses a collection of reproductions of famous European Madonna paintings. The non-Catholic visitor learns that reliquaries are saints' shrines of all sizes that can be displayed anywhere from behind an altar in a massive gold frame to behind a pendant in a tiny glass locket. The idea of wearing a first-degree relic, usually a chip of a saint's bone, hidden in the back of a ring, has endless implications.

From Mount Saint Joseph take a westward drive on Highway 56 for 11 miles to the **Diamond Lake Resort.** Statewide catfish farming is on the rise because reclaimed surface mines are required to have settling ponds, which are appropriate places for raising fish. This farm is a successful, sophisticated business whose owners are more than happy to show people around. During the summer visitors ride a tram to see the whole operation. Open daily 8:00 A.M. to 5:00 P.M.; closed December through March. Call (270) 229–4961.

After the fish farm tour, you may be curious to know how the product tastes. The **Windy Hollow, Raceway Park, Restaurant and Museum** (270–785–4088) has a famous catfish buffet Friday and Saturday from 5:00 to 8:30 P.M. (and a big country-ham breakfast buffet on Sunday from 7:00 A.M. to 1:30 P.M. if fish isn't your dish). Every day is your lucky day at the pay lakes, and you don't even need a fishing license! Windy Hollow wins the contest for having the most going on at once: drag racing, water sliding, camping, pay-lake fishing, barbecuing, golf, and even old western movie viewing while you eat. Don't miss the cowboy museum. Yee-haw! From Owensboro follow Highway 81 south to Old 81 and exit west. Follow the signs.

Although the third weekend in October is the best time to visit **Reid's Orchard,** because it hosts a two-day harvest festival, any time during apple season in the fall is a good time to pick your own of whatever is ripe at that moment. The farm store offers cider, relishes, produce, and whatever else these industrious folks decide to make and sell. Call ahead (270–685–2444) for hours and information.

The **John James Audubon State Park** is about 20 miles west of Owensboro, along Highway 41 north of Henderson. Although Audubon is the most famous American painter of birds, he was a failure as a business executive. While he lived in this area, from 1810 to 1820, Audubon got involved in several entrepreneurial projects, all of which failed because instead of working, he spent his days in search of rare birds. With nothing left but his portfolio of bird paintings, his talent, and an idea, Audubon dragged his poor family all over the South while he painted and searched for a publisher. Eventually he found an engraver in London, England, who printed his 435 hand-colored plates as *The Birds of America.* A complete bound set of the original folios and numerous individual prints are on display in the Audubon Memorial and Nature Museum, as is the largest collection of Audubon memorabilia in existence, including many of his original paintings, journals, correspondence, and personal items. Another treasure in the museum is a rare 3-by-5-inch daguerreotype of the elderly Audubon taken by the famous early photographer Matthew Brady.

The whole northern half of the park was donated as a nature preserve, with the stipulation that it be treated as a bird sanctuary and that the old-growth beech and sugar maple woods be preserved. Ask the park naturalist what wild and amazing flora and fauna can be seen. The park also sponsors spring and fall migration bird walks.

Adjacent to the museum is the Nature Center, which features a glass-enclosed Nature Observatory and a Discovery Center with exhibits on bird biology and psychology. Daily programs are offered in the summer, and special events are sprinkled throughout the rest of the year. Hours are 10:00 A.M. to 5:00 P.M. daily. Admission to the museum and Nature Center is $4.00 for adults, $3.00 for children ages six to twelve, or a family charge of $10.00. Call (270) 826–2247 for more information.

More Good Lodging in Western Kentucky

CADIZ
Lake Barkley State Resort Park, Off Highway 68; (270) 924–1131.
Two lodges and cottages; golf and fitness center. $44 to $168.

DAWSON SPRINGS
Pennyrile Forest State Resort Park, Highway 109; (270) 797–3421. Lodge and cottages. $42 to $118.

GILBERTSVILLE
Kentucky Dam Village State Resort Park, Highway 62 at Highway 641 on Kentucky Lake; (270) 362–4271. Lodge and cottages; golf course. $42 to $140.

GRAND RIVERS
Grand Rivers Inn, 1949 JH OBryan Avenue, 42045; (270) 362–4487. Rooms and cottages; 1/4 mile from lake. $42 to $54.

HENDERSON
L&N Bed and Breakfast, 327 North Main Street, 42420; (270) 831–1100. Historic home overlooking the river. $65 to $75.

Victorian Quarters Bed & Breakfast, 109 Clay Street, 42420; (270) 831–2778. Scenic mansion overlooking the Ohio River. Three rooms; $85 to $95.

Super 8 Motel of Henderson, 2030 Highway 41N, 42420; (270) 827–5611. About $45.

HOPKINSVILLE
Fairfield Inn, 345 Griffin Bell Drive, 42240; (877) 233–9330.

KUTTAWA
Davis House,
528 South Willow Way,
42055; (270) 388–4468.
Two-story Victorian
bed-and-breakfast on
Lake Barkley. About $65
per night.

MAYFIELD
Super 8 Motel,
1100 Links Lane, 42055;
(270) 247–8899. $50
and up.

Susan B. Seay's Magnolia
Manor, 401 South Seventh,
42066; (270) 247–4108.
B&B in a 1900 Greek
Revival–style mansion.

OWENSBORO
Executive Inn Rivermont,
One Executive Boulevard,
42303; (270) 926–8000. $55
and up.

Helton House
Bed and Breakfast, 103 East
Twenty-third Street, 42303;
(270) 926–7117. Mission-
style home in a tree-lined
neighborhood. $60 to $80.

Holiday Inn, Highway 60
West; (270) 685–3941.
Indoor pool, sauna,
children's play area. $61
and up.

PADUCAH
1857's, 127 Market House
Square, 42001;
(800) 264–5607 or
(270) 444–3960. A three-
story brick lodging on the
National Register of His-
toric Places. Some pets and
children allowed. Pool table
and hot tub.

Fisher Mansion Bed and
Breakfast, 901 Jefferson
Street, 42001;
(270) 443–0716. Restored
1903 Victorian mansion.
Honeymoon suite includes
double Jacuzzi and private
dining.

JR's Executive Inn, One
Executive Boulevard,
42001; (270) 443–8000 or
(800) 866–3636. Luxury
riverside hotel. About $70.

Rosewood Inn Bed &
Breakfast, 2740 South
Friendship Road, 42003;
(800) 548–3840 or
(270) 554–6632. Two guest
rooms and two suites in a
country farmhouse. $65 to
$105.

Trinity Hills Farm Bed and
Breakfast and Stained Glass
Studio, 10455 Old
Lovelace Road, 42001;
(800) 488–3998 or
(270) 488–3999.
Handicapped-accessible,
country setting with goats
and peacocks. $100 up.

**MORE FUN PLACES TO EAT IN
WESTERN KENTUCKY**

BENTON
Catfish Kitchen,
136 Teal Run Circle, 42025;
(270) 362–7306. Lakeside
dining; great seafood and
homemade desserts.

CADIZ
Lake Barkley State Resort
Park, Off Highway 68;
(270) 924–1131. Spacious
dining room with fireplace;
regional specialties.

Vintage Grill, Main Street,
downtown Cadiz;
(502) 522–3009. Lots of
Mexican-style dishes;
American steaks and
burgers. Specialty coffee
shop attached.

CENTRAL CITY
Colonel's Grill,
143 West Broad Street,
42330; (270) 754–4233.
Hometown diner with fab-
ulous fried chicken and
pork chops, homemade
breads, and desserts. Packed
at lunchtime; closes at 3:00
P.M.

GRAND RIVERS
Miss Scarlett's Restaurant,
708 Complex Drive, 42045;
(270) 928–3126. Tradi-
tional Southern and
regional fare, with home-
made breads and soups.

Dockers Grille, Turtle Bay
Resort overlooking Lake
Barkley; (270) 362–8364.
Lunch and dinner; try the
"turtle burger."

HENDERSON
The Mill Restaurant,
526 South Main Street,
42420; (270) 831–2255.
Decorated with antiques
and stuffed animals;
includes a microbrewery.

Wolf's Restaurant and Tavern, 31 North Green Street, 42420; (270) 826–5221. Henderson's local hangout since the late 1800s; famous for its bean soup and corn bread.

HOPKINSVILLE
Coffeyville Cafe, 308 North Main Street, 42240; (270) 885–0451. Sandwiches and daily specials.

KUTTAWA
Kuttawa Harbor Marina, 1709 Lake Barkley Drive, 42038; (270) 388–9563. Famous for its "Rudyburger"; indoor and outdoor dining.

MURRAY
Firehouse Grill, 403 Chestnut Street, 42701; (270) 753–6190. Barbecue and steaks.

OWENSBORO
Old Hickory Pit, 338 Washington Avenue, 42301; (270) 926–9000. Smoked mutton and great desserts.

Old South Barbeque, 3523 Highway 54, 42301; (270) 926–6464. More barbecue and accoutrements.

Shady Rest Barbecue Inn, Highway 60 East, 42301; (270) 926–8234. Barbecue and burgoo (stew); fried pies for dessert.

PADUCAH
BB Whiskers, 2701 Irvin Cobb Drive, 42003; (270) 443–7076. Catfish and western Kentucky–style barbecue.

C.C. Cohen Restaurant and Bar, 103 Broadway, 42001; (270) 442–6391. Steaks and seafood with weekend entertainment.

Flamingo Row West, 2100 Broadway, (270) 442–0460. Famous for over twenty varieties of "stuffed bread." You can't miss the super-bright building facade made of handmade tiles. Outdoor dining.

Jeremiah's Restaurant and Brew Pub, 225 Broadway, 42001; (270) 443–3991. Twenty-ounce steaks and a large selection of ales.

Index

A

Abbey of Gethsemani, 59
Abraham Lincoln Birthplace
  National Historic Site, 161
Actors Theatre, 51
Adsmore Museum, 205
After Dinner Downtown Paducah, 198
Alfalfa Restaurant, 10
Alice Lloyd College, 88
Alvin Mountjoy House, 117
Amelia's Field Country Inn, 12
American Cave Museum and
  Hidden River Cave, 150
American Printing House
  for the Blind, 55
Amerson Farm Orchard, 17
Amos Shinkle Townhouse
  Bed and Breakfast, 128
Anderson Ferry, 125
Anna's Kitchen, 154
Antique Mall of Historic Danville, 30
Antique Mall on the Square, 120
Antique Market, 33
Appalachia—Science in the
  Public Interest (ASPI), 171
Appalachian Celebration, 109
Appalachian Cultural and
  Fine Arts Center, 77
Appalshop, 80
AQS National Quilt Show, 196
Arbor Rose Bed and Breakfast, 57
Architectural Salvage, 54
Ascension Episcopal Church, 40
Ashland, 102
Ashland, the Henry Clay Estate, 9
Ashland Area Art Gallery, 104
Atkinson-Griffin House, 163
Atomic Cafe, 9
Augusta, 132
Augusta Ferry, 133

Augusta General Store, 134

B

Bad Branch Nature Preserve, 80
Banana Festival, 187
Bar-B-Q Capital of the World, 219
Bardstown, 56
Bardstown Art Gallery, 58
Bardstown Historical Museum, 58
Barlow House Museum, 193
Barren River Canoeing, 148
Barren River Imaginative Museum
  of Science, 147
Barthell Mining Camp, 173
Barton's Foods, 96
Bat Cave, 106
Battle of Tebbs Bend, 163
Beargrass Creek State Nature
  Preserve, 48
Beattyville, 99
Beaumont Inn, The, 19
Beehive Tavern, The, 133
Behringer-Crawford Museum, 130
Bell County Chamber of
  Commerce, 72
Bell House, 40
Bellevue, 132
Ben E. Clement Mineral
  Museum, 202
Benham, 78
Bennett's Mill Bridge, 102
Benton, 181
Berea, 36
Bernheim Forest Arboretum and
  Nature Center, 56
Berry, Wendell, 119
Berryman's Tasty Treat, 40
Bert and Bud's Vintage Coffins, 184
Betty Thomas Teddy Bears, 176
Bi-Water Farm, 16

INDEX

INDEX

iron furnaces,
Boone Furnace, 106
Clinton Furnace, 105
Iron Hill Furnace, 106
Mount Savage Furnace, 106
Pactolus Furnace, 106
Princess Furnace, 105
Iron Rail Restaurant, 12
Iroquois park, 54
Issac Shelby Cemetery State
Historic Site, 30

J

J. D. Maggard's Cash Store, 79
Jack Jouett House, 27
Jack Thomas House, 160
Jackson, 99
Jacob Hiestand House, 163
Jefferson Davis Monument
State Historic Site, 211
Jenkins, 83
Jenny Wiley State Resort Park, 86
Jenny Wiley Summer
Music Theatre, 87
Jenny Wiley Trail, 86
Jesse Stuart State Nature
Preserve, 101
Jim Beam American Outpost and
Museum, 56
Jim's Music Shop, 204
Joe and Mike's Pretty Good Tours, 55
Joe Bologna's, 10
Joe Ley Antiques, 54
John A. Roebling Suspension
Bridge, 128
John B. Begley Chapel, 163
John C. C. Mayo Museum, 85
John Fitch's grave, 55
John James Audubon State Park, 222
Johnson Creek Covered Bridge, 139
Jones Visual Arts Center at Centre
College, 30

Joseph Byrd Brannen & Co., Antique
Furniture Reproductions, 135
Jot 'Em Down Store, 4
Judy Drive-In, 39

K

Keeneland Race Course, 6
Kente International, 54
Kentucky Art and Craft Gallery, 51
Kentucky Cardinal Cheese Store, 115
Kentucky Center for the Arts, 51
Kentucky Coal Mining Museum, 78
Kentucky Derby, 47
Kentucky Derby Museum, 48
Kentucky Folk Art Center, 109
Kentucky Hemp Museum, 219
Kentucky Highlands Museum, 103
Kentucky History Center, 44
Kentucky Horse Center, 11
Kentucky Horse Park, 3
Kentucky Museum, The, 143
Kentucky Opry, 183
Kentucky Railway Museum, 60
Kentucky Reptile Zoo, 93
Kentucky Ridge State Forest, 74
Kentucky Shakespeare Festival, 50
Kentucky's Country Music Highway, 88
Kessler's 1891 Eatery, 25
Kincaid Regional Theatre, 117
Kingdom Come State Park, 78
King's Quilting Studio, 197
Kirchoff's Bakery and Deli, 197
Kizito Cookies, 53
Knob Creek Farm, 161
Knobs Haven Retreat, 61
Kuttawa, 200

L

L&N Depot, 12
La Fonda Restaurant, 20
Labrot & Graham, The Bourbon
Homeplace, 26

INDEX

Rabbit Hash General Store, 124
Rail City Hardware, 104
Railway Museum of Greater
    Cincinnati, 130
Raintree Inn Bed & Breakfast, 170
Rebecca-Ruth Candy, Inc., 43
Red Bird Mission Crafts, 75
Red Mile Harness Track, The, 5
Red River Gorge, 91
Red River Historical Museum, 99
Reelfoot Lake, 189
Reid's Orchard, 222
Renfro Valley, 177
Rhodes Hall Art Gallery, 61
Richmond, 35
Rick's White Light Diner, 44
Ridge Runner Bed and Breakfast, 73
Ridge Trail, 71
Ringos Mills, 139
River Heritage Museum, 197
Riverview at Hobson Grove, 145
Robert Penn Warren Museum, 213
Robinson Forest, 100
Rock Hotel Trail, 74
Rockcastle Adventures, 176
Rockcastle River Runners, 176
Roe Wells School, 96
Rooster Run General Store, 53
Rough River State Dam
    Park, 159–60
Royal Spring, 13
Rudy's Restaurant, 185
Russell, 104
Russell Springs, 168
Russellville, 214
Ruth Hunt Candies, 42

S

Saint Catharine Motherhouse, 64
Saint Joseph Catholic Church, 148
Saint Joseph Proto-Cathedral, 58
Saint Rose Proto-Priory, 64

Samuel May House, 88
Sandford House Bed and
    Breakfast, 129
Sarah Bush Johnson Lincoln
    Memorial, 157
sassafras tree, 219
Schlabach's Bakery, 212
Schmidt's Coca-Cola Museum, 155
Schneider's Sweet Shop, 132
School House Inn, The, 78
Science Hill, 46
Scotland Yard, The, 47
Scott County Tourism, 13
Scuba Center, 99
Seaman's Church Institute, 197
Seldon Scene Farm, 23
Seldon-Renaker Inn, The, 113
Shaker Tavern, 216
Shaker Village of Pleasant Hill, 22
Shelbyville, 46
Sheltowee Trace, 95
Sheltowee Trace Outfitters, 172, 176
Shooting Star Nursery, 45
Siegel Pottery, 119
Simpson County Archives
    and Museum, 149
Sky-Vue Drive-In, 39
Slade, 92
Smith's Grove, 148
Snowberry Hill, 47
Somerset, 167
South Union, 216
South Union Post Office, 216
South Union Shaker Village, 214
Southern Deposit Bank, 214
Spalding Hall, 58
Speed Art Museum, 50
Spirit of Jefferson, 49
Spratt Stoneworks, 96
Springfield, 64
Stab, 170
Stanford, 32

INDEX

About the Author

Zoé Ayn Strecker is a sculptor and writer who lives and works near the Kentucky River in Mercer County.